THE CATHOLIC UNIVERSITY OF AMERICA
CANON LAW STUDIES
No. 298

The Minister of Holy Communion

A Historical Synopsis and a Commentary

A DISSERTATION

SUBMITTED TO THE FACULTY OF THE SCHOOL OF CANON LAW OF THE CATHOLIC UNIVERSITY OF AMERICA IN PARTIAL FULFILLMENT OF THE REQUIREMENTS FOR THE DEGREE OF DOCTOR OF CANON LAW

BY

REVEREND DANIEL E. SHEEHAN, J.C.L.
PRIEST OF THE ARCHDIOCESE OF OMAHA

THE CATHOLIC UNIVERSITY OF AMERICA PRESS
WASHINGTON, D. C.

NIHIL OBSTAT:

CLEMENS V. BASTNAGEL, S.T.L., J.U.D.

Censor Deputatus

Washingtonii, D. C., die 4 octobris, 1950.

IMPRIMATUR:

GERALDUS T. BERGAN, D.D.

Archiepiscopus Omahensis

Omaha, die 7 octobris, 1950.

MURRAY & HEISTER

WASHINGTON, D. C.

PRINTED BY

TIMES AND NEWS PUBLISHING CO.

GETTYSBURG, PA., U. S. A.

TABLE OF CONTENTS

TABLE OF CONTENTS (Continued)

TABLE OF CONTENTS (Continued)

FOREWORD

The greatest gift which Christ could give to His Church was Himself. This gift came to the Church through the Sacrament of the Holy Eucharist. From the very beginning the Church realized its tremendous responsibility for the proper care and administration of this Most Excellent Sacrament. One aspect of this solicitude is seen in the legislation which the Church provided for the administration of Holy Communion.

In the present dissertation there will be delineated, in a brief and limited manner, the history of the legislation and the practice of the Church pertaining to the minister of Holy Communion, along with a canonical commentary on the pertinent legislation in the Code of Canon Law. The present study does not purport to be a liturgical work, and hence the liturgical aspects of the subject are entered into only briefly and only in so far as the liturgical aspect is a consequence of the canonical interpretation. This work in no wise intends to serve as a manual of ceremonies; rather, it seeks to place in its proper perspective the canonical legislation that relates to the minister of Holy Communion.

The law with regard to the ordinary and the extraordinary minister of Holy Communion will be examined with a special emphasis placed on the requirements of the law for the proper authorization of the minister for the lawful administration of Holy Communion. A special treatment is given in Chapter V to the law on the minister of Holy Communion to the sick, since there are definite and distinct provisions in the law with regard to the proper authorization of the minister of Communion to the sick. For an integrated handling of the subject there is added a final chapter which treats of certain incidental questions in the canonical legislation with respect to the time, the place, and the rite, for the administration of Holy Communion.

The writer wishes to express his sincere gratitude to his former Archbishop, the late James Hugh Ryan, and to the Most Reverend

Gerald T. Bergan, D.D., Archbishop of Omaha, for the opportunity to pursue advanced studies in Canon Law; to the Faculty of the School of Canon Law at the Catholic University of America, Washington, D. C., for their kind assistance and helpful guidance; and to all others who have aided in any way in the preparation of this work.

PART ONE

Historical Synopsis

CHAPTER I

Legislation Before the Council of Trent (1545-1563)

Article 1. The Minister of Holy Communion Before the Time of Gratian (1140)

Section 1. The Priest

The Holy Eucharist is a lasting Sacrament, and consequently the consecration (*confectio*) and the reception (*susceptio*) are separated from each other by an interval of time. For this reason there can be one minister for the consecrating and another for the dispensing of this Holy Sacrament. The present study is concerned with only the minister of the reception, the minister of Holy Communion.

The question of the minister does not concern the validity of the reception, for the Eucharist once consecrated remains the Body and Blood of Christ as long as the appearances of bread and wine are apt to contain within themselves the substances of bread and wine.[1] There is question here, not of any dogmatic concern, for the Eucharist would be validly received even under complete disregard of the law relative to the minister,[2] but rather of the lawfulness of the administration. This matter the Church can determine, so that with changing circumstances the discipline may vary.

The priest alone—and this includes the one who possesses the fullness of the priesthood through episcopal consecration—has the

---

[1] Pohle (1852-1922)-Preus (1871-1934), *The Sacraments* (authorized English edition based on the fifth German edition with some abridgements and additional references, 4 vols., St. Louis, 1917), II, *The Holy Eucharist,* 134 (hereafter cited *The Holy Eucharist*); Doronzo, *Tractatus Dogmaticus de Eucharistia,* Tom. I, *De Sacramento* (Milwaukee: Bruce, 1947), pp. 441-447.

[2] St. Thomas Aquinas (1225-1274), *Summa Theologica* (6 vols., Taurini: Marietti, 1937), Pars III, q. 78, a. 6 (hereafter cited *Summa*).

power of consecrating the Holy Eucharist. Only the priest can change bread and wine into the Body and Blood of Christ. This is a dogma of faith.[3] It naturally follows that the priest is also the ordinary minister for the dispensing of this sacrament. The Holy Eucharist was given to men by Christ at the Last Supper, and at that time Christ by His mandate, "Do this in remembrance of me," conferred on the Apostles the power of changing bread and wine into His Body and Blood. This power which the Apostles received has passed down to the bishops and priests in the Church, so that every priest through his ordination receives this tremendous power.[4] With the power of consecration naturally comes the right and the duty of dispensing this Heavenly Food to others. For the priest is the representative of Christ, His servant and the steward of His Mysteries.[5]

St. Thomas found three reasons for the priest's primary and pre-eminent right to dispense the Holy Eucharist. First, the priest consecrates in the person of Christ, and since the consecration of Christ's Body belongs to the priest, so likewise does the dispensing. Secondly, it is the priest who is the appointed intermediary between God and the people, and hence he should deliver the consecrated gifts to the people. Thirdly, out of reverence to this Sacrament only consecrated hands should touch it.[6] The priest has continually exercised this prerogative which he enjoys by divine right.[7] From the earliest days of the Church the primary right and duty of the priest to administer the Eucharist has always been evident.[8]

---

[3] Denzinger-Bannwart-Umberg, *Enchiridion Symbolorum Definitionum et Declarationum de Rebus Fidei et Morum* (ed. 21.-23., St. Louis: Herder and Co., 1937), nn. 430, 949 (hereafter cited *Enchiridion*).

[4] De Augustinis (+ 1899), *De Re Sacramentaria* (2 vols., Woodstock, Md., 1878), Vol. I, Pars II, art. 5, thesis xi, pp. 207 ff.; Doronzo, *Tractatus Dogmaticus de Eucharistia, De Sacramento,* pp. 737-741; Denzinger, *Enchiridion,* nn. 957, 961.

[5] I Cor., IV:1.

[6] *Summa,* Pars III, q. 82, a. 3.

[7] Luke, XXII:19.

[8] Cf. Bona (1609-1674), *Rerum Liturgicarum Libri Duo* (Romae, 1671), Cap. xvii (hereafter cited *Res Liturgicae*); Fortescue (1874-1923), *The Mass: A Study of the Roman Liturgy* (edited by H. Thurston, New York:

Section 2. The Deacon

The primitive teaching and practice of the Church both in the East and in the West, show that the priest was aided and supplemented in his ministry of the Holy Eucharist by the deacon. The diaconate is a ministerial order which the Apostles called into use in order to deal primarily with the temporal concerns of the Church.[9] The deacons had to prepare the materials for the corporate worship, and soon came to be associated in the service of the altar. They shared, by virtue of their ordination, in the sacramental gift of Orders, and consequently served in the sanctuary as a minister of the priest and the bishop, as their aid and instrument.[10]

There are many witnesses to the fact that deacons gave Holy Communion to the faithful from the first days of the Church down to our own time. In the early Church, St. Justin (100/10-163/7) wrote that deacons distributed the Holy Eucharist to the faithful during divine services, and also carried It to those who were absent.[11] Although St. Justin stated that the deacon gave Communion under both species, there was reflected at a very early time a special connection between the deacon and the chalice.

Tertullian (ca. 160-ca. 240) related that the people received Communion under both kinds, the celebrant giving the consecrated Bread, the deacon, the Chalice.[12] St. Cyprian (200-258) mentioned that it was the deacon who gave Communion to the unruly child

---

Longmans, Green and Co., 1937), pp. 36, 374 (hereafter cited *The Mass*); Duchesne (1843-1922), *Christian Worship: Its Origin and Evolution* (London, 1903), p. 186 (hereafter cited *Christian Worship*); Brightman (1856-1932), *Eastern Liturgies* (Oxford, 1896), p. 25. All of this testimony is based on overwhelming evidence in the Fathers and in other early Christian writers.

[9] Acts of the Apostles, VI.

[10] Gasparri (1852-1934), *Tractatus Canonicus de Sanctissima Eucharistia* (2 vols., Parisiis, 1897), II, n. 1097 (hereafter cited *De Eucharistia*).

[11] *Apologia* I, cc. 65, 67—Quasten, *Monumenta Eucharistica et Liturgica Vetustissima* (Bonnae: Petrus Hanstein, 1935), pars I, n. 17, 20 (sumptus est a Latina interpretatione Ottonis). (Hereafter cited *Monumenta Eucharistica*).

[12] Tertullianus, *De Corona*, c. 3—Migne (1800-1875), *Patrologiae Cursus Completus, Series Latina* (*MPL*) (221 vols., Paris, 1844-1864), II, 79, 80.

which received only under the appearance of wine, and who then accompanied the bishop in giving Communion to the people, the bishop going first with the consecrated Bread, and the deacon following him with the Precious Blood.[13]

This was also the practice in the East. In the important oriental canonical work, *Constitutiones Apostolorum,* which purported to be the work of St. Clement of Rome (+ 97), but which is now known to have been compiled in Syria toward the end of the fourth or at the beginning of the fifth century,[14] there are contained some important liturgical rules. The early liturgy is described thus:

> Et episcopus quidem tribuat oblatam dicens; Corpus Christi: et qui recipit, respondeat: Amen: diaconus vero teneat calicem ac tradendo dicat; Sanguis Christi, Calix vitae, et qui bibit respondeat: Amen. Psalmus autem tricesimus tertius dicatur, dum reliqui omnes communicant.[15]

The first *Ordo Romanus* (ca. 680) shows that the deacon had an important part in assisting the priest in giving out Communion at Rome.[16] The antiquity of this practice is indicated by St. Lawrence's (+ 258) charge to Pope Sixtus (257-258): "Experire utrum idoneum ministrum elegeris, cui commisisti Dominici sanguinis dispensationem."[17]

While the deacon enjoyed the privilege of distributing Holy Communion in all parts of the Church, it is evident that this function was always considered as extraordinary and supplementary to that of the priest. The very fact that he carried the chalice and followed the priest in the act of giving Communion indicates in itself that the deacon had the second place. This de-

[13] *De Lapsis,* nn. 17, 25—*MPL,* IV, 485.

[14] Van Hove (1872-1947), *Commentarium Lovaniense in Codicem Iuris Canonici,* Tom. I, *Prolegomena* (2. ed., Mechliniae: Dessain, 1945), p. 129 (hereafter cited *Prolegomena*).

[15] *Constitutiones Apostolorum,* VIII, 15, 16—Funk (1840-1907), *Didascalia et Constitutiones Apostolorum* (2 vols., Paderbornae, 1905), I, 518, 519.

[16] I, 20—*MPL,* LXXVIII, 947.

[17] Cited by St. Ambrose (+ 397), *De Officio,* Lib. I, Cap. 41—*MPL,* XVI, 84.

pendent and secondary rôle can be clearly seen from the *Constitutiones Apostolorum.* In Lib. VIII, n. 28, the text reads:

> Diaconus non benedixit: non dat benedictionem, accipit vero ab episcopo et presbytero; non baptizat, non offert; ipse vero cum episcopus aut presbyter obtulit, dat populo, non tanquam sacerdos, sed tanquam ministrans sacerdotibus.[18]

This text clearly shows the deacon's instrumental rôle in his capacity of minister to the priest.

The secondary rôle of the deacon is shown also in the *Traditio Apostolica,* a pseudo-apostolic collection of the Western Church, written about the early part of the third century.[19] In describing the ceremonies of first Communion it stated that, when there were not enough priests available, the deacon administered the chalices of water, milk and wine.[20] The inference is clear. The deacon was a substitute for the priest when the priest was not available, for the function of assisting the bishop at first Communion rightfully belonged to the priest.

Throughout the early ages of the Church there was repeated conflict between the priests and the deacons for supremacy in ecclesiastical affairs, both spiritual and temporal. So it was hardly to be expected that there would be a complete accord in this matter. The deacons could and did give Communion, but their rights were restricted. The I Ecumenical Council of Nicaea (325) forbade deacons to give Holy Communion to the priests.[21] Pope Gelasius I (492-496) in his *Epistola ad universos Episcopos per Lucaniam, Brutos et Siciliam Constitutos* reminded the deacons of their position as a minister of the priest and the bishop, and told

---

[18] Funk, *Didascalia et Constitutiones Apostolorum,* I, 531.

[19] Van Hove, *Prolegomena,* pp. 125, 126.

[20] Quasten, *Monumenta Eucharistica,* pars I, p. 31 (based on the Hauler edition of the *Traditio Apostolica,* Leipzig, 1900).

[21] Can. 18—J. Hardouin (1646-1729), *Acta Conciliorum et Epistolae Decretales ac Constitutiones Summorum Pontificum* (12 vols., Parisiis, 1714-1715), I, 331 (hereafter cited Hardouin), and J. Mansi (1692-1767), *Sacrorum Conciliorum Nova et Amplissima Collectio* (53 vols. in 60, Parisiis, 1901-1927), II, 675 (hereafter cited Mansi).

them that their rights over the Body of Christ were dependent on the priest and the bishop.[22]

The so-called IV Council of Carthage restricted the deacon in a similar manner. The purported collection of its acts is a systematic collection of canons derived from the Greek and Gallic Councils along with some decretals of the Roman Pontiffs, made during the middle of the fifth century in Gaul, most likely at Arles.[23] Canon 38 forbade the deacon to distribute the Body of Christ in the presence of the priest, unless it was necessary and the priest ordered him to do so.[24]

According to St. Thomas, the deacon maintained for many centuries his right to administer the Chalice to the laity, but his rights in regard to the Body of Christ were limited.[25] The old association of the powers of the deacon with the Chalice remained important, for the power of the deacon diminished as Communion under one kind became more frequent.[26]

However, in France in the ninth and tenth centuries, as a reaction to abuses in regard to the administration of the Eucharist, even the administration of Holy Viaticum was restricted to the priest. Hincmar (806-882), Archbishop of Rheims (845-882), ordered his priests to give Viaticum *"per se, et non per quemlibet."*[27] More than a century later (990) the Council of Anse (near Lyons) in similar language commanded that only the priest was to give Holy Viaticum.[28]

These severe restrictions were not universal, for in the twelfth century the Council of Westminster (1138) in England put dea-

---

[22] Tit. VIII—Thiel (1826-1908), *Epistolae Romanorum Pontificum a Sancto Hilario (461-468) usque ad Sanctum Hormisdam (514-523)*, (Brunsbergae, 1868), p. 366 (hereafter cited Thiel).

[23] Van Hove, *Prolegomena*, p. 152, 153; Cicognani, *Canon Law* (2. ed., trans. by J. M. O'Hara and F. Brennan, Westminster, Md.: Newman Book Shop, Reprint, 1947), p. 222.

[24] Mansi, III, 954; Hardouin, I, 981. The same law is found in the Synod of Elvira (305), c. 32—Mansi, II, 11.

[25] *Summa*, Pars III, q. 82, a. 3.

[26] Pohle-Preuss, *The Holy Eucharist*, p. 262; Fortescue, *The Mass*, p. 375.

[27] *Capitulary of Hincmar of Rheims*, II, can. 10—Mansi, XV, 480; *MPL*, CXXV, 779.

[28] Can. 1—Mansi, XIX, 101.

cons on the same level as priests in the administration of Viaticum.[29] Perhaps the restrictions in France were occasioned by the excessive abuses prevalent there at that time, but, whatever the reason, the deacon was given greater liberty elsewhere as the time of the *Decretum* of Gratian approached.

Section 3. The Laity

In the early days of the Church the laity were allowed to take the Eucharist to their homes and to communicate themselves. This practice arose during the times of persecution, during the period in which there was no public reservation of the Blessed Sacrament. Due to the dangers and uncertainties of the times, Christians could not know when they might be arrested and put to death. For this reason they took the Holy Eucharist to their homes and reverently guarded It, so that they might assure themselves of the consolation of Viaticum in the event that they were apprehended.

While the early Christians most certainly did receive the Holy Eucharist during their divine services, nevertheless the carrying of the Blessed Sacrament to their homes was apparently a universal practice in the early Church.[30]

Lay people gave Communion not only to themselves, but for a good reason they gave It also to others. Dionysius of Alexandria (248-264/265), in a letter written to Pope Fabian (236-250), related that he sent a boy to a dying man, Serapion, to give him Viaticum. Serapion upon realizing that he was near death had sent his nephew for the priest that he might receive the last sacraments. Being sick, the priest himself could not come, so he sent the boy with the Holy Eucharist to give It to the dying man.[31]

---

[29] Can. 2—Wilkins (1685-1745), *Concilia Magnae Britanniae et Hiberniae* (4 vols., London, 1737), I, 415; Mansi, XXI, 511.

[30] Tertullianus, *Ad Uxorem,* Lib. II, cap. 5—*MPL,* I, 1296; St. Cyprianus, *De Lapsis,* c. 26—*MPL,* IV, 486; Origen (185/186-254/255), *In Exodum,* XIII, c. 3—Migne, *Patrologiae Cursus Completus, Series Graeca* (MPG) (161 vols. in 164, Parisiis, 1856-1866), XII, 391.

[31] Eusebius (263-339), *Historia Ecclesiastica,* Lib. VI, c. 44—*Die griechischen Christlichen Schriftsteller der ersten drei Jahrhunderte* (7 vols. in 10). II, Pars II (*Eusebius Werke, Historia Ecclesiastica,* ed. Schwartz, Leipzig, 1903), p. 625.

Inasmuch as even a boy might be called to administer Viaticum, it is not surprising that minor clerics were sometimes allowed to carry the Holy Eucharist, especially during the days of the persecutions. They were not allowed to distribute Holy Communion during Mass. The early councils were very explicit in their prohibition of the observance of any such practice and of the rise of any such custom.[32] But, although minor clerics could not give Communion during public worship or at solemn services, they did frequently carry the Eucharist to the absent. This function was entrusted to acolytes on many occasions.[33] A classic example is that of St. Tarsicius (+ 255?), an acolyte who was martyred while trying to take Communion to some Christians who were in prison in Rome.[34]

Although the practice of the lay administration of the Eucharist had begun for reasons of safety and security during the persecutions, it continued for some time. While he looked upon it as an exceptional practice, still as late as the fourth century St. Basil, Metropolitan of Caesarea (370-379), did not condemn it. He saw the private administration of Communion as a general practice in the absence of priests and deacons, especially among the monks in Alexandria and Egypt. Nevertheless he made an attempt to explain the procedure as implying the reception of Communion from the hands of the priest, inasmuch as he shared with the communicants a number of Hosts at one and the same time.[35]

That this practice was still widespread in Rome in the fourth century is known from the testimony of St. Jerome (ca. 342-420). In referring to the dispositions for the worthy reception of Holy

---

[32] Council of Laodicea (343/381), can. 21—Mansi, II, 569; Hardouin, I, 785. On this point, consult Witasse (1660-1716), *Tractatus Theologici* (6 vols., Venetiis, 1783), Tom. IV, *De Augustissimo Eucharistiae Sacramento*, q. vii, a. 2.

[33] Innocentius I (402-417), Epist. ad Decentium, cap. V—Jaffé, *Regesta Pontificum Romanorum ab condita Ecclesia ad annum post Christum natum MCXCVIII (1198)* (2. ed., cura G. Wattenbach, F. Kaltenbrunner [ad annum 590], P. Ewald [anno 590-882], S. Löwenfeld [anno 882-1198], 2 vols., Lipsiae, 1885-1888), in 311 (hereafter cited Jaffé): Mansi, III, 1028. Cf. De Augustinis, *De Re Sacramentaria*, Vol. I, Pars II, art 5, p. 212.

[34] *Martyrologium Usuardi Monachi*, Aug. 15—*MPL*, CXXIV, 366.

[35] *Epist. XCIII ad Caesariam—MPG*, XXXII, 483.

Communion, he wrote: "Ipsorum conscientiam convenio, qui eodem die post coitum communicant. . . . Quare ad martyres ire non audent? quare non ingrediuntur Ecclesias? An alius in publico, alius in domo Christus est? Quod in ecclesia non licet, nec domi licet."[36]

The practice of taking the Eucharist in the hands and the consequent possibility of communicating oneself were forbidden by the Councils of Saragossa (380) and the I Council of Toledo (400). Although these councils were directed primarily against Priscillianism, a gnostic, manichaean heresy which, having originated in Spain in the fourth century, maintained that Christ had no real body, so that its adherents abstained from consuming the Sacred Host upon receiving It, nevertheless these canons also ruled out the reservation of the Eucharist in the home and the private reception of It there from lay hands.[37] While the elimination of the private reservation and reception of the Holy Eucharist was but an indirect result of this legislation, nevertheless it was effectively gained.[38]

After that time the administration of Holy Communion by anyone other than a priest or a deacon was considered either an abuse or an exceptional case. Minor clerics no longer enjoyed any right in this matter, for if any custom had arisen it had been abolished. In a case of extreme necessity, when even a layman could rightfully carry the Blessed Sacrament, a minor cleric was to be preferred if a choice arose between a layman and a cleric.[39]

There were exceptional cases, but concomitantly with each of them the presence of a serious reason warranted an exceptional procedure. St. Ambrose (+ 397) commended the faith of trav-

---

[36] *Epistola XLVIII ad Pammachium,* n. 15—*MPL,* XXII, 506; *Corpus Scriptorum Ecclesiasticorum Latinorum* (*CSEL*) (68 vols., Vindobonae: F. Tempsky, 1866—), LIV, 377.

[37] Council of Saragossa (380), can. 3: "Eucharistiam gratiam si quis probatur acceptam in ecclesia non sumpsisse, anathema sit in perpetuum."—Mansi, III, 634; I Council of Toledo (400), can. 14—Mansi, III, 1000; Hardouin, I, 991.

[38] Bona, *Res Liturgicae,* Lib. II, Cap. XVII, n. 7.

[39] Schmalzgrueber (1663-1735), *Ius Ecclesiasticum Universum* (5 vols. in 12, Romae, 1843-1845), Lib. III, tit. 3, nn. 12-13 (hereafter cited Schmalzgrueber).

elers who, because of the dangers involved in travel in those days, took the Eucharist with them in order to be able to receive Viaticum if the need arose.[40]

In places where it was feared that no priests would be available, either because of the remoteness of the locality or also because of the raging of a persecution, the private reception of Communion was still practiced.[41] The monks of the East were still communicating themselves in the ninth century. They adhered to this practice to avoid association with the Iconoclast heretics.[42]

The spirit of piety and devotion reflected in the lives of virgins recently consecrated to God likewise was a factor that was deemed to give rise to an exceptional case. As late as the twelfth century such virgins were permitted to retain the Holy Eucharist for devotional Communions for eight days after the ceremony of their consecration.[43]

In this matter abuses arose at various times. Efforts to combat them followed as a result. In the seventh and eighth centuries serious abuses existed in France. Not only men, but also women, dared to usurp the prerogatives of the priesthood. They assumed priestly vestments, and even attempted to distribute Communion during Mass.

In the early days women had communicated themselves just as the men had done, but the women were never allowed in the service of the altar. The Council of Laodicea (343/381) had forbidden that practice.[44] Again in the next century Pope Gelasius (492-496)

---

[40] *De Excessu Fratris—MPL,* XVI, 1304.

[41] "Communion at home, a very frequent custom in the time of the persecutions, was maintained among solitaries in monasteries where there were no priests, and, generally, in the case of those who lived at a great distance from a church, even after the Church was free from persecution. In 519, Dorotheos, the bishop of Thessalonica, fearing that persecution was about to descend upon his flock, caused the elements for Communion to be distributed among them in basketsful."—Duchesne, *Christian Worship,* p. 249, footnote 3. Duchesne borrowed this text from Thiel, p. 902, n. 2.

[42] Theodore of Studium (+ 826), *Epist. I,* n. 57; *Epist. II,* n. 209—*MPG,* XCIX, 1115; XCIX, 1661.

[43] Martène (1654-1739), *De Antiquis Ecclesiae Ritibus* (4 vols., Rotomagi, 1700-1706), Lib. I, Cap. V, art. 1, n. 5.

[44] Can. 44: "Non oportet mulierem ad altare ingredi."—Mansi, II, 571.

reminded women that they were barred from ministering at the altar, and in consequence could not presume to take over any duties that belonged to men.[45]

In view of these specific prohibitions, it is clear that the deaconesses were also forbidden to administer Holy Communion in church. There were excesses and extravagances in regard to their position, especially among the heretical sects. The 19th canon of the I General Council of Nicaea (325) saw fit to remind the Paulinianist deaconesses especially, but also all other deaconesses, that they were not to arrogate to themselves any clerical prerogatives.[46]

The *Contitutiones Apostolorum* show that in the East[47] there was a definite rite of ordination for the deaconesses. This rite is found in the *Constitutiones Apostolorum* between the ordination rite of the deacon and that for the subdeacon.[48] This implies that at one time in the East they most likely constituted an ecclesiastical order.

Certainly the deaconesses were never considered to have the powers of the deacon. This is clear from the enumeration of their functions and duties in the Eastern liturgical work, Lib. VIII of the *Constitutiones Apostolorum*. There it was stated:

> Diaconissa non benedicit, sed nec peragit quidquam eorum quae presbyteri aut diaconi faciunt, dumtaxat ianuas custodit, et presbyteris quando baptizantur mulieres ministrat propter decorum.[49]

---

[45] *Epist. ad universos episcopos per Lucaniam, Brutos, et Siciliam Constitutos,* Tit. 26—Thiel, pp. 376, 377.

[46] Mansi, II, 678.

[47] The Western Church repudiated the idea that these women received the sacrament of Orders. The so-called ordination was acknowledged as nothing more than an avowal of chastity. Any ordination of deaconesses was specifically forbidden by the following councils: the I Council of Orange (441), c. 26—Hefele (1809-1893)—Leclercq (1869-1945), *Histoire des Conciles* (10 vols. in 19, Paris, 1907-1938), III, 446; the Council of Epaon (517), c. 21—Mansi, VIII, 561; and the II Council of Orleans (533), c. 18—Mansi, VIII, 837.

[48] Lib. VIII, Cap. XIX, XX—Funk, *Didascalia et Constitutiones Apostolorum,* I, 525.

[49] Cap. XXVIII, n. 6—Funk, *Didascalia et Constitutiones Apostolorum,* I, 531.

In this *ex professo* furnished explanation of the activities of the deaconesses there was no mention of the administration of the Eucharist; rather, it was excluded, since it was listed as one of the functions of the priest and the deacon, and deaconesses were forbidden to usurp those things which belonged to the priests and the deacons. If this had been one of the usual activities of the deaconesses, then mention of it would hardly have been omitted. One could rather expect that it would have been explicitly mentioned as an exception to the previous statement. Whether the deaconesses were allowed in the early days to carry the Eucharist to sick women is not absolutely certain. The existence of such a permission would not have been surprising, since in the early days all the faithful were allowed to take the consecrated Bread to their homes.[50]

In France the abuses of lay administration were combatted by means of provincial conciliar legislation in the seventh, eighth and ninth centuries. The Councils of Rouen (650)[51] Aix-la-Chappelle (816)[52] and Paris (829) took the lead in attacking the problem. The Council of Paris called attention to the grave violations of the Christian law and tradition which were prevalent in France at the time. Women were even putting on the sacred vestments to administer the Holy Eucharist to the people. The bishops of the province were ordered to put an end to these shameful abuses.[53]

Hincmar of Rheims (806-882) was very specific in his legislation. In one of his Capitularies he commanded that the priests of his archdiocese administer Communion to the sick *"per se, et non per quemlibet."*[54]

Pope St. Leo IV (847-855) took cognizance of this problem, and in the advice he offered for bishops to give to their priests he mentioned the abuse of the laity, especially on the part of

---

[50] Schroeder (1875-1942), *Disciplinary Decrees of the General Councils* (St. Louis: B. Herder, 1937), p. 113.

[51] Can. 2—Mansi, X, 1199; Bruns, *Canones Apostolorum et Conciliorum Saeculorum* IV-VII (2 vols., Berolini, 1839), II, 268.

[52] Lib. I, cap. 82—Mansi, XIV, 201.

[53] Council of Paris (829), Lib. I, cap. 45—*Monumenta Germaniae Historica, Leges in 4,* Sectio III, *Concilia,* Tom. II, pars II (ed. A. Werminghoff, Hannoverae, 1908), pp. 639, 640 (hereafter cited *MGH*).

[54] *Capitularia,* II, Can. 10—Mansi, XV, 480; *MPL,* CXXV, 779.

women in administering Holy Communion.[55] Roman conciliar legislation strove to put down similar abuses. The Council of Rome (853) in canon 33 stated: "Quamobrem nulli laicorum liceat in eo loco ubi sacerdotes reliquive clerici consistunt, quod presbyterium nuncupatur, quando missa celebratur consistere."[56]

After this turbulent period the abuses of lay people, especially of women, in attempting to administer the Holy Eucharist were under control. In exceptional cases the laity were allowed to administer the Sacrament, but such opportunities were very rare. One such opportunity is noted in the Council of Westminster (1138), just two years before the *Decretum* of Gratian. In canon 2 the Council decreed: "Sancimus etiam ut ultro octo dies Corpus Christi non reservetur neque ad infirmos nisi per sacerdotem aut per diaconum aut necessitate instante per quemlibet cum summa reverentia deferatur."[57] This appears to have been more of a concession than was deemed lawful in other places, especially in France. In an elastic sort of way it reflected the utmost that the Church yielded with regard to the lay distribution of Holy Communion at the time of Gratian.

ARTICLE 2. THE MINISTER OF HOLY COMMUNION IN THE *Decretum* OF GRATIAN (1140)

Section 1. The Ordinary Minister

The law on the distribution of Holy Communion had crystallized by the time of Gratian (1140), and the discipline of the Church has not varied since that time. This is a very clear indication of the unfailing zeal of the Church in doing everything possible to insure reverence to this Most Excellent Sacrament and to prevent, if possible, any and all abuses in regard to It. The law of Gratian was that the priest was to administer the Holy Eucharist, but that the deacon could do so if certain conditions were verified. The rights of lay people were severely restricted.[58]

[55] *Fragmenta Epistolarum ex registro Leonis Papae IV*, cc. VI, VII—Mansi, XIV, 891.

[56] Mansi, XIV, 1008.

[57] Wilkins, *Concilia Magnae Britanniae*, I, 415.

[58] Cc. 13, 18, D. XCIII; C. 29, D. II, *de cons.*

Gratian did not use the specific terminology of "ordinary" and "extraordinary" minister as it is in use today, but the same concepts were clearly defined. The terminology itself dates from a later period. But there was a clear-cut distinction between the primary and independent right and duty of the priest to give Communion and the supplementary and secondary right of the deacon in carrying out this function. The priest was thus the ordinary minister, as he is today, while the deacon could act only when the necessity arose. His function was extraordinary, as it is today. It was only the benevolent interpretation of the glossators and commentators that allowed lay people any possibility of functioning in this capacity.

First to be considered is the right of the priest to dispense the Holy Eucharist as that right was reflected in the *Decretum.* The primary right of the priest was indicated positively in the declared duty and obligation of the priest, and negatively in the indicated limitations which restricted the right of the deacon.[59] All these limitations were in favor of the priest relative to his native and unlimited right in this regard. The right of the priest as it is negatively established may first be investigated.

In the first place it was categorically stated that the deacon was not to give Communion or bless the Chalice. The ancient law as enacted in the Council of Laodicea was restated.[60] The *Glossa Ordinaria* explained that *"panem dare"* meant to give Communion to the faithful. So the priest who consecrated was also the one who was to distribute the Eucharist, unless the exceptions provided for in other canons were present. The strictness of this canon was of course mitigated in accordance with the clear meaning and interpreation of the other laws in the same matter.

There was a definite acknowledgment that the deacons had the power of Orders, but there was also the insistence that they keep within the bounds of the power committed to them. While they were indeed ministers of the altar, so that they could bestow

---

[59] C. 29, D. II, *de cons.;* c. 18, D. XCIII.

[60] "Non oportet panem dare nec calicem benedicere."—C. 16, D. XCIII.

solemn baptism and give Holy Communion, yet they could do so only under certain conditions.[61]

The *Glossa Ordinaria* in giving the background and occasion of this indicated that deacons had usurped the office of bishop and priest, and had baptized and given Communion on their own authority.[62] The usurpation resulted not simply from the fact that they administered the sacraments, but from the consideration that they had done so on their own authority. The Glossator then explained under what conditions the deacon could act without being accused of usurping the rights of the priest. But always in the presence of the priest, even though there existed an urgent need, the deacon had to receive from the priest the order to act.[63]

The matter so carefully explained by the Glossator in reference to c. 13, D. XCIII, was stated as the law in c. 18 of the same Distinction.[64]

The primary right of the priest was further indicated in the limitation that was placed on the deacon by c. 14, D. XCIII. This law forbade deacons to give Communion to the priests, for the priest who had the power to offer the sacrifice certainly should not receive Communion from the hand of one who did not possess this power.

Ioannes Teutonicus (+ 1245) in a gloss under "*Corpus Christi tradere*" furnished a cross reference to a canon in the *Second Part of the Decretum*.[65] This canon dealt with simony

[61] "Diaconos propriam constituimus observare mensuram, nec ultra tenorem paternis canonibus deputatum quidpiam temptare permittimus, et nihil eorum suo ministerio penitus applicare, quae primus ordinibus proprie decrevit antiquitas. Absque episcopo vel presbytero baptizare non audeant, nisi praedictis ordinibus fortassis longius constitutis necessitas extrema campellat. Quid etiam laicis Christianis facere plerumque conceditur. Sacri Corporis praerogationem sub conspectu episcopi seu presbyteri (nisi his absentibus) ius non habeant exercendi."—C. 13, D. XCIII, taken from the decretals of Pope Gelasius I.

[62] *Casus* ad c. 13, D. XCIII.

[63] *Glossa Ordinaria* ad c. 13, D. XCIII, s.v. *necessitas*.

[64] "Presente presbitero diaconus eucharistiam corporis Christi populo, si necessitas cogit, iussus eroget." This text derived from the so-called IV Council of Carthage (398).

[65] C. 12, C. I, q. 1.

and the punishments for it. The Glossator there raised the question regarding the manner in which priests, when cut off from the body of Christ, could fulfill the duties of the sacerdotal office. The priest as minister of the Eucharist was under consideration. It was asked if he was able, when under anathema, to administer the sacrament of the Eucharist. Could he lawfully fulfill his duties under the law? The query clearly postulated that the duty in question belonged to the priestly office, that it was a function given to the priest by the law.

These arguments, although indirect, reflected the predominant rôle that attached to the priest in the administration of Holy Communion. They indicated that the Eucharist as a sacrament that needed to be dispensed to the faithful was a priest's responsibility, and that any help he obtained in carrying out this function was of a dependent and supplementary character in relation to his own primary right and obligation.

The eleventh century was the age of Berengarius (1000-1088) and of his errors concerning the Real Presence. Consequently one finds developed at that time a very precise statement of the doctrine and the practice of the Church in regard to the Holy Eucharist. The importance of the Eucharist doctrine made it imperative for Gratian to include many specific laws and statements on this doctrine in the *Third Part* of his *Decretum.* Incorporated therein is much which is of a doctrinal rather than of a disciplinary nature.

But Gratian also included very important disciplinary laws, for he sensed the desire of the Church to impress upon its members the importance of the Eucharistic doctrine by means of very express laws in regard to the use and the care of the Holy Eucharist. So it was with very strict language that there was imposed on the priest the obligation of carrying the Eucharist to the sick. In the event of non-compliance he laid himself open to the risk of being deprived of his clerical standing. He was under constraint to fulfill this obligation personally; he was not free to discharge his duty through the ministry of the laity.[66]

[66] "Igitur interdicit per omnia sinodus, ne talis temeraria presumptio ulterius fiat; sed omnimodis presbyter per semitipsum infirmum communicet. Quod si aliter fecerit, gradus sui periculo subiacebit."—C. 29, D. II, *de cons.*

(attributed by Ivo, Burchard, and Gratian to the Council of Rheims [630], cap. 1, but drawn most likely from the Council of Rouen [650], can. 2).

Ioannes Teutonicus severely censured the foolish and witless priest who gave the Holy Eucharist to lay people, even to women, when It was to be carried to the sick.[67] Only a real necessity could excuse the priest, as the gloss under the words "*per semetipsum*" indicated.[68] The priest was personally burdened with the care and the reverent dispensing of this Sacrament, since he was the primary and ordinary minister for the administration of the Holy Eucharist. Consequently there was a clear realization that the function of taking Holy Communion to the sick belonged to the priest.

Section 2. The Extraordinary Minister

The deacon by his Orders was entitled to share in the ministry of the altar, but always in a dependent rôle. The canons of *Distinction XCIII,* wherein Gratian treated of this matter, fall under his *Dictum* which reminded the deacons that they are subject to the priests.[69] These laws received mention above, where the superior right of the priest was duly established, but they should be recalled again for the sake of showing also the deacon's rights. The *Glossa Ordinaria* on these canons of D. XCIII, as also on c. 29, D. II, *de cons.*, dealt with the exceptions to the law as stated in the *Decretum.* It is mainly from the glosses that one will succeed in determining when and under what circumstances the deacon was conceded the right to administer Holy Communion.

It was in c. 13, D. XCIII, that Gratian basically reminded the deacons of the limits of their powers, and of the conditions under which these powers might be used. In view of the importance of this law the *Glossa Ordinaria* offered a valuable commentary. The Glossator stated that when there was a real necessity, and when no bishop or priest was present, the deacon could on his own authority carry the Holy Eucharist to the sick.[70]

---

[67] *Glossa Ordinaria* ad c. 29, D. II, *de cons.* s.v. *casus.*

[68] "Per semetipsum—vel per diaconum, si necesse est."

[69] *Dictum* post c. 12, D. XCIII. "Ut ex premissis auctoritatibus apparet, diaconi debent obedientiam presbiteris, sicut et presbiteri episcopis."

[70] *Glossa Ordinaria* ad c. 13, D. XCIII, s.v. *necessitas.*

This was not to be considered an extravagant concession, for the deacon acted *"iure suo"* in carrying out this function. If the priest or bishop was present, then the situation was entirely changed, for regardless of the reason the deacon could then act only if he had been ordered by the priest. The presence of a group of people who desired to receive Holy Communion when there was lacking a sufficient number of priests to take care of them in a reasonable time was considered a justifying cause for the deacon to act.[71]

Canon 18 stated the law as it was explained by the glosses on canon 13.[72] Ioannes Teutonicus explained the meaning of the law by means of his gloss on the word *"presente."* He there indicated that the deacon could act *"iussus vel non iussus,"* provided only that the inability of the priest to act was verified. This law evidently meant, just as was seen in regard to canon 13, that the deacon could dispense the Holy Eucharist to the sick and also in church whenever necessity called for it, that is, only when there was no priest or bishop present to fulfill the function. If a priest or the bishop was present, the deacon could act only under command from either of them. Rufinus (+ 1190) stated it in this way:

> Ius non habent exercendi sub conspectu, i.e. presentia episcopi vel presbyteri, nisi ab eis iussus, alias autem nullo modo ius habent hoc faciendi, nisi his absentibus.[73]

Thus, while the deacon's rôle was supplementary, and for its exercise always contingent on some real need which existed in the absence of the priest, he acted *"iure suo"* if no priest was available. As this power was rightfully his whenever a sufficient need arose, the deacon could act. And from the example given by the glosses it is clear that the necessity did not have to be extreme.[74]

---

[71] *Loc. cit.*

[72] "Presente presbytero diaconus eucharistiam corporis Christi populo, si necessitas cogit, iussus eroget."

[73] *Summa Decretorum* (ed. Heinrich Singer, Paderborn, 1902), ad cc. 13 et 18, D. XCIII.

[74] *Glossa Ordinaria* ad c. 13, D. XCIII, s.v. *necessitas.*

Section 3. The Exceptional Minister

The right of the laity to distribute Holy Communion had been severely restricted from the time of the fourth century. Gratian stated an old law which prohibited this practice.[75] Lay distribution was called a detestable and horrible abuse which could not be tolerated. The priest could not allow a lay person to carry the Holy Eucharist, for a lay person was not allowed even to enter the sanctuary or to approach the altar. For this prohibition Gratian borrowed another old law from the I General Council of Nicaea (325), according to which lay persons had been forbidden to enter that part of the church where the clergy assisted at divine services.[76] However, as Rufinus pointed out, this prohibition had applicable force exclusively at the time of divine services, so that a lay person was not barred from access to the *presbyterium* at other times, for example, when Communion was to be taken to the sick in an emergency.[77]

While the law was very strict in its literal meaning, the Glossator in his comment on the words *"per semetipsum"* stated that the priest had to give Communion personally, unless the factor of necessity as explained above made the act allowable for the deacon, or unless a case of dire emergency pointed out the need that Holy Communion be carried to the sick by a lay Catholic.[78] In his commentary Rufinus likewise stated that this duty was to be performed by the priest personally, unless there arose the need of carrying Holy Viaticum to the sick at a time when the priest himself suffered illness. Under such conditions even a boy could take Communion to the sick person.[79] There was recalled the incident of the boy who had carried Holy Viaticum to the dying Serapion.[80]

This very liberal interpretation was not accepted by a later glossator, probably Ioannes de Phintona (+ ca. 1281), in his

---

[75] C. 29, D. II, *de cons.*

[76] C. 30, D. II, *de cons.*

[77] *Summa Decretorum,* ad c. 30, D. II, *de cons.*

[78] Per semetipsum—vel per diaconum, si necesse est, . . . vel per laicum catholicum."—*Glossa Ordinaria* ad c. 29, D. II, *de cons.* s.v. *per semetipsum.*

[79] *Summa Decretorum,* ad c. 29, D. II, *de cons.*

[80] Eusebius, *Historia Ecclesiastica,* Lib. VI, c. 44—GCS, II, Pars II, p. 625.

comment on another canon of the *Decretum* of Gratian.[81] In the *Additio* to this canon the following question was raised: "Sed numquid a laico possum recipere Eucharistiam in necessitate cum sufficit contritio?" In answer this glossator referred to c. 47, D. II, *de cons.*: "Credere in eum, hoc est panem vivum manducare. Qui credit in eum manducat eum."[82] The answer obviously indicated that in preference to receiving Holy Communion from a lay person the dying penitent should make a spiritual communion. This reflected quite a different attitude than that of Rufinus and of the gloss on c. 29, D. II, *de cons.*, and could be looked upon as excessively strict.

Cardinal Hostiensis (+ 1271) in his brief reference to this point did not take into consideration any exceptional or extraordinary contingencies, for he simply stated that Communion could be carried to the sick only by priests or by deacons.[83] This was the law as it was stated in Gratian. If there was in existence any other usage as warranted by particular local or personal circumstances, such a usage stood indeed as an exception rather than as the rule.

ARTICLE 3. THE PROPER MINISTER OF HOLY COMMUNION

Section 1. The Right of the Parish Priest

Every priest through his ordination (*vi ordinationis*) has the power of administering the sacrament of the Holy Eucharist. This function cannot properly be called an act of jurisdiction. Nevertheless, in the course of time the exercise of this power came to be regulated. In the Church as a divine institution and as a completely self-contained society, government and order must be duly preserved in the administering of the sacraments. "To feed the sheep" is not the indiscriminate duty of any and every priest; he who has been entrusted with a special *"cura animarum"*

---

[81] C. 42, C. XXIV, q. 1.

[82] Cf. St. Gregorius Magnus (590-604), *Dialogi,* Lib. III—*MPL,* LXXXVII, 127.

[83] Henricus de Segusio, *In Quinque Libros Decretalium Commentaria* (5 vols. in 3, Venetiis, 1581), III, tit. 44, n. 1 (hereafter cited *Commentaria*).

is the one who has a definite right and obligation in this regard, for he is the "*proprius sacerdos*" designated for the care of a particular portion of Christ's flock. So it was that the parish priest came to be entrusted with the right, and in some cases with the exclusive right, of administering Holy Communion to those who were placed under his care.[84]

With the exception of the enactment of the I Council of Carthage (348), there is very little in the early ages of the Church on the parochial aspect of the administration of Holy Communion.[85] Indeed, one could hardly expect to find much legislation on this point while parishes were only in the formative stages. For as long as Mass was said in the chapels and the oratories of the wealthy which existed without dependence on the baptismal churches, and as long as the people were free to attend Mass anywhere they pleased, one could hardly assume as extant any practice which reflected a strict regulation in regard to the administration of Communion. The people certainly felt free to receive Communion where they went to Mass.[86]

The administration of Holy Communion became a parochial function as the duty of attendance at Mass became defined within more restricted limits. In the sixth century the Council of Agde (506) allowed the faithful to fulfill their obligation of assisting at Mass through their attendance at the Holy Sacrifice in rural oratories on all days except the major feasts. On such days they had to go to the cathedral or to their parochial church.[87]

[84] Suarez (1548-1617), *Opera Omnia* (28 vols., ed. C. Berton, 1856-1878, Vol. XXI, 1866), *Tertia Pars Summae Theologicae,* Disp. LXXII, Sect. II, n. 2—*Opera Omnia,* XXI, 579, 580.

[85] Can. 7: "Statuat gravitas vestra, unusquisque clericus, vel laicus, non communicet in aliena plebe absque litteris episcopi sui, et omnes episcopi responderunt, in hoc clero et laicis convenientissime provideri."—Mansi, III, 156.

[86] Stutz, "The Proprietary Church as an Element of Medieval Ecclesiastical Law," *Studies in Medieval History, Medieval Germany (911-1250)* (translated by Geoffrey Barraclough, 2 vols., Oxford: Blackwell, 1938), II, 47-54.

[87] C. 21—Mansi, VIII, 328; Hardouin, II, 1000; cf. I Council of Orleans (511), c. 25—Mansi, VIII, 355; Hardouin, II, 1011. For more detailed information on this point consult Feldhaus, *Oratories,* The Catholic University of America Canon Law Studies, n. 42 (Washington, D. C.: The Catholic University of America, 1927), pp. 39 ff.

Soon the requirements became more exacting. It was forbidden to go to any but the parochial church on certain feast days and Sundays. This is shown by the *Paleae* inserted in the *Decretum* of Gratian (1140), especially the two which were attributed to the spurious Council of Nantes, which was believed to have been held at the end of the ninth century.[88]

According to these laws the priest could not allow the faithful from another parish to assist at Mass on Sundays or feast days unless they could show proper permission.[89] These *Paleae* were indeed of uncertain origin, yet they enjoyed a widespread application in the shaping of ecclesiastical discipline.[90] Regardless of their actual lack of authenticity, they seemed to wield an effective influence, for by the end of the twelfth century the obligation of the people to assist at Mass in the proper parish, at least on certain days, had become a duty which was enforceable as a well-founded parochial right, at least to such an extent that Bernard of Pavia (+ 1213) could write: "Habet autem hic ius ecclesia in parochia sua, videlicet, ut populous pro divinis officiis illuc debeat convenire, et maxime in maioribus solemnitatibus."[91]

These restrictions indicative of the proper place for attendance at Mass necessarily strengthened the parochial nature of the administration of Holy Communion. Of course the connection between these two functions was quite necessary. But the reason for the restriction was to be sought, not exclusively in the reservation of the place of attendance at Mass for its own sake, but also, as Thomassinus (1619-1695) inferred, in the ever-present risk that someone might be fraudulently admitted to Holy Communion.[92]

---

[88] Fournier (1885-1935)—Le Bras, *Histoire des Collections Canoniques en Occident depuis les Fausses Décrétales jusqu' au Décret de Gratien* (2 vols., Paris: Recueil Sirey, 1931-1932), I, 259.

[89] Cc. 4, 5, C. IX, q. 2.

[90] Regino of Prüm (+ 915), *Libri Duo de Synodalibus Causis,* Lib. II, cap. 61—*MPL,* CXXXII, 203; Burchard (+ 1025), *Decretorum Libri Viginti,* lib. II, cap. 91, 92—*MPL,* CXL, 642.

[91] *Summa Decretalium* (ed. E. A. T. Laspeyres, Ratisbonae, 1860, lib. III, tit. 25, n. 104.

[92] "Suberat et alia ratio: Ut ne videlicet quos proprius parochus sacris interdixerat, aut ad tempus abstinuerat, ii parocho ab alio fraudulenter et inpune admitterentur ad synaxin et ad communionem."—*Vetus et Nova*

In the *Decretum* of Gratian there was no direct indication that the parish priest enjoyed exclusive prerogatives in the administration of Holy Communion. But in it there was evidence of the Church's solicitude for the sick, and in the laws taken from particular councils the priest was warned to have the Blessed Sacrament always prepared, so that he might take It to the dying.[93] Another law found in the *Decretum* reminded the priest that it was his personal obligation to care for the sick, and that he should not allow the Eucharist needlessly to be carried by lay people. Compliance with this law was ordered under threat of severe penalty.[94]

In 1215 the IV General Council of the Lateran enacted the first general legislation which gave evidence of the parochial right in the administration of Holy Communion.[95] This was the first explicit reference to the *"proprius sacerdos"* in regard to the administration of Holy Communion. There had indeed been legislation which ordered the reception of the Eucharist on certain feasts, or a certain number of times a year, but without any reference to the proper priest as the agent of Its administration.[96]

So, for the first time the law granted to the proper priest definite and certain discretionary powers relative to the administration of at least the Easter Communion. Whether the parishioner should fulfill the precept or temporarily defer its fulfillment was left to the judgment of the parochial priest. It is true that the law did not specify any set place for the reception of this Communion,

---

Ecclesiae Disciplina circa Beneficia et Beneficiarios (10 vols., Magontiaci 1787), Pars I, lib. II, cap. 24, n. 5 (hereafter cited *Ecclesiae Disciplina*).

[93] Cf. c. 93, D. II, *de cons.*

[94] C. 29, D. II, *de cons.*

[95] Can. 21: "Omnis utriusque sexus fidelis, postquam ad annos discretionis pervenerit, onmia sua solus peccata saltem semel in anno fideliter confiteatur proprio sacerdoti, et iniunctam sibi poenitentiam propriis viribus studeat adimplere, suscipiens reverenter ad minus in Pascha Eucharistiae sacramentum, nisi forte de proprii sacerdotis consilio ob aliquam rationabilem causam ad tempus ab huiusmodi perceptione duxerit abstinendum: alioquin et vivens ab ingressu ecclesiae arceatur, et moriens Christiana careat sepultura."—c. 12, X, *de poenitentiis et remissionibus,* V, 38.

[96] Cf. cc. 16, 17, 19, D. II, *de cons.*

but the right as accorded to the pastor[97] indicated that he was to have knowledge of the fulfillment of the Easter duty, which knowledge could most readily be gained if the fulfillment of this duty was undertaken in the proper parish church.

Bernard of Parma (+ 1266) in the gloss on this canon stated that the *"proprius sacerdos,"* that is, the *"curator parochialis,"* was he who had the right under the law, and also the accompanying duty, of securing the fulfillment of this obligation. This right he held to the exclusion of any other priest, secular or religious.[98] The same glossator explained at some length that even the privileges which the Mendicants had received from the Pope himself were of no avail if their use implied any prejudice to the right of the *"propius sacerdos."* The possession of the privilege notwithstanding, they could not invoke its use apart from the permission of the proper priest.[99]

However, Panormitanus (1386-1453) taught that residential bishops or papal legates, also their penitentiaries, and even their vicars general, could give the necessary permission in place of the parochial priest.[100] He referred to a gloss of Ioannes Andreae (+ 1348) on another canon, in which the latter maintained that a bishop's granted permission had valid effect for the lay people,

---

[97] While the term "pastor" as it is known today came into use with the celebration of the Council of Trent (1545-1563), Hostiensis in his comment on this law made it clear who the "proprius sacerdos" was. He was the one to whom the parochial care (*cura*) was committed, and who, either in his own person or by means of a vicar, was bound to maintain residence within the parish. His *"cura"* connoted the duty of watchfulness and solicitude for the souls which he was to lead to salvation, and hence it involved not only the duty of administering the sacraments, but also the tasks of instructing, of visiting, of guiding, of correcting—in a word, of doing whatever was requisite for gaining the salvation of the souls entrusted to him. —Hostiensis, *Summa Aurea* (Venetiis, 1570), lib V, tit. 38, c. 12.

[98] *Glossa Ordinaria* ad c. 12, X, *de poenitentiis et remissionibus,* V, 38, s.v. *alieno sacerdoti.*

[99] "Nec papa, per talem indulgentiam intendit praeiudicare proprio sacerdoti."—*Casus* ad c. 12, X, *de poenitentiis et remissionibus,* V, 38.

[100] Nicholaus de Tudeschis (Abbas Panormitanus), *Commentarium in Quinque Libros Decretalium* (5 vols. in 7, Venetiis, 1588), Lib. V. tit. 38, c. 12 (hereafter cited Panormitanus).

similarly as it had valid effect when he issued it in favor of his own officials.[101]

Ioannes Andreae referred to the same question in another gloss. There he stated that, although the permission of the pastor was necessary in order that any other priest might perform one of the reserved parochial functions, such as the administration of Holy Communion, yet the bishop also could grant the same permission. This held inasmuch as the entire diocese was constituted as the parish of the bishop. The bishop could beyond all doubt grant such a permission when the parish was vacant, and it appeared altogether admissible for him to grant the same permission also when the parish was occupied. Still the Glossator cautiously insinuated that it seemed preferable for the people not to approach the bishop with their request for this permission under the latter circumstances.[102]

The provisions of the law as enacted in the canon *"Omnis utriusque sexus"* concerning the reception and the administration of Holy Communion were embodied in the canons of later councils, which called attention once more to these regulations, and thus sought to gain greater compliance with them. The Council of Padua in 1339 forbade any priest, chaplain or cleric to enter the parish of another to administer the sacraments. Permission was likewise needed for the person to receive the sacraments from any priest other than the proper parish priest. The obligation was placed on both parties, the minister and the recipient alike.[103] The Council of Cologne in 1310 was quite specific. Canon 20 stated: "Statuimus item, ut nullus parochianus ab alio quam a suo vero plebano communionem recipiat, nisi de hoc privilegiis authenticis sit munitus."[104]

St. Thomas (1225-1274) in the *Supplement* to the *Summa*

---

[101] *Glossa Ordinaria* ad c. 2, *de poenitentiis et remissionibus,* V, 10, in VI°, s.v. *suo subdito.*

[102] *Glossa Ordinaria* ad c. 1, *de privilegiis et excessibus privilegiatorum,* V, 7, in Clem., s.v. *presbyteri.*

[103] C. 12—Mansi, XXV, 1137.

[104] Mansi, XXV, 242. See also the Council of Paris (1212-1213), cap. 10—Mansi, XXII, 822; the Council of Avignon (1282), c. 5—Mansi, XXIV, 442; the Council of Avignon (1337), c. 4—Mansi, XXV, 1089.

indicated just how definitely the administration of Holy Communion had become a parochial function. He found it necessary to affirm the validity of the sacrament when it was administered by someone other than the parish priest.[105]

The rights of the proper priest were further strengthened by the General Council of Vienne (1311-1312). This Council threatened with an *ipso facto* ensuing excommunication any religious who administered Holy Communion without the permission of the proper priest.[106] This law was indeed quite comprehensive in its literal meaning, but its import seemed not entirely clear. Ioannes Andreae in his gloss immediately narrowed the potential sphere of its application. He interpreted the phrase *"sacramentum Eucharistiae ministrare"* as pointing to the distribution of Holy Communion *"in die paschae."*[107] Certainly he did not intend to exclude Viaticum, for that function was definitely a parochial function.[108]

This law of the General Council of Vienne was directed against religious, and thus the enacted penalty applied only to them. Religious were required to obtain permission from the parish priest, in fact a *"specialis licentia,"* or else suffer the threatened excommunication. The Glossator identified the parochial priest as the one in whose parish the faithful held residence.[109] But he seemed hesitant in determining whether for the granting of the requisite special permission there was need of expressly adverting not only to the person of the recipient, but also the person of the religious who was to be the minister, as also to the nature of the sacrament he was to administer. He deemed such a comprehensive form of permission advisable. Nevertheless he reflected his own opinion in the following statement: "Crederem

---

105 *Supplementum,* q. 8, a. 4, ad 2.

106 Can. 16: "Religiosi, qui clericis aut laicis sacramentum unctionis extremae vel eucharistiae ministrare, matrimoniave solemnizare, non habita super his parochialis presbyteri licentia, . . . praesumpserint, excommunicationis incurrant sententiam ipso facto, per sedem apostolicam duntaxat absolvendi."—c. 1, *de privilegiis et excessibus privilegiatorum,* V, 7, in Clem.

107 *Glossa Ordinaria, ibid.,* ad *Casum.*

108 Council of Aix-la-Chapelle (836), cap. 5—*MGH, Leges in 4,* Sectio III, *Concilia,* Tom. II, pars II, 711-712.

109 *Glossa Ordinaria, ibid.,* s.v. *parochialis.*

tamen quod ex quo de sacramento fit specificatio, licet non exprimatur nomen parochiani cum datur licentia, parochiano evitetur poena."[110]

Section 2. The Privileges of Religious

Previous to the IV General Council of the Lateran (1215) there was little reference to any interference on the part of religious in the matter of parochial ministrations. An exception to the general practice was granted in their favor by Pope Paschal II (1099-1118) when in 1113 he decided in favor of the Benedictine Abbey of St. Vaast at Arras over the Canons of Arras in whose parish the Abbey was located. Paschal stated that it was unreasonable for the people who had been admitted all year long to the religious chapel to be excluded on feast days from Holy Communion. He further allowed any that would want to receive Holy Communion in the religious chapel to feel free to do so.[111]

On the other hand, Honorius II (1124-1130) confirmed the right of the parish church, especially with reference to the Easter season. And Eugene III (1145-1154) in 1150 decreed that, as a sign of the right of the parish church, a parish priest should distribute Holy Communion at Easter time in the Chapel of the Abbey of St. Victor in the Diocese of Tarascon in Southern France.[112]

However, during the period from the thirteenth to the sixteenth century there was much conflict between the parish priests and the new Mendicant Orders. The monasteries previously had infringed on the rights of the parish only passively, if at all, but with the rise of the Mendicants difficulties arose. These new Orders with their mixed contemplative and active life very often, in their zeal, overstepped the limits and privileges of the office. Needless to say, the guilt was not all one-sided, but this fact only added bitterness to the conflict. The controversy became so heated that in 1321 Pope John XXII (1316-1334) had to in-

---

[110] *Glossa Ordinaria, ibid.*, s.v. *specali.*

[111] Paschalis II, const. *"Dissensio, quae,"* 7 nov. 1113—Jaffé, n. 6359; *MPL*, CLXII I, 333.

[112] Cited by Browe, "Die Kommunion in der Pfarrkirche," *Zeitschrift für Katholische Theologie* (Innsbruck, 1877-), LIII (1929), 504.

tervene. Ioannes de Polliaco (Jean Pouilly, died after 1322), a master of theology at the University of Paris, claimed that neither God nor anyone else could dispense from the obligation of receiving the Easter Communion in the parish church. The Pope condemned this teaching as erroneous, false and contrary to the Catholic faith.[113]

It was the practice of the Popes always to uphold the right of the parish priest in regard to the Paschal Communion, but at the same time they conceded ample liberty to the Friars in administering Communion outside of the Paschal season. Benedict XII (1334-1342) insisted that the Communion of precept was not to be administered by any religious unless they had the permission of the parish priest.[114] In the faculties given by Pope Paul III (1534-1549) to the religious Orders which were being organized in his time, specific exception was made to the administration of the Eucharist on Easter Sunday. Holy Communion could be administered to all who asked to receive It, except on this one particular day.[115]

With reference to those who lived at the religious house the ruling was difficult. Religious could on the very day of Easter itself administer the Easter Communion to those who were lodged at the monasteries, such as the domestics, the poor and the sick. This special privilege, traditionally observed at the Benedictine monasteries, was safeguarded by the Council of Vienne (1311-1312).[116] This right had previously been acknowledged by Innocent IV (1243-1254) in his constitution *"Qui Leum."*[117]

[113] Const. *"Vas electionis,"*—21 iul. 1321—c. 2, *de hereticis,* V, 3, in Extravag. com.; Denzinger, *Enchiridion,* n. 493.

[114] *Bullarium Franciscanum* (4 vols., ed. J. H. Sbaralea, Romae, 1759-1768), IV, 60.

[115] Paulus III, const. *"Dudum felicis,"* 25 iul. 1535—*Bullarum Diplomatum et Privilegiorum Sanctorum Romanorum Pontificum Taurinensis Editio* (24 vols., et Appendix, Augustae Taurinorum, 1857-1872), VI, 192 (hereafter cited *Bull. Rom.*); const. *"Licet debitum,"* 18 oct. 1549—*Bull. Rom.,* VI, 399.

[116] Can. 16—c. 1, *de privilegiis et excessibus privilegiatorum,* V, 7, in Clem.

[117] 3 febr. 1244—Potthast (1824-1898), *Regesta Pontificum Romanorum inde ab anno post Christum natum NCXCVIII ad annum MCCCIV* (2 vols., Berolini, 1874-1875), n. 11240.

This immunity was not restricted to the monasteries alone but was extended also to the infirmaries and hospitals conducted by the religious. The General Council of Vienne took cognizance of the existence of hospitals exempted from the parochial care, and ordered that where these existed they were to be continued in that status, inasmuch as legal prescription had set in against the parish priest. However, if the parochial priest had continued serving the hospital, then his rights were confirmed.[118]

In many cases custom may have furnished the reason in the first place for the exemption that arose. Van Espen (1646-1728) noted that frequently in individual cases the origin of the custom derived from an agreement between the parish priest and those who had charge of the hospital. When it was found that such an arrangement would be to the advantage of both parties, it was quite natural for an agreement to be reached.[119] Many times it was the factor of custom rather than the enactment of any law or the possession of any privilege that enabled Rome to settle disputes between pastors and hospitals or their chaplains regarding the question of the hospital's exemption.[120]

It was canon 16 of the Council of Vienne that made this exemption quite specific. It is to be remembered that the hospitals were conducted for the most part by religious. Consequently the Council freed from the obligation of obtaining any special permission for the administration of the sacraments all those religious who held from the Holy See the privilege to care for the domestics, the poor, or the sick who were lodged at their institution.[121]

Despite the close association of the Tertiaries with the Orders, the parish priest retained the right to give them Communion on

---

[118] Can. 7—c. 2, *de religiosis domibus, ut episcopo sint subiectae,* III, 11, in Clem.

[119] *Ius Ecclesiasticum Universum* (10 vols., Venetiis, 1769) lib. II, tit. VI, cap. III, n. 42.

[120] Bouix, *Tractatus de Parocho* (3. ed., Paris, 1880), p. 653.

[121] Can. 16; "Sane, religiosis illis, quibus est ab apostolica sede concessum, ut familiaribus suis domesticis, aut pauperibus, in hospitalibus suis degentibus, sacramenta possint ecclesiastica ministrare, nullum ex praemissis volumus quoad hoc praeiudicium generari."—c. 1, *de privilegiis et excessibus privilegiatorum,* V, 7, in Clem.

Easter Sunday.[122] In fact, the Tertiaries of St. Francis de Paul (+ 1507) were to receive Communion in their parish church on four great feasts. They were to receive in the parochial church on Christmas, on Pentecost, on the feast of the Assumption, as well as on Easter Sunday.[123]

By reason of their privilege, many religious could administer Holy Communion to the faithful in their own churches on all days except Easter Sunday. From 1474 to 1563 there existed among the religious Orders a general intercommunication in their mutual privileges.[124] As a result of this the extant privileges became very widespread. This meant that at the time of the Council of Trent (1545-1563) the pastor had lost his exclusive right to administer Holy Communion at all other times than on the day of Easter itself.

Section 3. The Exclusive Right of the Parish Priest to Administer Holy Communion to the Dying

Along with the pastor's obligation of administering the Easter Communion, his obligation of administering Holy Viaticum also came to be reserved. As indicated earlier, the Church was very solicitous for the welfare of the sick and strove to see that no one would die without the consolations that were to be derived from the reception of Holy Viaticum. For this reason Gratian included in his *Decretum* a canon which ordered the priest to have the Eucharist always ready with a view to taking Holy Communion to the dying.[125]

He likewise included in his *Decretum* the text of a law which insisted that the fulfillment of the obligation to receive Holy Communion when in danger of death was to be cared for by the priest personally, unless it became impossible for him to exercise that care through his personal act.[126] This was certainly not

---

[122] Leo X (1513-1521), const. "*Nuper,*" I mart. 1518—*Bull. Rom.*, V, 689.

[123] Alexander VI (1492-1503), const. "*Ad ea,*" 1 maii 1501—*Bull. Rom.*, V, 392.

[124] Cf. *Bull. Rom.*, V, 212; V, 212-223; V, 471, VI, 144; VII, 471; VII, 584; VII, 923; XI, 608; etc.

[125] C. 93, D. II, *de cons.*

[126] C. 29, D. II, *de cons.*

novel legislation, for many particular councils had stressed the duty of the parish priest in taking care of the sick.[127]

So desirous was the Church that no one should die without the reception of Holy Viaticum, that even during the time of a general interdict the priest could give Viaticum, although he was not to administer extreme unction.[128] Likewise, Gregory IX (1227-1241), in order that the Eucharist might always be ready for administration, allowed the rectors of churches to say Mass once a week during such an interdict.[129] The Glossator in the *casus* on this law indicated that it was the concern of the parochial priest to see that the Eucharist was kept ready for administration during the time of an interdict.[130] This in itself furnished evidence that the administration of Holy Viaticum was regarded as a parochial function.

The jurisprudence of the time was quite unanimous in agreeing that the parish priest had the right and the duty of carrying the Eucharist to the sick. Hostiensis (+ 1271) pointed out that it was the parochial priest, the one who was held to residence in the parish, who had the obligation of administering to the people in their needs. He was to carry the Eucharist to the sick, and was to do so with reverence and respect. He was to instruct his people to be devout and respectful in the presence of the Blessed Sacrament. But most of all he was to spare no effort in order to make sure that none would die without the reception of Holy Viaticum.[131]

Panormitanus (1386-1453) propounded the same view. The *"sacerdos parochialis"* was obliged to exercise a special care for the sick. He was never presumptuously to leave the city without first having visited the sick in order to make sure that no one would die without having received the last sacraments.[132]

---

[127] Council of Aix-la-Chapelle (836), *De Vita et Doctrina Inferiorum Ordinum,* cap. 5—*MGH, Leges in 4,* Sectio III, *Concilia,* Tom. II, pars II, 711-712; Council of Anse (990), c. 1—Mansi, XIX, 101; Council of Avignon (1282), c. 5—Mansi, XXIV, 422.

[128] C. II, X, *de poenitentiis et remissionibus,* V, 38.

[129] C. 57, X, *de sententia excommunicationis,* V, 39.

[130] *Casus* ad c. 57, X, *de sententia excommunicationis,* V, 39.

[131] *Commentaria,* lib. III, tit. 41, c. 10; lib. III, tit 44, c. 1; lib. V, tit. 38, c. 12.

[132] Panormitanus, lib. III, tit. 41, c. 1.

Religious Orders were quite restrained in the matter of administering Holy Viaticum. The caution exercised by them can be understood in view of the emphatic regulations of Leo X (1513-1521). In 1516 he forbade Regulars to administer to the sick and dying even after the pastor had denied them his priestly service. Priests religious could administer the sacraments only if they could prove a just cause for their doing so, this cause being sworn to under seal of a notary or in the presence of two witnesses. Leo X further ordered that the administration of the sacraments to lay people who served in a monastery was to be limited to the time when they were actually under the obedience of the religious superior.[133]

The privileges as accorded to religious Orders also give evidence of this prevailing attitude. For example, the faculties given by Pope Paul III (1534-1549) to the Jesuits in 1549 illustrate the practice of the Church. The Jesuits were specifically forbidden to give Communion *"in articulo mortis"* unless they had the permission of the proper pastor, or unless there was an urgent need or an emergency.[134]

---

[133] Const. *"Dum intra,"* 19 dec. 1516—*Fontes,* n. 72.
[134] Const. *"Licet debitum,"* 18 oct. 1549—*Bull. Rom.,* VI, 399.

CHAPTER II

Legislation from the Council of Trent (1545-1563) to the Code of Canon Law (1918)

ARTICLE 1. THE MINISTER OF HOLY COMMUNION BY REASON OF ORDINATION

Section 1. The Ordinary Minister

The discipline of the Church in regard to the minister of Holy Communion was definitely settled prior to the celebration of the Council of Trent (1545-1563). This was to be expected, for the Church was traditionally solicitous to exercise the utmost vigilance lest there creep in any disrespect in the administration of this Most Excellent Sacrament. The period beginning with the Council of Trent effected no drastic changes; rather it was a period of stabilization and of the definitive perfecting of that which was already the law and practice. A development of the canonical reasoning relative to the established practice was a notable characteristic of the period.

The current law was stated succinctly by the Council of Trent in these words: "Semper in Ecclesia Dei mos fuit ut laici a sacerdotibus communionem acciperent; sacerdotes autem celebrantes se ipsos communicarent, qui mos, tamquam ex traditione apostolica descendens, iure ac merito retineri debet."[1] The office of the priest as the *ex officio* designated and ordinary minister of Holy Communion was acknowledged as a sacred heirloom which derived from Apostolic tradition, and consequently, with all justice and reason, the power and dignity of this office were for the future to be accorded the same reverent and respectful recognition.

According to Suarez (1548-1617), the right which the priest possesses by reason of his ordination implies an exclusive authority over the administration of Holy Communion. The priest is given

[1] Sess. XIII, *de Eucharistica,* c. 8.

ordinary powers over the Body of Christ. These powers are ordinary and proper, and extend over Christ's real Body as well as over His Mystical Body. The priest by his ordination has this power *ex iure divino;* it is not given to any other. He has these powers so exclusively that no one inferior to a priest can ever give Holy Communion without the commission of the priest.[2]

The arguments of St. Thomas[3] are quoted and developed by the commentators of the period.[4] Laymann stated that the ordinary power of giving Holy Communion to the Christian people belongs to the priests alone *"ex Christi institutione,"* since priests alone by their ordination receive the power of consecrating. Consequently it is *"valde rationabile"* that the office of dispensing this sacrament should belong to priests. Likewise it belongs to the office of the priest to offer gifts and oblations to God in behalf of the people; it should therefore also be the office of the priest to return gifts from God to the people. The greatest of all God's gifts and mysteries is the Holy Eucharist.[5]

These same reasons of appropriateness and fitness for the administration of Holy Communion by the priest were used again at the end of the nineteenth century by Gasparri (1852-1934), a fact that illustrates the constant tradition of the Church in this doctrine and practice.[6]

This constant tradition was again emphasized in the twentieth century in an official document of the Church. Leo XIII (1878-1903) in his Encyclical *Mirae caritatis* of May 28, 1902, reaffirmed the ancient law and practice with these words: "Sacerdotes, enim, quibus Christus Redemptor Corporis et Sanguinis sui mysteria conficiendi ac dispensandi tradidit munus. . . ."[7]

---

[2] *Tertia Pars Summae Theologicae,* Disp. LXXII, Sect. I, nn. 4, 5—*Opera Omnia,* XXI, 576, 577.

[3] *Summa,* Pars III, q. 82, a. 3.

[4] Cf. Laymann (1574-1635), *Theologia Moralis in quinque libros partita* (5 vols. in 1, Venetiis, 1719), Lib. V, Tract. IV, cap. VII, n. 1 (hereafter cited Laymann); Schmalzgrueber, Lib. tit. 41, n. 10; Gasparri, *De Eucharistia,* II, n. 1069.

[5] Laymann, Lib. V, Tract IV, Cap. VII, n. 1.

[6] Gasparri, *De Eucharistia,* II, n. 1069.

[7] *Codicis Iuris Canonici Fontes,* cura Emi Petri Card. Gasparri editi (9 vols., Romae: Typis Polyglottis Vaticanis, 1923-1939; [Vols. VII, VIII, IX,

The Council of Trent had stated that the priest in celebrating Mass was to communicate himself.[8] But could a priest give Communion to himself when he was impeded from saying Mass? If no other priest was available, and if no irreverence or scandal intervened, he could certainly give Viaticum to himself and even the Communion of devotion.[9] De Lugo (1583-1660) regarded this common opinion as being involved in many difficulties. Yet, though he felt that a priest who thus received the Communion of devotion at his own hand exchanged, as it were, his priestly status for a lay status in the act of reception, he eventually conceded the admissibility of this manner of communicating on the part of a priest as an act which could not with certainty be stigmatized as sinful.[10]

The reason why a priest may administer Communion to himself was elucidated further by Barbosa (1589-1649). He explained that there was no intrinsic reason which precluded the minister and the recipient of the Eucharist from being identified in one and the same person. In the act of contracting marriage the two Christian parties administer to themselves the sacrament of matrimony; likewise prelates make themselves the recipients of their own indulgences. A person, it is true, cannot beget himself, and hence likewise can not achieve his own spiritual birth through baptism of himself. Similarly no one can exercise confessional

---

ed. cura et studio Emi Iustiniani Card Serédi]), n. 648 (hereafter cited *Fontes*).

[8] Sess. XIII, *de Eucharistia*, c. 8.

[9] Laymann, Lib. V, Tract. IV, Cap. VII, n. 6; Suarez, *Tertia Pars Summae Theologicae*, Disp. LXXII, Sect. III, n. 3—*Opera Omnia*, XXI, 587; St. Alphonsus M. de Ligorio (1696-1787), *Theologia Moralis* (ed. L. Gaudé, 4 vols., Romae, 1905-1912), Lib. VI, n. 238; Ballerini (1805-1881)-Palmieri (1829-1909), *Opus Theologicum Morale* (3 ed., 7 vols., Prati, 1898-1901). Tract. X, Sect. IV, n. 93 (hereafter cited Ballerini-Palmieri); Gasparri, *De Eucharistia*, II, n. 1081; Lehmkuhl (1834-1918), *Theologia Moralis* (12. ed., 2 vols., Friburgi Brisgoviae, 1914), II, n. 183; Genicot (1856-1900)-Salsmans (1873-1944), *Theologiae Moralis Institutiones* (6. ed., 2 vols., Bruxellis, 1909), II, n. 182.

[10] De Lugo, *Disputationes Scholasticae et Morales* (editio nova accurante Fournials, 8 vols., Pariis, 1868-1869), *Tractatus de Eucharistia*, Disp. XVIII, Sect. I, nn. 28-33 (hereafter cited as De Lugo).

jurisdiction over himself to administer the sacrament of penance to himself. But the act of feeding oneself holds no inner contradiction within itself. The act of communicating oneself is simply the act of administering spiritual food to oneself. So with equal reason a priest can be both the minister and the recipient of the spiritual food which the Blessed Eucharist is in all truth and reality.[11]

Section 2. The Extraordinary Minister

From the beginning of the Church the deacon had been the auxiliary and subsidiary minister of Holy Communion. Once his ministry was quite useful and necessary, as it was his duty to carry the Chalice of the Sacred Blood when Communion was given under both species. Later he could exercise this function of administering Communion only when necessity arose. The deacon's status in this regard was not altered by the Council of Trent. He remained the extraordinary minister of Holy Communion. Through his ordination to the diaconate he acquired this secondary ministry, which was to be exercised under the commission of the priest. He was to be the aid or instrument of the priest in the administration of Holy Communion, when he was either expressly or at least presumably authorized by the priest to exercise this function.[12]

The Council of Trent called attention to the fact that from the very manner of Christ's institution of the Holy Eucharist It falls under the power and authority of the priest.[13] Yet it has not been made necessary, by any demand inherent in the divine law, that the priest give this sacrament to the faithful with his own hand. This duty may be committed to others. Christ was primarily concerned with the consecration of the Eucharist when he gave his command to the Apostles.[14] The Church may decide how this

---

[11] Barbosa, *De officio et Potestate Parochi Descriptio* (ed. U. Giraldi a S. Cajetano, Romae, 1774), Pars II, Cap. XX, n. 23.

[12] Gasparri, *De Eucharistia,* II, n. 1079; also De Lugo, Disp. XVIII, Sect. I, n. 12.

[13] Sess. XIII, *de Eucharistia,* c. 8; sess. XXIII, *de ordine,* c. 1.

[14] Luke, XXII:19.

sacrament is to be dispensed to the faithful according to the needs of the faithful and the exigencies of the time.[15]

Suarez saw no deformity in the authorization of the deacon to administer Holy Communion as long as the deacon acted under the authority of the priest.[16] Without this authorization the deacon certain acted illicitly, and according to the older authors he also incurred an irregularity.[17] But at a later time Ballerini (1805-1881) pointed out that the incurring of this irregularity remained factually a doubtful issue, since the deacon did not perform any act which was certainly beyond the powers inherent in his ordination to the diaconate.[18] Gasparri concurred in this opinion.[19]

The law as incorporated in the *Decretum* of Gratian remained the basic law. The deacon could administer Communion in a case of necessity if he had the commission of the priest. In the presence of a priest this commission needed to be given expressly, but in his absence it could rightfully be presumed. Yet in all cases a true necessity was postulated.[20]

What nature or character did the postulated necessity call for? As Woywod (1880-1941) pointed out, the pre-Code commentators in practice interpreted necessity in the sense of a cause or a reason. By *necessitas* they referred to an occasion which served to justify the action of the deacon.[21]

St. Alphonsus considered the question of this required necessity at some length. He stated that some authors demanded the presence of an extreme necessity, so that the deason's ministry could be employed only in the event that his services were indispensable for the administration of Holy Viaticum. Others, he noted, required only a grave necessity, which he identified with

---

[15] Laymann, Lib. V, Tract. IV, Cap. VII, n. 2.

[16] Suarez, *Tertia Pars Summae Theologicae,* Disp. LXXII, Sect. I, nn. 6, 7 —*Opera Omnia* XXI, 577.

[17] St. Alphonsus, *Theologia Moralis,* Lib. VI, n. 234; Laymann, Tract. V, Cap. VII, n. 3.

[18] Ballerini-Palmieri, Tract. X, Sect. IV, n. 85.

[19] *De Eucharistia,* II, n. 1079.

[20] Cc. 13, 18, D. XCIII.

[21] Woywod, *A Practical Commentary on the Code of Canon Law* (fifth, revised edition, 2 vols., New York: J. Wagner, Inc., 1939), I, 403 (hereafter cited *Practical Commentary*).

the notion of great utility and convenience for the faithful. Such a necessity was present if on a feast day a large number of persons who wished to receive Holy Communion suffered a delay in consequence of the priest's unaided distribution, or if some of the faithful reasonably presented themselves for the reception of Holy Communion while the priest was busy with the hearing of confessions, or the preaching of a sermon, or the giving of a catechetical instruction.[22]

Although St. Alphonsus pointed with emphasis to the universal agreement which held that in case of extreme necessity when a priest was not present the deacon was both authorized and obliged to take Viaticum to a dying person, he seemed willing to accept the milder opinion, for he did not register any specific objection to it.[23]

Because of the greater number of priests as compared with their number in the early days of the Church, Barbosa (1589-1649) had thought that the deacon could not administer Holy Communion unless there existed a most grave cause and at the same time an urgent necessity. This meant that the deacon could act only *"in articulo mortis"* upon the previous order of the bishop or of the priest if either was present. But the normally required permission was rightfully to be presumed if the priest was absent, unable, or unjustly unwilling to take Viaticum to the dying person.[24]

Witasse (1660-1716) followed the lead of Barbosa. He likewise adopted the more rigid opinion that only an extreme emergency justified the act of distribution by the deacon, for the ancient prerogative of the deacon in this regard had become obsolete. Such an extreme emergency existed when Holy Viaticum had to be taken to a dying person who without the deacon's services would have been deprived of this grace.[25]

Even before Witasse and Barbosa presented this doctrine, Laymann (1574-1635) had admitted the partial validity of the arguments later stressed by these two authors. Laymann granted

[22] *Theologia Moralis,* Lib. VI, n. 237.

[23] *Loc. cit.*

[24] *De Officio et Potestate Parochi Descriptio,* Pars II, Cap. XX, n. 4.

[25] *De Augustissimo Eucharistiae Sacramento,* p. 462.

that the greater number of priests available, as also the fact that Communion was being distributed only under one species, called much less frequently than in former times for the deacon's service in the administering of Communion. Despite this admission he held to the common opinion, namely, that not an extreme emergency but only a grave cause was requisite for the allowable distribution of Communion on the part of a deacon whenever a priest was not available.[26]

This opinion was held commonly by the commentators before the advent of the present Code. The deacon by his ordination was the extraordinary minister of Holy Communion, and all that was required was a grave cause in connection with the non-availability of a priest who could conveniently care for the legitimate needs of the faithful.[27]

It is certain that the deacon was not entitled to act unless there was a necessity. This is clear from the response of the Sacred Congregation of Rites given February 25, 1777, to a question asked by Augustine Motuski of the Order of Friars Minor of the Observance of St. Francis. He had asked whether one who was only in the Order of the diaconate was allowed to administer Holy Communion outside of the case of necessity. The response was in the negative, with the admonition that it was to be so observed.[28] This response did not touch the question of grave or of extreme necessity; it simply implied that some necessity was required.

Another response of the same Congregation pertained to the question of the necessity postulated as a condition if the deacon was rightfully to administer the Holy Eucharist. This response of the Sacred Congregation of Rites to the Most Reverend Charles Jeantet, Coadjutor Apostolic Vicar of Tonkin, French Indo-China, touched primarily on rubrical considerations, but the reply

---

[26] Lib. V, Tract. IV, Cap. VII, n. 2.

[27] Suarez, *Tertia Pars Summae Theologicae,* Disp. LXXII, Sect. I, n. 8—*Opera Omnia,* XXI, 578; Schmalzgrueber, Lib. III, tit. 41, n. 11; Gasparri, *De Eucharistia,* II, n. 1079; Gury (1801-1866), *Compendium Theologiae Moralis* (ed. tertia ab H. Dumas, 2 vols., Parisiis, 1881), II, n. 289; Genicot-Salsmans, *Theologiae Moralis Institutiones,* II, n. 181; Ballerini-Palmieri, Tract. X, Sect. IV, n. 89; Lehmkuhl, *Theologiae Moralis,* II, n. 180.

[28] *Fontes,* n. 5815.

is important for the matter at hand. It was asked if a deacon *"ex mandato sui vicarii,"* when taking Viaticum to the sick, could perform the usual ceremonies for giving Communion to the sick. The answer was significant: "Deficiente presbytero et vicarii Apostolici concurrente licentia, affirmative in omnibus."[29]

This reply of the Sacred Congregation dealt fundamentally indeed with the right of the deacon to give Communion. Apart from the question of the ceremonies involved, the reply stated that, with the vicar's permission in the absence of any available priest, the deacon could give Holy Viaticum. Did this mean that the deacon could act at the commission of his superior even though no grave cause existed? The raising of this question furnishes occasion for adverting to an opinion which had been repudiated by Suarez and St. Alphonsus. The opinion had been advanced by Sylvester Prieras (+ 1523) when he stated that the command of the bishop or of the priest was sufficient in itself to warrant the distribution of Communion by the deacon even though no grave need was present.[30] It does not appear that the response which was given in 1858 upheld the opinion of Sylvester Prieras. It must be remembered that the question in itself prescinded from the cause or the necessity, so that the phrase *"ex mandato sui vicarii"* did not necessarily imply that the deacon acted on the order of his superior apart from the existence of a grave reason. Rather, the case indicated that a very grave reason was present. The non-availability of priests to administer Holy Viaticum was always considered by the authors as constituting a grave necessity. And that was precisely the background in which the case was presented.

If under permissive circumstances the deacon could provide for the needs of the faithful, then he could likewise provide for his own needs. All agreed that at the hour of death, in the event that a priest was not available, the deacon could administer Holy Viaticum to himself. Furthermore, the opinion which stood recognized for its greater probability of correctness held that a deacon could communicate himself in simple consideration for his legitimate

---

[29] S.R.C., *Tunkini Occidentalis,* 14 aug. 1858, ad I—*Fontes,* n. 5990.

[30] Suarez, *Tertia Pars Summae Theologicae,* Disp. LXXII, Sect. I, n. 8—*Opera Omnia,* XXI, 578; St. Alphonsus, *Theologia Moralis,* Lib. VI, n. 237.

devotion, provided of course that a priest was not available and that all occasion for scandal was obviated.[31]

Section 3. The Exceptional Minister

Since the Holy Eucharist is the Body and the Blood of Jesus Christ, It must be shown the greatest reverence and respect.[32] Its consecration and administration pertain essentially to the power of Orders.[33] But is there never any warrant for the administration of this Sacrament by the lower clerics or the laity? May not clerics below the diaconate and also the laity under certain conditions give Holy Communion to themselves or to others? The Council of Trent did not consider this practical question, but the post-Tridentine commentators gave it their discussion.

As indicated by Laymann,[34] the law remained as it was explained in the *Glossa Ordinaria* on the *Decretum* of Gratian. With no priest or deacon available, a lower cleric or a Catholic layman could take Viaticum to a dying person.[35]

Suarez[36] and St. Alphonsus[37] explained more fully the rational basis for the law. As a result it was commonly held that in a case of extreme necessity, that is, in an emergency occasioned by the *articulus mortis,* a lay person or a minor cleric could give Holy Viaticum to himself or to another. To act licitly, a lay person or such a cleric could undertake this exceptional procedure only if priest and deacon alike were not available, and even under such

---

[31] Suarez, *Tertia Pars Summae Theologicae,* Disp. LXXII, Sect. III, n. 3—*Opera Omnia,* XXI, 587; Laymann, Lib. V, Tract. IV, Cap. VII, n. 6; DeLugo, Disp. XVIII, Sect. I, n. 35; St. Alphonsus, *Theologia Moralis,* Lib. VI, n. 238; Ballerini-Palmieri, Tract. X, Sect. IV, n. 93; Gasparri, *De Eucharistia,* II, n. 1081; Genicot-Salsmans, *Theologiae Moralis Institutiones,* II, n. 182.

[32] Leo XIII, ep. encycl. *Mirae caritatis* 28 maii, 1902—*Fontes,* n. 648.

[33] Conc. Trident., sess. XXIII, *de ordine,* c. 1; sess. XIII, *de Eucharistia,* c. 8.

[34] *Theologia Moralis,* Lib. V, Tract. IV, Cap. VII, n. 6.

[35] *Glossa* ad c. 29, D. II, *de cons.,* s.v. *per semetipsum.*

[36] *Tertia Pars Summae Theologiae,* Disp. LXXII, Sect. I, n. 6; Sect. III, n. 3—*Opera Omnia,* XXI, 577; XXI, 687.

[37] *Theologia Moralis,* Lib. VI, n. 237.

circumstances the act had always to remain free of the occasion of scandal.[38]

De Lugo (1583-1660) insisted that the opposite doctrine held sway in his time. He stated that both the law and the practice in the Church, in consideration especially of the greater number of men in the priesthood, made any more liberal opinion very difficult to maintain. He admitted that the opinion of Suarez and of Laymann enjoyed some favor of probability by reason of their authority, but he contended that the opinion which denied this right to laymen under any and all conditions unless there acceded the explicit permission of the Holy See constituted the more tenable opinion. The special permission which had been granted to Mary, Queen of Scots, by Pope Sixtus V convinced De Lugo that a special concession of the Pope was necessary even in the most urgent cases.[39]

However, authors of the period held that even the local ordinary could authorize laymen and minor clerics to administer Holy Viaticum during plagues, general pestilences, or other general emergencies.[40] A response of the Sacred Congregation for the Propagation of the Faith indicated that the local ordinary could permit the laity to administer the Holy Eucharist under certain conditions. On July 21, 1841, this Sacred Congregation, in response to a question proposed by the Vicar Apostolic of Tonkin, French Indo-China, stated that as long as the Blessed Sacrament was not exposed to irreverence or danger, confessors condemned to death were to be allowed to take the Holy Eucharist in their

---

[38] St. Alphonsus, *loc. cit.;* Suarez, *loc. cit.;* Laymann, *Theologia Moralis,* Lib. V. Tract. IV, Cap. VII, n. 6; Barbosa, *De Officio et Potestate Parochi Descriptio,* Pars II, Cap. XX, n. 30; Schmalzgrueber, Lib. III, tit. 41, n. 13; Benedictus XIV, *De Synodo Dioecesana* (2 vols., Rome, 1806), Lib. XIII, Cap. XIX, n. 27; Ballerini-Palmieri, Tract. X, Sect. IV, n. 90; Gasparri, *De Eucharistia,* II, n. 1080; D'Annibale (1815-1892), *Summula Theologiae Moralis* (3. ed., 3 vols., Romae, 1889-1892), III, n. 395; Lehmkuhl, *Theologia Moralis,* II, n. 183.

[39] *De Eucharistia,* Disp. XVIII, Sect. I, nn. 24, 25.

[40] Benedictus, XIV, *De Synodo Dioecesana,* Lib. XIII, Cap. XIX, n. 16; Gasparri, *De Eucharistia,* II, n. 1080; D'Annibale, *Summula Theologiae Moralis,* III, n. 395; Lehmkuhl, *Theologia Moralis,* II, n. 183.

own hands and secretly give themselves Communion, lest their priests also be apprehended.[41]

ARTICLE 2. THE PROPER MINISTER OF HOLY COMMUNION

Section 1. Authorization for Lawful Administration of Holy Communion

a. The Pastor by Reason of His Office

The discretionary power of the pastor in the administration of the Easter Communion had been established by the IV General Council of the Lateran (1215).[42] The General Council of Vienne (1311-1312) had further strengthened the parochial right by establishing an automatic penalty of excommunication against any religious who presumed to administer Holy Communion without the permission of the proper pastor.[43]

The *Glossa Ordinaria* had restricted the applicability of this excommunication to the case in which the religious on their own account and without the needed authorization administered Holy Communion on Easter Sunday.[44] This excommunication applied solely to religious. Hence, even apart from the consideration of the many granted and shared privileges which qualified the pastor's exclusive right to administer the Holy Eucharist, that pastoral right was exposed to many potential violations in consequence of the lack of strong penal sanctions that could operate as a deterrent.

The Council of Trent (1545-1563) was to strengthen the right of the pastor considerably. The Council, to effect the reform in the Church that was so much needed, sought to establish a vigorous parochial organization as the basis of the spiritual well-being of the faithful. It insisted on a definite territorial and personal relationship between the pastor and those who were under his care.

---

[41] *Collectanea S. Congregationis de Propaganda Fide* (2 vols., Romae: Typis Polyglottis Vaticanis, 1907), I, n. 928 (hereafter cited *Collectanea*); *Fontes*, n. 4789.

[42] C. 12, X, *de poenitentiis et remissionibus*, V, 38.

[43] C. 1, *de privilegiis et excessibus privilegiatorum*, V, 7, in Clem.

[44] *Casus* ad c. 1, *de privilegiis et excessibus privilegiatorum*, V, 7, in Clem.

Where there was no definite parochial boundary, and where the pastor did not have a definite group of the faithful under his care, the bishop was to effect such an arrangement. There were to be definite and distinct parishes, each with its own pastor. It was from this pastor alone that the parishioners could lawfully receive the sacraments.[45]

The Council emphasized this personal relationship between the pastor and his parishioners, and stressed the consequent exclusive right of the pastor to administer the sacraments.[46] This right of the pastor gave rise to a correlative duty on the part of the people. This reciprocal right and duty consisted in the mutual necessity for the pastor to administer the sacraments only to his own parishioners, and for them to receive them only from him.[47]

Suarez accordingly drew the following conclusion. Along with the power of Orders, for the licit administration of Holy Communion all priests, both religious and secular, needed to possess jurisdiction with respect to the one to whom the Sacrament was to be administered, or they needed to obtain the permission of the one who possessed this jurisdiction.[48] Pastors and others who held offices to which was attached the care of souls had this authority from their office. It was ordinary authority. The pope, the bishop, the pastor, and the religious superior had a right and a duty, as prescribed by the constitution of the Church, to care for the spiritual needs of some of Christ's flock. They were obliged to feed the sheep—each being responsible for a definite group of Christ's fold. For anyone else to usurp this prerogative constituted a grave perversion of due order and authority.[49]

The exclusive right of the pastor to administer Holy Com-

---

[45] Conc. Trident., sess. XXIV, *de ref.*, c. 13.

[46] This right of the territorial pastor was frequently upheld by the Holy See. Cf. for example, S.C.C., *Romana,* 27 aug. 1667—*Fontes,* n. 2802; *Asculana,* 7 iun. 1698—*Fontes,* n. 2962; S.C. de Prop Fide (C.G.), 13 iun. 1662—*Fontes,* n. 4450.

[47] De Luca (1614-1683), *Theatrum veritatis et iustitiae* (16 vols. in 4, Romae, 1706), *De Parocho,* disc. XXII, nn. 8, 9.

[48] *Tertia Pars Summae Theologicae,* Disp. LXXII, Sect. III, n. 2—*Opera Omnia,* XXI, 586.

[49] Suarez, *op. cit.,* Disp. LXXII, Sect. II, nn. 35—*Opera Omnia,* XXI, 580, 581.

munion was not circumscribed in the law in such a manner as to make it applicable solely to the Paschal Communion or to Holy Viaticum. Authors from the time of the Council of Trent made this clear. St. Alphonsus, for example, stated that the needed permission to give Communion could more easily be presumed if the Communion was not one of precept. This certainly implied that a permission was necessary in every case.[50]

As was pointed out by Giraldi of St. Cajetan (1692-1775) in his additions to Barbosa's work, the pastor's right stood confirmed not only against claims alleged by religious, but against the claims pretended by any other priest as well. The older law was definitely extended by the Council of Trent to forbid any priest to usurp the pastor's prerogative of administering Holy Communion.[51] Consequently Gasparri wrote that the distribution of Holy Communion was a function which *"iure proprio"* belonged to the pastor alone, whether the Communion was one of devotion or one of obligation.[52] It was a violation of the pastor's right in a matter of serious importance for anyone to administer the Holy Eucharist at any time without proper authorization.[53]

The pastor had not only the right to administer Holy Communion to the faithful under his care, but he had also an obligation to do so as often as his subjects reasonably asked to receive It, and especially at any time of necessity or when his subjects were obliged by a precept.[54] Outside of the case of necessity the denial did not inherently connote a grave sin if the petition was not fully reasonable, or if it was such that it interfered with the due order in the parish.[55]

---

[50] *Theologia Moralis*, Lib. VI, n. 235.

[51] *De Officio et Potestate Parochi Descriptio*, Pars II, Cap. XX, n. 7, *additio*.

[52] *De Eucharistia*, II, n. 1080.

[53] Ballerini-Palmieri, Tract. X, Sect. IV, n. 83.

[54] St. Alphonsus, *Theologia Moralis*, Lib. VI, n. 233; Suarez, *Tertia Pars Summae Theologicae*, Disp. LXXII, Sect. III, n. 1—*Opera Omnia*, XXI, 586; Bouix, *Tractatus de Parocho*, p. 565; Wernz (1842-1914), *Ius Decretalium* (2. ed., 6 vols. Romae et Prati, 1906-1913), Tom. II, Pars II, p. 1043.

[55] Gasparri, *De Eucharistia*, II, n. 1082; Lehmkuhl, *Theologia Moralis*, II, n. 184.

The obligation of the pastor to administer Holy Communion was rooted in the virtue of justice; the same kind of duty which rested upon any other priest was a task that looked to its fulfillment as a demand made by the virtue of charity.[56] Nevertheless it was commonly held that in the face of great danger to himself the pastor did not need to administer Holy Communion personally, but could procure the fulfillment of the obligation through another. Likewise, since the reception of Holy Viaticum was not an absolute necessity for salvation, the obligation to administer It could cease when great danger threatened the agent in his act of administering It.[57]

Barbosa, basing his argument on the Council of Trent, Session XIII, *de Eucharistia,* c. 6, held that the pastor was obliged personally to take Holy Communion to the sick, even during the time of a general pestilence.[58] Bouix (1808-1870), in following the teaching of Pope Benedict XIV (1740-1758) in this matter, considered the pastor to be under obligation to administer Holy Viaticum during the time of a general danger, unless in doing so he would have been prevented from administering the necessary sacraments of baptism and penance.[59]

The matter was quite fully treated by Fagnanus (1598-1678). This author cited a declaration of Pope Gregory XIII (1572-1585) which approved a particular decree of the Sacred Congregation of the Council on October 12, 1576. This earlier decree had stated that the pastor was held solely to the administration of the sacraments of baptism and of penance during a time of pestilence, and that he had the option of procuring the fulfillment of this obligation either in person or through another, for the pastor had also the concomitant obligation of not exposing the healthy members of his parish to any danger of pestilential infection.

---

[56] Lehmkuhl, *Theologia Moralis,* II, n. 185; Gury, *Theologia Moralis* II, n. 291.

[57] St. Alphonsus, *Theologia Moralis,* Lib. VI, n. 233; Gury, *loc. cit.;* Gasparri, *De Eucharistia,* II, n. 1082; Fagnanus, *Commentaria in Quinque Libros Decretalium* (4 vols., Venetiis, 1697), Lib. III, tit. 4, c. 17, n. 37 (hereafter cited *Commentaria*).

[58] *De Officio et Potestate Parochi Descriptio,* Pars II, Cap. XX, n. 31.

[59] Bouix, *Tractatus de Parocho,* p. 568; Benedictus XIV, *De Synodo Dioecesana,* Lib. XIII, Cap. XIX, n. 7.

Again, on October 26, 1576, the same Pontiff through another decree made it clear that, even though the pastor was willing to administer to the sick, it was better for the general welfare of the parish that this be done by another. On December 23rd of the same year Gregory XIII again ordered that the pastor, inasmuch as he was not obliged to observe residence during the time of a pestilence, was likewise not held in person to administer even the sacraments of baptism or of penance. Hardly, then, could one regard the pastor to be held to administer the Holy Eucharist under similar extenuating circumstances.[60]

b. The Minister by Reason of Delegation

The right to administer Holy Communion could be delegated by the one who had the ordinary authority. This delegation, which accorded the faculty or the permission to administer the sacrament, did not necessarily have to be of an express character. A presumed or an interpretative permission sufficed. The lawful presumption of a granted permission sufficed for the administration of the Holy Eucharist, for no previous sharing of jurisdiction over the recipient was required, as was the case with the sacrament of penance.[61]

To illustrate this point, authors discussed the question of whether a *"sacerdos simplex,"* a priest not approved by the ordinary for the hearing of confessions, could be delegated for the administering of Holy Communion. Barbosa[62] and Leurenius (1646-1723)[63] followed the thought of De Lugo when they maintained that the Council of Trent did not adversely affect or limit the authority of the pastor for allowing a "simple priest" to administer the Holy Eucharist within his parish church or in his parish. The proper pastor could select any priest. It was pointed out that jurisdiction was not necessary for the valid administration of Holy Communion as it was necessary for the hearing of con-

---

[60] *Commentaria,* Lib. III, Tit. 4, c. 17, nn. 37-45.

[61] De Lugo, Disp. XVIII, Sect. II, nn. 37, 39.

[62] *De Officio et Potestate Parochi Descriptio,* Pars II, Cap. XX, n. 6.

[63] *Forum Beneficiale sive Questiones et Responsa Canonica* (2 vols., Venetiis, 1742), Sect. III, Cap. II, n. 5.

fessions, and that there was no reason why the ordinary's approval as based on an examination regarding the priest's qualifications for the hearing of confessions should be required. The pastor was simply allowing a *"sacerdos simplex"* to exercise a power which he fully possessed through his previous ordination to the priesthood.[64]

For the legitimate administration of Holy Communion not only a formal or express permission but also a reasonably presumed permission proved sufficient. The presumption was of course not a reasonable presumption if it was known to stand in opposition to the express will of the pastor.[65] If the pastor was absent, or if he was unable to administer the Holy Eucharist, then in a case of extreme necessity any priest, secular or religious, could presume permission. If the pastor unjustly refused permission, or unjustly refused to administer Holy Viaticum, then the faculty would be presumed by some other priest as having been conceded to him by the bishop, by the pope, or by the law itself.[66]

The use of presumed permission became quite common. Devoti (1744-1820) wrote that in his time permission to administer Holy Communion could be presumed on any occasion except for the Paschal Communion and Holy Viaticum.[67] Santi (1830-1885) maintained that with the exception of the two cases mentioned by Devoti, the administration of the Eucharist could hardly be looked upon as reserved to the pastor. Unless some other hindrance intervened, any priest could give Holy Communion to the faithful without seeking permission except for the Easter Communion and Holy Viaticum.[68] Wernz (1842-1914) made the same observation. He stated that the pastor had the exclusive

---

[64] De Lugo, Disp. XVIII, Sect. II, n. 39.

[65] Ballerini-Palmieri, Tract. X, Sect. IV, n. 84.

[66] Ballerini-Palmieri, *loc. cit.;* Suarez, *Tertia Pars Summae Theologicae,* Disp. LXXII, Sect. I, n. 9—*Opera Omnia,* XXI, 579; Laymann, Lib. V, Tract. IV, Cap. VII, n. 2; Barbosa, *De Officio et Potestate Parochi Descriptio,* Pars II, Cap. XX, n. 2.

[67] *Institutionum Canonicarum Libri Quatuor* (3 vols., Venetiis, 1827), Lib. II, Tit. II, Sect. III, n. xxxxvii.

[68] *Praelectiones Iuris Canonici* (2. ed., 5 vols. in 1, Ratisbonae, 1892), Lib. III, tit. 29, n. 10.

right and duty to administer Holy Communion on Easter Sunday and the Holy Viaticum.[69]

This wide presumption of permission was based on a statement made by the Council of Trent with relation to the Mass. The Council has stated its desire that the faithful who were present at Mass should receive Holy Communion in order to derive the fullest benefit from this Most Holy Sacrifice.[70] Since the Church desired that the faithful receive Holy Communion at the Mass they attended, it was easy to see how there could and did arise the custom of presuming permission to give Holy Communion each time Mass was celebrated. It was reasonable to assume that the pastor wished what was the very evident mind of the Church.[71]

The Sacred Congregation of the Council confirmed this custom on May 17, 1747. In a public oratory established by the ordinary, Holy Communion could be given independently of the pastor during the actual celebration of Mass.[72]

The Church was much slower to grant full authorization for the distribution of Holy Communion in a private oratory. Pope Benedict XIV in 1751 had written that permission for the use of a private oratory did not necessarily include the permission to distribute Holy Communion.[73] And on February 10, 1906, the Sacred Congregation of Rites had declared that it was lawful to distribute Holy Communion to only such persons as were mentioned in the indult which granted the privilege of the private oratory.[74] But this policy was changed by Pope Pius X (1903-1914). On May 8, 1907, Pope Pius X decreed through the Sacred Congregation of Rites that, *"salvis iuribus parochialibus,"* the indult of the use of a private oratory included the faculty

---

[69] *Ius Decretalium,* Tom II, Pars II, p. 1042.

[70] "Optaret quidem sacrosancta synodus, ut in singulis missis fideles adstantes non solum spirituali affectu, sed sacramentali etiam Eucharistiae perceptione communicarent, quo ad eos sanctissimi huius sacrificii fructus uberior proveniret; . . . "—Sess. XXII, *de sacrificio missae,* c. 6.

[71] Santi, *Praelectiones Iuris Canonici,* Lib. III, tit. 29, n. 10.

[72] S.C.C., *Comen.,* 17 maii 1749, ad 4—*Fontes,* n. 3605.

[73] Ep. encycl. *Magna cum,* 2 iun. 1751, § 24—Fontes, n. 413.

[74] *ASS,* XL (1906-1907), 173.

of giving Holy Communion to the faithful assisting there at Mass.[75] The pastor's right to administer the Easter Communion remained intact, but otherwise Communion could thenceforth be distributed whenever Mass was celebrated in a private oratory.

c. The Priest Religious by Reason of Privilege

The Council of Trent did not alter the position of religious in regard to the administation of the Holy Eucharist. The law of the Council of Vienne (1311-1312) remained. By the common law any religious who knowingly presumed to give Holy Communion without the permission of the pastor contracted the censure of excommunication.[76] This permission could be obtained from the pope, from the bishop, or from the pastor, and it could readily be presumed except in the case of a Communion of precept, namely the Easter Communion and Holy Viaticum.[77]

The problem involved the administration of Communion to seculars. The Council of Trent took cognizance of the authority and the responsibility of the religious superior in the spiritual care of those who pertained to the religious family. The religious superiors at the houses of clerical communities certainly could administer the sacraments to those who were of their own household.[78]

Another fundamental point was the fact that the Council of Trent did not abolish the privileges which had been given to religious for the administration of Holy Communion to seculars in the churches of the religious. The privilege of administering Holy Communion in their churches to all the faithful on all days except Easter Sunday had been given to the Franciscans on July 1, 1555, by Pope Paul IV (1555-1559),[79] and this privilege was later specifically extended to all Regulars by Pope St. Pius V

---

[75] S.R.C., *Urbis et Orbis,* 8 maii 1907—*Decreta Authentica Congregationis* Sacrorum Rituum (5 vols. et 2 Appendices, Ex Typographia Polyglotta, 1898-1927), n. *4201* (hereafter cited *DA*); Fontes, n. 6357.

[76] C. 1, *de privilegiis et excessibus privilegiatorum,* V, 7, in Clem.

[77] Barbosa, *De Officio et Potestate Parochi Descriptio,* Pars II, Cap. XX, n. 7; Schmalzgrueber, Lib. III, tit. 29, n. 15.

[78] Sess. XXV, *de regularibus,* c. 1.

[79] Const. *Ex clementi,* § 7—*Bull. Rom.,* VI, 492.

(1566-1572).[80] This grant of Pius V was made after the close of the Council of Trent, but it implied mainly the confirmation of a faculty which most of the religious already possessed. While the Council of Trent had severely restricted the right of Regulars to absolve,[81] no such restriction was effected regarding the privilege to administer Holy Communion.

Who could rightfully be considered free from the parochial jurisdiction? The correct answer to this question was indeed a matter of importance, for to such persons the religious could administer Holy Communion at any and all times. The Council of Trent indicated that all those who were engaged in the actual service of the monastery, who resided therein, and who lived under the obedience of the religious superior were exempt from parochial jurisdiction in view of their actual subjection to the religious superior.[82] This necessarily included the members of the community. It also established a usable norm for determining what laymen, if any, could receive all the sacraments from the religious.

The status of servants at monasteries accordingly needed a more specific determination. Gregory XIII (1572-1585), in his Constitution *Circumspecta* of November 25, 1580, demanded that all three of the following conditions be verified if the servants were to be regarded as subjects of the religious superior: 1) the fact of the servants' actual residence at the monastery; 2) the fact of their actual occupation with the monastery, and 3) the fact of their actual subjection in obedience to the religious superior. The obedience here contemplated was not the obedience which was necessitated by a vow of religion, but simply the subjection to the will of the superior.[83]

Benedict XIV later stressed the same criteria,[84] in line with the policy of the Sacred Congregation of the Council.[85]

---

[80] Const. *Etsi mendicantium,* 16 maii 1567, n. XXIII, § 5—*Fontes,* n. 121.

[81] Sess. XXIII, *de ref.*, c. 15.

[82] Sess. XXIV, *de ref.*, c. 11.

[83] Footnote to *Fontes,* n. 1954.

[84] *Institutiones Ecclesiasticae* (3 vols., Romae, 1784), Cap. LV, n. 7.

[85] S.C.C., iun. 1587—Pallottini, *Collectio omnium conclusionum et resolutionum quae in causis propositis apud Sacram Congregationem Cardinalium S. Concilii Tridentini interpretum prodierunt ab eius institutione*

By apostolic privilege some religious Orders which were engaged in hospital work were exempt from the jurisdiction of the local pastor, and hence the chaplains who served these Orders could administer all the sacraments.[86] No such privileges were enjoyed by the ordinary religious house. If anyone became sick while staying there, the sacraments could not be administered without the permission of the pastor of the territory within which the monastery was located.[87]

Section 2. The Minister of the Paschal Communion

The exclusive right of the pastor in the matter of the Paschal Communion had been established by the IV General Council of the Lateran in 1215.[88] The Council of Trent in no way changed this discipline, for it reminded all the faithful that they were to communicate at Easter time in accord with the precept of the Church's law.[89] The referred to precept could be no other than that of which mention was contained in canon 21 of the IV Lateran Council, as the parallel in regard to the obligation of annual confession clearly indicated.[90]

---

anno MDLXIV ad annum MDCCCLX, distinctis titulis alphabetico ordine per materias digesta (18 vols., Romae, 1868-1895), s.v. *sacramentum,* I, n. 14 (hereafter cited Pallottini) ; S.C.C., *Vratislavien.,* 25 ian. 1738—*Thesaurus Resolutionum Sacrae* Congregationis Concilii (167 vols., Romae, 1718-1908), VIII, 17 (hereafter cited *Thesaurus*).

[86] This was especially true of hospitals established for the poor, and of asylums erected for the lepers. For example, Pius IV (1555-1559) gave the chaplains of the Order of St. Lazarus the right to administer the sacraments to all their hospitals and leper asylums. Cf. Const. *Inter assidua* 18 maii 1565—*Bull. Rom.,* VII, 365. Likewise, on January 4, 1572, in the Bull, *Licet ex debito,* Pius V (1566-1572) approved the Congregation of the Brothers of St. John of God for hospital work, and provided that in all their hospitals a priest was to have care of the brothers and patients under the direct jurisdiction of the local ordinary (*Bull. Rom.,* VII, 960).

[87] S.C.C., *Monopolitana,* 27 sept. 1670—Ferraris, *Prompta Bibliotheca Canonica, Iuridica, Moralis, Theologia, necnon Ascetica, Polemica, Rubricistica, Historica* (9 vols., Romae, 1885-1899), s.v. *Eucharistia,* n. 19 (hereafter cited *Bibliotheca*) ; cf. also, Pallottini, s.v. *parochus,* § II, n. 34.

[88] Can. 21—c. 12, X, *de poenitentiis et remissionibus,* V, 38.

[89] Sess. XIII, *de Eucharistia,* can. 9.

[90] Sess. XIV, *de poenitentia,* can. 8.

Laymann (1574-1635), when writing in the century after the Council of Trent, stated that the law of the Decretal *"Omnis utriusque sexus,"* namely canon 21 of the IV Lateran Council, was still in effect. He presented it as the common doctrine that the Easter Communion could be lawfully administered only by the pastor, or with his permission. In other words, the Council of Trent had in no way derogated from the law of the earlier enactment.[91] A century later, Schmalzgrueber (1663-1735) wrote that in his day no contrary custom was to be tolerated.[92]

Pope Benedict XIV on June 2, 1751, reiterated the force of the Decretal *"Omnis utriusque sexus,"* and at the same time reminded Regulars that, despite the privileges they had received from Pope Paul IV and Pius V, they were limited in the use of these privileges in such a manner that they could not give Communion in their churches on Easter Sunday.[93]

The right of the pastor to administer the Paschal Communion was rather generally observed in consequence of the censure that Clement V (1305-1314) had attached to the act of the unlawful administration of the Paschal Communion.[94] But by reason of the extension of time granted by Pope Eugene IV (1431-1447) for the fulfillment of the Easter obligation[95] some problems arose. The Holy See repeatedly declared that the benefit of the exclusive right of the pastor did not extend to the whole period, but that it related only to Easter Sunday, and to that Communion which satisfied the obligation of the precept.

A reply given by the Sacred Congregation of the Council on January 23, 1586, was cited by Fagnanus. In this reply it was stated that, while Regulars could administer Holy Communion during the Easter season, they could not give Communion on the Paschal day itself, *"etiam devotionis causa."*[96] Barbosa cited a decision of the same Sacred Congregation given on March 2,

---

[91] *Theologia Moralis,* Lib. V, Tract. IV, Cap. VII, n. 3.

[92] *Ius Ecclesiasticum Universum,* Lib. III, tit. 29, n. 15.

[93] Ep. encycl. *Magna cum,* 2 iun. 1751, § § 21, 22—*Fontes,* n. 413.

[94] C. 1, *de privilegiis excessibus privilegiatorum,* V, 7, in Clem.

[95] Const. *Fide digna,* 8 iul. 1440—*Fontes,* n. 53.

[96] Fagnanus, *Commentaria,* Lib. V, Tit. 38, c. 12, nn. 42, 43.

1619, which likewise expressly forbade religious to give Holy Communion in their churches on Easter Sunday.[97]

The policy of the Church in the seventeenth century was very clearly indicated by Innocent X (1664-1665). In his Constitution *Exponi Nobis* of February 7, 1665, he confirmed and approved a decision of the Sacred Congregation of the Council as issued on July 9, 1644. In this response the Archbishop of Bordeaux was told that he could not forbid Regulars to administer the sacraments from Palm Sunday to Whitsunday, but he could forbid them to administer Communion on Easter Sunday, even though the Paschal precept had been or still would be satisfied in the parish church on some other day of the Easter season.[98]

However, in the nineteenth century the rigor of the law was relaxed when the excommunication for administering Holy Communion was restricted to the administration of Holy Viaticum alone.[99] This indicated a definite trend, and on Nov. 28, 1912, Pius X (1903-1914) removed the prohibition of administering Communion on Easter Sunday in non-parochial churches.[100]

Section 3. The Minister of Holy Viaticum

The right of the pastor to administer Holy Communion to the dying had become firmly established at the time of the Council of Trent. The Council in its brief reference to the subject recommended and reaffirmed the law and practice as estabished by the earlier councils of the Church.[101]

Suarez (1548-1617), writing some forty or fifty years after the Council of Trent, noted that it was the common teaching of all that the administration of Viaticum belonged to the proper

---

[97] *De Officio et Potestate Parochi Descriptio,* Pars II, Cap. XX, n. 10; also, S.C.C., *Suessana,* 14 ian. 1736—*Thesaurus,* VII, 166.

[98] *Bull. Rom.* XV, 362; similarly, S.C.C., 21 maii 1627; 26 apr. 1653; 31 ian. 1653—Pallottini, s.v. *Sacramentum,* I, nn. 2, 5, 6.

[99] Pius IX (1846-1878), const., *Apostolicae Sedis,* 12 oct. 1869, § II, n. 14—*Fontes,* n. 552.

[100] *Acta Apostolicae Sedis, Commentarium Officiale* (Romae, 1909-), IV (1912), 726 (hereafter cited *AAS*).

[101] Sess. XIII, *de Eucharistia,* c. 6.

pastor.[102] De Lugo (1583-1660) stated: ". . . quod tamen videtur contra sensum fidelium et contra doctrinam communem theologorum, qui universaliter dicunt omnes fideles debere accipere viaticum ultimum de manu, vel consensu, parochi vel praelati, *nulla facta exceptione.*"[103]

The Church always has been most solicitous for the welfare of the faithful, and especially so at the time of their death. Several popes saw fit to remind the pastor of his obligation of a special care with regard to the dying. Innocent X (1644-1665),[104] and Clement XII (1730-1740),[105] and especially Benedict XIV (1740-1758) stressed the right and duty imposed on the pastor by reason of his office. In his Constitution *Firmandis,* Benedict emphasized the right of the parish priest under the law of the Council of Trent to administer Holy Viaticum to his parishioners who were critically ill.[106] Again, in his Encyclical *Inter omnigenas,* Benedict XIV reminded the pastor that he must administer Viaticum *"quamprimum"* to the sick who are in danger of death, lest any of them die without the graces conferred through the reception of Holy Viaticum. However, in order to administer Holy Viaticum the pastor was not allowed to celebrate Mass in the home of the sick except in rare cases of exceptional circumstances.[107] The reason why the pastor alone should be competent to administer Viaticum was given by Benedict. Since the pastor was the one who administered the Paschal Communion, he could better than anyone else know whether or not the individual was a notorius sinner, and whether or not he should be given Holy Viaticum.[108]

The strict parochial nature of the right to administer Viaticum was of such rigidity that authors from the time of the Council of Trent down to the present Code left no room for the sup-

[102] *Tertia Pars Summae Theologicae,* Disp. LXXII, Sect. II, n. 12—*Opera Omnia,* XXI, 585.

[103] Disp. XVIII, Sect. I, n. 31.

[104] Const. *Cum sicut,* 19 dec. 1648—*Fontes,* n. 232.

[105] Litt. ap. *Compertum,* 24 aug. 1734; litt. ap. *Concredita Nobis,* 13 maii 1739—*Fontes,* nn. 296, 300.

[106] 6 nov. 1744, § 9—*Fontes,* n. 349; cf. also, const. *Omnium sollicitudinum,* 12 sept. 1744, § 14, dub. XII, §§ 26-40—*Fontes,* n. 348.

[107] Ep. encycl. *Inter omnigenas,* 3 febr. 1744—*Fontes,* n. 339.

[108] Ep. encycl. *Ex omnibus,* 16 oct. 1756, § 8—*Fontes,* n. 441.

planting of that law through any contrary custom.[109] While the law of the Council of Vienne, which demanded the "special permission" of the pastor, was still in effect, the permission to administer Viaticum was not to be presumed unless there was an extreme necessity.[110] If the pastor was either absent, or unable or unjustly unwilling to administer Holy Viaticum, then permission was justly presumed by any priest, or even by a deacon.[111]

Pius IX (1846-1878) upheld the right of the pastor to administer Holy Viaticum when in his Constitution *Apostolicae Sedis* he enacted an automatic excommunication, reserved to the Holy See, as incurred by religious who presumed to administer Viaticum without the permission of the pastor.[112] In regard to the Last Sacraments, this was a reiteration of the law of the Council of Vienne (1311-1312), which had been in effect until that time.[113]

The excommunication established by Pius IX was directed against religious in the strict sense who with full knowledge administered Holy Viaticum without the permission of the pastor. By Holy Viaticum was meant the Communion which the dying were obliged to receive by reason of divine precept. No longer was a "special permission" required, as had been necessary in the law of the Council of Vienne, but a general, a tacit, or even a prudently presumed permission was deemed sufficient, at least in its nature of a factor that precluded the incurring of the threatened penalty.[114]

---

[109] St. Alphonsus, *Theologia Moralis,* Lib. VI, n. 240; Schmalzgrueber, Lib. III, tit. 29, n. 15; Devoti, *Institutionum Canonicarum Libri Quatuor,* Lib II, Tit. II, Sect. III, n. 47; Santi, *Praelectiones Iuris Canonici,* Lib. III, tit. 29, n. 10; Wernz, *Ius Decretalium,* Tom. II, Pars II, p. 1042; Gasparri, *De Eucharistia,* II, n. 1077.

[110] St. Alphonsus, *Theologia Moralis,* Lib. VI, n. 240; Schmalzgrueber, *loc. cit.*

[111] Barbosa, *De Officio et Potestate Parochi Descriptio,* Pars II, Cap. XX, n. 23; St. Alphonsus, *loc. cit.*

[112] 12 oct. 1869, § II, n. 14: "Excommunicationi latae sententiae Romano Pontifici reservatae subiacere declaramus: Religiosos praesumentes clericis aut laicis extra casum necessitatis Sacramentum extremae unctionis aut Eucharistiae per Viaticum ministrare absque parochi licentia."—*Fontes,* n. 552.

[113] C. 1, *de privilegiis et excessibus privilegiatorum,* V, 7, in Clem.

[114] Pennacchi (+ 1898), *Commentaria in Constitutionem Apostolicae* Sedis (2 vols., Romae, 1883), I, 1029, 1030; Gasparri, *De Eucharistia,* II,

Religious could lawfully give Viaticum in a case of necessity. Necessity was interpreted as the unavailability of the pastor to care for the dying.[115] Religious remained free to give Viaticum to other members of the coummunity and to servants living within the religious house. All who dwelled therein were exempt from the jurisdiction of the pastor.[116]

Unless religious possessed a specific privilege which granted them jurisdiction over the students, it was thought according to the more probable opinion then current that they contracted the excommunication if they gave Viaticum to any of the students in their colleges as long as they did so outside of a case of necessity or minus the requisite permission of the pastor.[117]

As was the case with regard to the right of administering the Paschal Communion, so also with relation to the similar right of administering the Holy Viaticum, the Holy See was approached with questions that called for the solution of doubts. These questions concerned the various classes of persons relative to whom the factor of a contested jurisdiction needed closer specification. It was generally agreed that domestic servants as also Tertiaries who dwelled within the monastery were under the jurisdiction of the clerical religious superior. But if they became ill outside the monastery, then the pastor of the territory was to care for them.

On June 20, 1609, the Sacred Congregation of Rites had declared that the administration of the sacraments to Tertiaries *in articulo mortis* belonged to the priests entrusted with the care of souls in that territory, that is, when the Tertiaries during such sickness were confined to their own homes.[118] The same was true of the servants if they were affected with a dangerous illness

---

n. 1078; Lega, *Praelectiones in Textum Iuris Canonici de Iudiciis Ecclesiasticis, Libr.* II, Vol. IV, *De Iudiciis Criminalibus in Genere et in Specie* (Romae, 1901), n. 8 (hereafter cited *De Iudiciis Criminalibus*); Lehmkuhl, *Theologia Moralis,* II, n. 1239.

[115] Lehmkuhl, *loc. cit.;* Gasparri, loc. *cit.*

[116] Lega, *De Iudiciis Criminalibus,* n. 8; Pennacchi, *Commentaria in Constitutionem Apostolicae Sedis,* I, 1028.

[117] Lega, *loc. cit.;* Pennachi, *loc. cit.*

[118] S.R.C., *Spoletana Terrae de Visso,* 20 iun 1609—*Fontes,* n. 5248.

outside the monastery. The religious could not administer Viaticum to these servants, even though they had lived habitually within the monastery.[119]

The Holy See repeatedly declared that apart from an express privilege religious could not administer Holy Viaticum to other seculars whose life became endangered the while they resided at the monastery. Nor could they administer Viaticum to seculars who were staying in the monastery in consequence of their sickness. The pastor within whose territory the monastery was located had this right.[120]

Not even soldiers wounded in battle could be given Holy Viaticum without the permission of the pastor within whose limits the monastery was located.[121] Outside parishioners (*peregrini*) who contracted a dangerous illness while staying at a monastery were more probably not subject to the exclusive jurisdiction of the territorial pastor. He was not their *proper* pastor, and hence the religious could give them Viaticum if the need arose for Its administration to them.[122]

The pastor's right was also at times challenged by the cathedral chapter. In a number of cases the chapter questioned the pastor's right to administer Holy Viaticum to the canons who during their sickness were cared for in the territory of the pastor. In these cases the Holy See consistently upheld the right of the pastor.[123]

---

[119] S.C.C., 14 apr. 1685—Pallottini, s.v. *parochus,* § II, n. 35; S.C.C., 28 aug. 1683—Adone, *Synopsis Canonico-Liturgica* (Neapoli, 1886), n. 765; S.C.C., *Ulixbonen.,* 17 sept. 1742—*Thesaurus,* II, 231.

[120] S.C.C., 19 sept. 1637; 17 nov. 1691; 21 mart. 1654; 17 nov. 1717—Pallottini, s.v. sacramentum, § I, nn. 8, 9; s.v. *parochus,* § II, nn. 32, 34; S.C. Ep. et Reg., 21 iul 1876—*Acta Sanctae Sedis* (41 vols., Romae, 1865-1908), X (1877), 405 (hereafter cited *ASS*).

[121] S.C.C., 13 febr. 1694—Pallottini, s.v. *sacramentum,* § I, n. 10.

[122] St. Alphonsis, *Theologia Moralis,* Lib. VI, n. 240; Ballerini-Palmieri, Tract. X, Sect. IV, n. 97.

[123] S.R.C., *Montis Regalis,* 17 mart. 1663 ad 4—*Fontes,* n. 5537; S.C.C., *Mantuana,* 16 mart. 1680—*Fontes,* n. 2854; *Tiburtina,* 12 maii 1685—*Fontes,* n. 2886; *Tolentinaten.,* 11 sept. 1694—*Fontes,* n. 2944; *Novarien.,* 27 aug. 1695—*Fontes,* n. 2950; *Narnien.,* 26 sept. 1699—*Fontes,* n. 2971; S.R.C., *S. Severi,* 13 maii, 18 dec. 1756, ad 7—*Fontes,* n. 5799.

PART TWO

Canonical Commentary

CHAPTER III

The Ordinary Minister of Holy Communion

ARTICLE 1. THE PRIEST BY REASON OF HIS ORDINATION

As was to be expected, what had been the universal teaching and practice of the Church found its way into the Code of Canon Law.[1] The priest has the exclusive right to consecrate the Holy Eucharist.[2] Consequently to the priest rightly belongs the primary right of administering this sacrament to others. The priest alone has the greater power of changing bread and wine into the Body and Blood of Christ. So to the priest primarily and fundamentally should belong the lesser and dependent power of dispensing these Mysteries to others.[3]

The power of Orders which the priest receives pertains directly to and exists as subservient to the sacrament of the Holy Eucharist. This power is related not only to the consecration of this sacrament but also to its administration. For this reason authors note that the priest is the *ordinary minister* not only in the sense of the usual or customary minister, but as the natural, or essential, or primary minister for the dispensing of Holy Communion.[4]

Since the power of administering Holy Communion comes to the priest by reason of his ordination, it is certainly *de iure divino, non mere ecclesiastico.*[5] While Coronata does not deny

[1] Canon 845, §1.—Minister ordinarius sacrae communionis est solus sacerdos.

[2] Denzinger, *Enchiridion,* nn. 430, 949.

[3] Cappello, *Tractatus Canonico-Moralis de Sacramentis* (3 vols. in 6, Vol. I, 4. ed., Romae: Marietti, 1945), I, n. 297 (hereafter cited *De Sacramentis*).

[4] Vermeersch-Creusen, *Epitome Iuris Canonici* (3 vols., 6. ed., Romae-Mechlinae: H. Dessain, 1937-1946), II, n. 111 (hereafter cited *Epitome*); Van Hove, *Tractatus de Sanctissima Eucharistia* (2. ed., Mechlinae: H. Dessain, 1941), p. 151 (hereafter cited *De Eucharistia*).

[5] Cappello, *De Sacramentis,* I, n. 297.

that the priest's right to administer Holy Communion derives from the divine law, he states that the priest alone is the ordinary minister because of the traditional practice of the Church rather than in consequence of any such requirement from the divine law itself.[6] This he seeks to prove from the statement of the Council of Trent: "Semper in Ecclesia Dei mos fuit ut laici a sacerdotibus communionem acciperent; sacerdotes autem celebrantes seipsos communicarent; qui mos a traditione Apostolica descendens iure ac merito retineri debet."[7]

The early post-Tridentive commentators saw this text as indicating the antiquity rather than the origin of the priest's prerogative. They wrote of an exclusive authority which the priest exercised over the administration of Holy Communion by reason of his ordination. According to Suarez (1548-1617), the priest by ordination has ordinary powers over the Body of Christ; these powers derive *"ex iure divino"* and are not given to any other. These powers are so exclusive that no one inferior to a priest can ever give Communion to another apart from the commission of the priest.[8] Laymann (1574-1625) saw the primary right of giving Holy Communion to the Christian people as belonging to priests alone *"ex Christi institutione,"* since priests alone by their ordination receive the power of consecration.[9]

The priest will usually receive Holy Communion in connection with his own celebration of Mass, but a priest who does not celebrate Mass may give Communion to himself. To do this lawfully, it is required that there be no other priest available and willing to administer Holy Communion, and also that there be no danger of scandal. All commentators agree that a priest may give Holy Viaticum to himself. But over and above that, he may likewise give Communion to himself to satisfy his private devotion.[10]

---

[6] Coronata, *Tractatus Canonicus de Sacramentis* (3 vols., Romae: Marietti, 1943-1946), I, 269 (hereafter cited *De Sacramentis*).

[7] Sess. XIII, *de Eucharistia*, c. 8.

[8] *Tertia Pars Summae Theologicae*, Disp. LXXII, Sect. I, nn. 4, 5—*Opera Omnia*, XXI, 576, 577.

[9] *Theologia Moralis*, Lib. V, Tract. IV, Cap. VII, n. 1.

[10] Vermeersch-Creusen, *Epitome*, II, n. 113; Coronata, *De Sacramentis*, I, 272; Van Hove, *De Eucharistia*, p. 155; Augustine, *A Commentary on*

The divine law always demands that scandal be avoided. It can be easily obviated here by a word of explanation to the faithful should there be anyone present. But in most cases this difficulty would not arise since the priest would give Communion to himself privately and secretly.[11] A sick priest may have occasion to give Holy Communion to himself when he feels that he cannot muster enough strength to celebrate Mass. But it is not necessary that he be unable to say Mass before he can lawfully communicate himself.[12]

Even if a deacon were present, the priest should give Holy Communion to himself rather than receive It from the hand of the deacon. The *Decretum* of Gratian contained a canon forbidding the deacons to administer Communion to the priests.[13] This canon referred to a situation in which there were priests available, so the situation was not exactly similar to the case at hand. However, it does show that the mind of the Church is that in the administration of Communion to priests the ordinary minister of Holy Communion (which is the priest himself) is not to be supplanted by the supplementary minister.

This argument is strengthened by the law of Code in that it requires a grave cause for the lawful administration of Holy Communion by the deacon.[14] With the priest himself ready and able to give Communion to himself, one can hardly recognize a grave cause as authorizing the deacon to act. Consequently authors hold that the priest should give Holy Communion to himself rather than call on the assistance of the deacon.[15]

The usual ceremonies in the administration of Holy Commun-

---

the New Code of Canon Law (8 vols., Vol. IV, 6. ed., St. Louis: Herder, 1931), IV, 215 (hereafter cited *Commentary*); Cappello, *De Sacramentis*, I, n. 307; Iorio, *Theologia Moralis* (3. ed., 3 vols., Neapoli: D'Auria, 1946-1947), III, n. 120. Gasparri, *De Eucharistia*, II, n. 1081; Lehmkuhl, *Theologia Moralis*, II, n. 183; St. Alphonsus, *Theologia Moralis*, Lib. VI, n. 238; *et alii*.

[11] Cappello, *De Sacramentis*, I, n. 307.

[12] Cappello, *De Sacramentis*, I, n. 307.

[13] C. 14, D. XCIII.

[14] Canon 845, § 2.

[15] Coronata, *De Sacramentis*, I, 272; Cappello, *De Sacramentis*, I, n. 307; Vermeersch-Creusen, *Epitome*, II, n. 113

ion ouside of Mass would be omitted when a priest is to give Communion to himself. Kneeling at the foot of the altar in surplice and stole the priest would say the *Confiteor, Misereatur* and *Indulgentiam.* He would then reverently receive the Sacred Host and thereupon immediately leave the altar without reciting the usual prayers.[16]

ARTICLE 2. AUTHORIZATION FOR THE LAWFUL ADMINISTRATION

Section 1. Nature of the Authorization

Every priest by reason of his ordination has the power of administering Holy Communion. But for the lawful exercise of this power there is required a proper authorization. This is true of all the sacraments, the Holy Eucharist being no exception. The administration of the sacraments was directly and immediately entrusted by Christ to the Church, and only through the Church to the priests who are the ministers of the Church. Consequently, along with the power of Orders, for the lawful administration of the sacraments the priest needs a due concession of this faculty from the Church.[17] For the administration of baptism in a case of necessity, and likewise of the sacrament of matrimony, this faculty is of a general concession. For the other sacraments, and this includes the Holy Eucharist, the faculty is granted by means of the concession of jurisdiction through an ecclesiastical office or by means of a particular delegation or deputation.[18]

"To feed the sheep" is not the indiscriminate duty of any and every priest; only he who has been entrusted with a special *"cura animarum"* has a definite right and obligation. He is the one designated to care for a particular portion of Christ's flock. He will lawfully administer the sacraments to those who are in his care.[19]

The Council of Trent had insisted on a definite territorial and personal relationship between the pastor and the parishioners

---

[16] Cappello, *De Sacramentis,* I, n. 307.

[17] Coronata, *De Sacramentis,* I, n. 59.

[18] Cappello, *De Sacramentis,* I, n. 49.

[19] Suarez, *Tertia Pars Summae Theologicae,* Disp. LXXII, Sect. II, n. 2—*Opera Omnia,* XXI, 579, 580.

under his care. The exclusive right of the pastor to administer the sacraments to his parishioners was based on this relationship.[20] Consequently authors of the post-Tridentine period wrote that the lawful administration of Holy Communion demanded in the minister the power both of Orders and of jurisdiction with respect to the one to whom the sacrament was to be administered, or, in defect of jurisdiction, the permission of the one who possessed this jurisdiction. The pope, the bishop, the pastor, the religious superior, all had this jurisdiction along with the right and duty of caring for a definite group of Christ's fold. For anyone else to violate their right was looked upon as a grave perversion of due order and authority.[21]

Modern authors use the same terminology. Although the administration of Holy Communion is an exercise of the power of Orders, for the lawful administration of Holy Communion they too demand that the minister have some pastoral power or jurisdiction with respect to the recipient, or have obtained the faculty from one who has such jurisdiction.[22] The distribution of Holy Communion as one of the most effective means of sanctification possessed by the Church should necessarily be a substantial element in the pastoral office. But this function is not of such a nature that it cannot be delegated to others. This is widely done by the law itself.[23]

---

[20] Sess. XXIV, *de ref.*, c. 13.

[21] Suarez, *Tertia Pars Summae Theologicae,* Disp. LXII, Sect. II, nn. 3, 5; Disp. LXII, Sect. III, n. 2—*Opera Omnia,* XXI, 580, 581, 586; De Lugo, Disp. XVIII, Sect. II, n. 36; St. Alphonsus, *Theologia Moralis,* Lib. VI, n. 235; Barbosa, *De Officio et Potestate Parochi Descriptio,* Pars II, Cap. XX, n. 7, *additio;* Gasparri, *De Eucharistia,* II, n. 1080.

[22] Vermeersch, *Epitome,* II, n. 111; Cappello, *De Sacramentis,* I, n. 297; Aeartnys-Damen, *Theologia Moralis* (13. ed., 2 vols., Taurini-Romae: Marietti, 1939), II, n. 9; Merkelbach, *Summa Theologiae Moralis* (3. ed., 3 vols., Parisiis: Desclée, de Brouwer et Cie, 1939), III, n. 86; Sabetti-Barrett, *Compendium Theologiae Moralis* (27. ed., New York: Pustet, 1919), n. 686; Zubizarreta, *Theologia Dogmatico-Scholastica* (3. ed., 4 vols., Bilbao: Eléxpuru Hños., 1937-1939), IV, n. 435; Jone, *Moral Theology* (translated and adapted to the Code and Customs of the United States of America by Urban Adelman, Newman Book Shop; Westminster, Maryland, 1945), n. 499.

[23] Canons 846, § § 1 and 2; 848, § 2; 849, § 1.

The fact that authorization to give Holy Communion is so widespread by reason of the law itself makes it difficult for Coronata to see how any longer one may say that jurisdiction is required for the lawful administration of the Holy Eucharist. He admits that the pre-Code law demanded jurisdiction with respect to the subject, or permission from one who had such jurisdiction. But he claims that the present law, especially in canons 846 § § 1 and 2, and 849, § 1, has taken away this restriction. He argues that the permission which is required of the rector of a church for the lawful administration of Communion does not involve a grant of jurisdiction, but simply illustrates the proper and just subordination which is due to the rector when a stranger wishes to administer a sacrament in the rector's church. He further maintains that, since the Code of Canon Law requires jurisdiction only for certain cases, namely, for the administration of Holy Viaticum, for the public carrying of Communion to the sick, and perhaps for the distribution of paschal communion, either jurisdiction is no longer required in any other circumstance, or it is conceded by the law itself to all priests alike, and consequently is not an important consideration.[24]

Certainly the distribution of Holy Communion is not an act of jurisdiction, nor does the dispensing of this sacrament depend upon jurisdiction for validity as does the sacrament of penance. Rather, jurisdiction is a basis for the authority to administer Holy Communion lawfully, and also for the authority to delegate this faculty to others. The fact that the faculty of administering Communion is delegated in certain cases by the law itself does not militate against the fact that the proper right is based upon the possession of a jurisdiction over the recipient on the part of the ordinary minister. The law itself is an expression of the will of the supreme legislator, who has universal and immediate jurisdiction over the whole body of the faithful, and every right to delegate others to share in the pastor's power.

---

[24] Coronata, *De Sacramentis, I,* 269, 270. As Coronata notes on page 270, footnote 3, in practice the difference of opinions does not amount to much. It simply reverts to whether or not the law is looked upon as conceding the necessary faculties, or whether the law does away with the need of a special faculty. In either case, the end result is the same.

Section 2. Authorization by Reason of Office

The administration of Holy Communion belongs by proper right to those who possess the pastoral power. Consequently, in the first place as lawful minister of this sacrament one must point to the local ordinary in his territory. This includes the residential bishop in his diocese and, for their respective territories, the vicar general, the abbot or prelate *nullius,* the apostolic administrator, and the vicar or prefect apostolic. Those who in default of any of the foregoing temporarily succeed to the government, either according to law or by virtue of approved religious constitutions, are also local ordinaries.[25] All the above mentioned lawully administer the Holy Eucharist, *iure proprio,* to any and all within the limits of their jurisdiction.[26]

Under the authority of the local ordinary the care of souls in each parish is entrusted to the pastor. The pastor and all who are regarded in law as equivalent to pastors are the proper ministers of Holy Communion to all within the territory of their parish, unless part of this territory or a number of the residents within it is withdrawn from the parochial authority by the ordinaryof the place.[27] The pastor in his parochial territory administers Holy Communion by reason of his office.[28]

Canon 451, § 2, makes the following the equivalent to pastors:

(a) Quasi-pastors;[29] (b) the actual vicar of a parish held in title by a moral person;[30] (c) the substitute vicar;[31] (d) the parish administrator;[32] (e) the curate lawfully constituted to act as pastor when the parochial office falls vacant;[33] (f) the adjutant

---

[25] Canon 198, § 1.

[26] Vermeersch-Creusen, *Epitome,* II, n. 111; Cappello, *De Sacramentis,* I, n. 290; Jone, *Moral Theology,* n. 499; Regatillo, *Ius Sacramentarium* (2 vols., Santander: Sal Terrae, 1945-1946), I, n. 306.

[27] Canon 462, § 2.

[28] Regatillo, *Ius Sacramentarium,* I, n. 306; Cappello, *De Sacramentis,* I,. n. 298.

[29] Can. 216, § 3.

[30] Can. 471.

[31] Can. 465, §§ 4 and 5; 474; 1923, § 2.

[32] Can. 472, 1°; 473.

[33] Can. 472, 2°.

vicar who is deputed with full powers.[34] All the foregoing are to be regarded as equal to the pastor in the matter of administering Holy Communion.

The rector of a seminary is the proper minister of Holy Communion for all who live at the seminary. As stated in canon 1368, the rector of a seminary holds the office of pastor in relation to all those who live at the seminary, exception being made only with reference to the sacraments of matrimony and penance.[35]

In all clerical religious institutes the superior is responsible for the pastoral care of the members.[36] Consequently in such institutes, for all the members and also for others who dwell there day and night, the *iure proprio* authorized minister of Holy Communion is the superior, either the major superior or the local superior.

Exempt lay institutes have a chaplain who has full pastoral care of the community.[37] The chaplains in these communities administer Holy Communion in their own right.[38]

Non-exempt lay religious are under the pastoral care of the local parish priest. But the local ordinary may appoint a chaplain and withdraw the community from the jurisdiction of the pastor.[39] The local ordinary may in a similar manner withdraw from the pastoral authority any hospitals or other houses of piety which are not exempt by law.[40] In such cases the chaplain is the proper lawful minister of Holy Communion.[41]

Section 3. Authorization by Reason of Delegation

The properly authorized minister of Holy Communion is he who has parochial jurisdiction over the person to whom this sacra-

---

[34] Can. 475.

[35] Regatillo, *Ius Sacramentarium,* I, n. 306.

[36] Coronata, *Institutiones Iuris Canonici* (2. ed., 5 vols., Taurini: Marietti, 1939-1947), I, 644.

[37] Bouscaren-Ellis, *Canon Law, A Text and Commentary* (Milwaukee: Bruce, 1946), p. 250; cf. can. 529; 514, § 3.

[38] Cappello, *De Sacramentis,* I, n. 298.

[39] Canons 464, § 2; 514, § 3.

[40] Canon 464, § 2.

[41] Regatillo, *Ius Sacramentarium,* I, n. 306; Cappello, *De Sacramentis,* I, n. 298.

ment is given. But since the act of distributing Communion is not an act of jurisdiction, the use of that term must be interpreted widely and must not be confused with that real jurisdiction which is so absolutely necessary in the administration of the sacrament of penance. The factor of jurisdiction as touching the administration of Holy Communion is not an element related to the validity of the administration. Rather, it is an element calculated for the preservation of due order in the administration of this sacrament. Consequently one can readily realize that the simple authorization which the pastor confers for the purpose of permitting a priest to administer Holy Communion is not an act of delegation in the canonical sense, but rather the granting of a permission to, or the sharing of a faculty with someone else. However, it is necessary; anyone who acts without this proper authorization acts unlawfully.[42]

This permission or faculty need not be granted in expressed words or signs. Since for the valid administration of Holy Communion no previous jurisdiction over the recipient is required as it is required for the sacrament of penance, even a reasonably presumed permission suffices. This permission may be explicit, implicit, tacit, presumed, general or particular. An explicit permission is one that is given in express words or signs. An implicit permission is one that is included in another. Permission is tacit when he who is able without grave inconvenience to impede the performance of an action does not do so. Presumed permission is that regarding which it can reasonably be judged that it would have been granted had the permission been asked for. Permission is general or particular depending upon whether or not it is granted for all cases or for some special contingency. Because of the nature of the faculty that is accorded to make the administration of Holy Communion lawful, any type of permission is lawful.[43]

In a case of great utility for the faithful, even for a single individual, any priest may reasonably presume permission to distribute Holy Communion. *A fortiori,* in any real necessity,

---

[42] De Lugo, Disp. XVIII, Sect. II, nn. 37, 38.

[43] Regatillo, *Ius Sacramentarium,* I, n. 307.

even though it is not extreme, there is found a sufficient reason for the lawful presumption of the permission necessary for the dispensing of this sacrament.[44] The right to presume permission in a case of necessity is confirmed by the law.[45]

The Code grants to all rectors of churches the faculty of administering Holy Communion. This must be gathered from canon 846, § 2, which acknowledges the authority of the rector as that which gives permission for the distribution of Communion in his church. If the rector can give permission to dispense the Holy Eucharist, he can certainly do so himself.[46]

Likewise from the law itself all priests assigned for service in a particular church are given permission to distribute Holy Communion in that church. This must be inferred from canon 846, § 2, according to which a *sacerdos extraneus* is the only one who needs a special permission, expressed or presumed. Since no special permission is required for the priest who is assigned to the church, one must infer that the faculty is indirectly conceded to him by the law itself.[47]

In virtue of this one may say that curates or assistants in a parish, the *vicari cooperatores,* need no further permission than that which is contained in the very act of their assignment to the parish. The Pontificial Interpretation Commission has clarified this matter by authoritatively explaining that a *sacerdos addictus* is a priest who while assigned to a definite church exercises the care of souls under the authority of the pastor.[48] As priests assigned to a definite church for exercising the care of souls under the direction of the pastor, *vicarii cooperatores* are qualified by the law to distribute Holy Communion, and hence need no further permission.

The most widespread concession of permission to administer Holy Communion is given in canon 846. The first paragraph

---

[44] Cappello, *De Sacramentis,* I, n. 299.

[45] Canon 848, § 2.

[46] Vermeersch-Creusen, *Epitome,* II, n. 111; Van Hove, *De Eucharistia,* p. 152.

[47] Regatillo, *Ius Sacramentarium,* I, n. 307; Van Hove, *De Eucharistia,* p. 152.

[48] *AAS,* XXXIV (1942), 102.

grants the faculty in connection with the Mass, the second paragraph concerns the administration of Communion outside of Mass.[49]

According to the Code every priest may distribute Holy Communion during his Mass, and if he celebrates the Mass privately, also immediately before and after that Mass. This holds for every private Mass, even that said in a private oratory, unless the local ordinary for a just cause has forbidden Communion to be distributed in a particular case.[50] This law makes any and every priest the lawful minister of Holy Communion whenever Mass is celebrated, with but one exception, to which the writer will advert later.

For many centuries it was doubted whether or not Holy Communion was to be distributed at Requiem Mass.[51] That question became definitely settled through a general decree of the Sacred Congregation of Rites as formulated on June 27, 1868. This decree was approved and confirmed by Pope Pius IX. It stated that Holy Communion could be given at Requiem Masses, even if the particles were consecrated at another Mass. It further stated that Holy Communion could be given immediately before or after Requiem Masses as well.[52]

Later the same Sacred Congregation was asked about the lawfulness of distributing Holy Communion at solemn or sung Masses of Requiem. On November 28, 1902, the Sacred Congregation replied that it was not the practice in Rome to give Communion at such solemn or sung Masses, but that, if for a reasonable cause Holy Communion was distributed, the deacon was not to sing the *Confiteor,* but rather was simply to recite it *alta voce.*[53]

---

[49] Canon 846, § 1.—Quilibet sacerdos intra Missam et, si privatim celebrat, etiam proxime ante et statim post, sacram communionem ministrare potest, salvo praescripto can. 869.

Canon 846, § 2.—Etiam extra Missam quilibet sacerdos eadem facultate pollet ex licentia saltem praesumpta rectoris ecclesiae, si sit extraneus.

[50] Canon 846, § 1.

[51] Cf. *DA,* nn. 1711, ad 2; 3177; *DAG,* nn. 3575, 3833, 4815, 4594.

[52] *Fontes,* n. 6026.

[53] *DA,* n. 4104.

This decree does not contain a strict prohibition. Now, in view of canon 846, § 1, there is certainly no reason to restrict the permission, given to every priest, by which he may administer Holy Communion at even solemn or sung Requiem Masses. The canon makes no distinction of this sort. There is hardly any special justifiying reason needed. As Cappello points out, the fact that even one of the faithful assisting at a chanted Requiem Mass should desire to receive Holy Communion would be in itself a sufficient justifying cause for the distribution of Holy Communion.[54]

The provisions of canon 846, § 1, extend also to the conventual or parochial Midnight Mass on Christmas. The priest who says Mass at midnight on Christmas is authorized to administer Holy Communion. Because of the specific mention of Holy Communion in paragraph 3 of canon 821, and the absence of any similar mention in paragraph 2 of the same canon,[55] it was considered doubtful whether Holy Communion could be given at Midnight Mass in any but religious or other pious houses which enjoyed the faculty of reserving the Blessed Sacrament.[56] A private decision, given to a bishop in the Philippine Islands in 1920, vindicated the distribution of Communion at the parochial and conventual Masses. This was authentically confirmed by the Pontifical Commission of Interpretation on March 16, 1936. The Commission stated that the priest who says Mass at Midnight on Christmas, whether according to law or in virtue of an apostolic indult, may administer Holy Communion unless the local ordinary has used his authority under canon 869 and for a just cause has

---

[54] *De Sacramentis,* I, n. 299.

[55] Canon 821, § 2. In nocte Nativatis Domini inchoari media nocte potest sola Missa conventualis vel paroecialis, non autem alia sine apostolico indulto.

[56] Vermeersch-Creusen, *Epitome,* II, n. 111.

Canon 821, § 3. In omnibus tamen religiosis seu piis domibus oratorium habentibus cum facultate sanctissimam Eucharistiam habitualiter asservandi, nocte Nativitatis Domini, unus sacerdos tres rituales Missas vel, servatis servandis, unam tantum quae adstantibus omnibus ad praecepti quoque satisfactionem valeat, celebrare potest et sacram communionem petentibus ministrare.

forbidden the distribution of Holy Communion in a particular case.[57]

Every priest is likewise authorized to give Communion immediately before and after private Mass. But what constitutes a private Mass? Liturgists, rubricists and canonists cannot agree on the precise meaning of this term. The meaning of the term "private Mass," as employed in the present law, is made somewhat clear by means of a decision of the Sacred Congregation of Rites which is listed as one of the sources of canon 846, § 1. In answer to a query the Sacred Congregation stated that priests fully vested for saying Mass could not distribute Holy Communion before or after a solemn Mass, a Missa cantata, or the conventual Mass.[58] As this is a source of canon 846, § 1, the law is understood as not granting the faculty to administer Holy Communion before or after the Masses mentioned, for the reason that they are not private Masses. Consequently authors argue that a private Mass is any Mass that is not a solemn, a sung, or a conventual Mass. In this sense the contrast is not between private and public, for a low Mass that is not a conventual Mass may be public in the sense that many of the faithful are in attendance. Rather, a private Mass is any non-conventual low Mass.[59]

The words, *etiam proxime ante et statim post,* point to the fact that the priest is already fully vested for the prospective celebration of Mass.[60] If there exists a reasonable cause for giving Communion before or after a non-private Mass, then the priest must first put off the vestments before he can fully dispense the sacrament. Van Hove (1872-1947) stated that a contrary custom which allows a priest when fully vested for Mass to distribute

---

[57] *AAS,* XXVIII (1936), 178.

[58] *Ordinis Fratris Minorem Provinciae Apuliae, 19 ian. 1906, ad iii—Fontes,* n. 6346.

[59] Regatillo, *Ius Sacramentarium,* I, n. 307; Cappello, *De Sacramentis,* I, n. 299; Coronata, *De Sacramentis,* I, 273; Woywod, Practical Commentary, I, n. 744. Some authors consider the parochial Mass—the *Missa pro populo* as required on days of obligation and suppressed feasts—not to be a private Mass. Cf. Augustine, *Commentary,* IV, 216, 217.

[60] Regatillo, *Ius Sacramentarium,* I, n. 307; Van Hove, *De Eucharistia,* p. 152.

Holy Communion before a *Missa cantata* can be sustained until the local ordinary disposes otherwise. Such a practice does exist in Belgium, he stated, and it is considered both reasonable and serviceable.[61] This practice is also found throughout the United States and can certainly be sustained.

The right to administer Holy Communion during, directly before or immediately after the Mass is a right given by the law itself, and hence no one may regard it as unimportant or make light of it. It goes without saying that this authorization cannot be taken away arbitrarily by anyone. The local pastor has no right to prohibit the distribution of Holy Communion when the visiting priest lawfully says Mass. Whenever a priest is allowed to say Mass in a church or in an oratory, he has by that very fact the implied permission to distribute Holy Communion. Neither on the occasion of a great festival, nor at the time a mission, nor even on Easter Sunday may a pastor or the rector of a church forbid the giving of Holy Communion by a visiting priest who has the permission to celebrate Mass.[62]

The Sacred Congregation of Rites on December 7, 1844, declared that it was not within the pastor's power to forbid the administration of Holy Communion right after Mass.[63] In this case the pastor thought that the disturbance and the noise occasioned by the departure of the people after the Mass implied an irreverence to the Blessed Sacrament. Even so the Sacred Congregation stated that it was beyond the authority of the pastor to oppose the customary practice. What was then the practice is now firmly established by the law. Therefore the authorization to administer Holy Communion directly before and immediately after as well as during Mass can be set down as a secure right that can not be taken away by the pastor, or by the rector of the church.

The local ordinary may forbid a priest to administer Holy Communion in connection with his Mass solely in a particular case and for a just and grave cause.[64] This power may be used *per*

[61] Van Hove, *De Eucharistia*, p. 152.

[62] Coronata, *De Sacramentis*, I, 273; Woywod, *A Practical Commentary*, I, n. 744; Cappello, *De Sacramentis*, I, n. 299.

[63] *DAG*, n. 4984.

[64] Canon 869.

modum actus only, and for a sound and weighty reason. The ordinary would exceed his authority were he by means of a diocesan statute or of a general decree to forbid the distribution of Holy Communion in such a case. The most he could do would be to issue a particular prohibition in view of the local circumstances which could be regarded as furnishing a just cause.[65]

The law of the Church also makes provision for the distribution of Holy Communion apart from Mass. A priest assigned to a particular church (*sacerdos addictus*) is considered to have thereat a habitual permission to distribute Communion. On the other hand, a priest who is not stationed at the church which he visits (*sacerdos extraneus*) may give Holy Communion outside of Mass with the permission of the pastor or of the rector of the church. This permission often may be presumed if no express prohibition has been issued by the rector of the church.[66] The law does not require any formal explicit grant of permission. It is satisfied with even less than an implicit permission. But it calls for at least a presumed permission, which obtains when it can reasonably be judged that the permission would have been granted on request.

The rector of a church may for a just cause deny permission to a visiting priest who wishes to distribute Holy Communion outside of Mass. This authority is given to him by the law, for no one can lawfully presume permission contrary to the reasonable prohibition of the rector. If the pastor or the rector would act in a manner which is patently unreasonable when he prohibits the distribution of Holy Communion, a priest could still administer Holy Communion with a safe conscience despite the seeming lack of permission, since the pastor's or rector's unreasonable refusal of permission evidently connotes the visiting priest's reasonable presumption of permission. But in such a case prudence must make sure to forestell all scandal likely to arise in consequence of any apparent disrespect of ecclesiastical authority.[67]

---

[65] Vermeersch-Creusen, *Epitome,* II, n. 111; Coronata, *De Sacramentis,* I, 273.

[66] Canon 846, § 2.—Etiam extra Missam quilibet sacerdos eadem facultate pollet et licentia saltem praesumpta rectoris ecclesiae, si sit extraneus.

[67] Coronata, *De Sacramentis,* I, 275; Cappello, *De Sacramentis,* I, n. 299.

It is within the competence of the rector of the church to regulate the time at which Holy Communion is to be distributed. This is to the advantage of the faithful, for regularity and due order in these matters serve their convenience best. Normally a visiting priest is obliged to heed such a regulation, for he cannot lawfully presume the permission of the rector while he acts contrary to the rector's reasonable wish as expressly manifested.[68] It is normally, but not absolutely, that the visiting priest is held by such a regulation, for there could well arise unusual circumstances which would make it lawful to deviate from the usual order. If the delay in waiting for the next regularly scheduled hour for the distribution of Holy Communion would constitute a grave hardship, or make it impossible for one or more of the faithful to receive Communion on some special occasion, then the visiting priest could lawfully administer the Holy Eucharist to them. The reason appears evident. Any prohibition under such unusual circumstances would have to be branded as unreasonable, and by that very token would make reasonable the visiting priest's presumption of permission.[69]

Section 4. Personal Disability

For the lawful administration of Holy Communion the authorized priest must be free of all personal impediments. Hence a priest may well lose his right to give Communion if he has incurred an excommunication,[70] a suspension,[71] or a personal interdict.[72] Any-

---

[68] Augustine, *Commentary,* IV, 217.

[69] Coronata, *De Sacramentis,* I, 275.

[70] Canons 2257 and 2261.

[71] Canons 2278 and 2279. A suspension *a divinis* specifically forbids the exercise of all acts inherent in the power of Orders, and consequently also the right to administer Holy Communion is taken away. The contracting of a general suspension entails also the contracting of the suspension *a divinis.* More specific suspensions, such as the *suspensio ab ordinibus,* the *suspensio a sacris ordinibus,* the *suspensio a certo et definito ordine exercendo,* the *suspensio a certo et definito ministerio,* likewise deprive a priest or a deacon of the right to administer the sacraments. A *suspensio a iurisdictione,* or a *suspensio ab officio,* could likewise nullify a pastor's *iure proprio* right to administer Holy Communion, but authorization for the lawful administration could certainly be given to one who had incurred such a penalty. Cf.

one who has incurred such a penalty is forbidden to administer Holy Communion.[73] The administration of Holy Communion would of course not lack in its validity. But because of the presence of the penalty the act of administering Holy Communion would be gravely illicit, and an irregularity[74] would be incurred unless one of the exceptions provided for in the law could be invoked.[75]

If such a penalty has been incurred automatically, but its observance has not become necessitated through a declaratory sentence or in consequence of the fact that the delict is notorious, then the penalty need not be observed in the external forum when its observance would result in scandal or if it would endanger the reputation of the individual.[76] In the absence of a declaratory sentence and also of notoriety in the delict which gave rise to the contracted penalty, the priest could still lawfully administer Holy Communion whenever his declining to do so would certainly cause consternation or untoward wonderment among the faithful.

The purpose of the law in forbidding one who has incurred a penalty to administer the sacraments is definitely not the fact that thereby it should become impossible or exceedingly difficult for the faithful to receive the sacraments. Consequently in canon 2261, §§ 2 and 3, there are indicated certain conditions under which ordinary excommunicates, and even the excommunicati vitandi and those whose excommunication was attended with a declaratory or a condemnatory sentence, can nevertheless lawfully administer the

---

Rainer, *Suspension of Clerics,* The Catholic University of America Canon Law Studies, n. 111 (Washington, D. C.: The Catholic University of America, 1937), pp. 76-87.

[72] Canons 2268 and 2275.

[73] Canons 2261; 2275; 2284.

[74] Canon 985. "Sunt irregulares ex delicto: . . . 7°. Qui actum ordinis, clericis in ordine sacro constitutis reservatum, ponunt, vel eo ordine carentes, vel ab eius exercitio poena canonica sive personali, medicinali aut vindicativa, sive locali prohibiti."

[75] Canons 2232, § 1; 2261, §§ 2 and 3.

[76] Canon 2232, ø 1. For a lengthy explanation of this canon, cf. Conran, *The Interdict,* The Catholic University of America Canon Law Studies, n. 56 (Washington, D. C.: The Catholic University of America, 1930), pp. 51 ff.

sacraments. These regulations apply to suspended and personally interdicted priests as well.[77]

Those who have simply contracted an excommunication, or have become suspended or personally interdicted apart from any attendant declaratory or condemnatory sentence, can lawfully administer the sacrament of the Holy Eucharist as often as the faithful legitimately ask It of them. Moreover, when thus administering the Holy Eucharist, the minister is not obliged to inquire why the petitioner wishes to receive.[78] Ordinarily the absence of other priests will be the reason why the faithful would call such a minister. But that is not the only reason. The law requires not a grave cause, but only a just cause,[79] that is, any cause which makes a deviation from the law the more reasonable thing. As Augustine (1872-1943) stated, "any reason may be called just which promotes devotion or wards off temptations or is prompted by real convenience, for instance, if one does not want to call another."[80]

Hyland gives as examples of a just cause the intention of approaching Holy Communion with greater purity of soul, and the intention of receiving the Holy Eucharist more frequently.[81]

Moreover the request of the faithful need not be explicit; an implied or reasonably presumed request proves sufficient.[82] If a priest knew that a number of the faithful desired to receive Holy Communion the while no other priests were present, he could present himself ready to give Communion to them. Such a course of action would be justified on any day, not merely on Sundays or on other days of obligation. When the good of souls demands the

---

[77] Canons 2275, § 2, and 2284.

[78] Canon 2261, § 2.

[79] Canon 2261, § 2.—Fideles, salvo praescripto § 3, possunt ex qualibet iusta causa ab excommunicato Sacramenta et Sacramentalia petere, maxime si alli ministri desint, et tunc excommunicatus requisitus potest eadem ministrare neque ulla tenetur obligatione causam a requirente percontandi.

[80] *Commentary,* IV, 182.

[81] *Excommunication,* The Catholic University of America Canon Law Studies, n. 49 (Washington, D. C.: The Catholic University of America, 1928), p. 92.

[82] Vermeersch-Creusen, *Epitome,* III, n. 463; Cocchi, *Commentarium in Codicem Iuris Canonici* (8 vols., Vol. VIII, 4. ed., Taurinorum Augustae: Marietti, 1938), VIII, 182.

administration of Holy Communion and no other priest is present, then an implicit or presumed request on the part of the faithful will prove sufficient to warrant the distribution of Holy Communion to them.[83]

Excommunicati vitandi, and also priests whose excommunication, suspension, or personal interdict was attended with a condemnatory or declaratory sentence, can administer the Holy Eucharist only to those who are in danger of death, and even then only if no other priests are present.[84] With the phrase *periculum mortis* the Code points to the case in which death may presumably ensue even though the probability of recovery is not at all entirely excluded. A person need not be dying (*in articulo mortis*), and death need not be imminent, before the danger of death can really exist. A *periculum mortis* can still be present even when there is greater likelihood of recovery than there is probability that death will ensue.[85]

The danger of death may arise from intrinsic causes, such as sickness, old age, or wounds, or from extrinsic causes, such as an impending serious operation, or imminent combat for a soldier. In a case of positive doubt whether or not the person is in danger of death, the doubt should be resolved in a person's favor. Even if a priest administered Holy Viaticum to one who was erroneously believed to be in danger of death, his action would be lawful despite the absence of any real danger.[86]

In the light of the conditions as set down in canon 2261, § 3, there appears to be no reason why Communion could not be given several times if the conditions are verified. The law does not restrict the minister in question to a single administration of Holy Viaticum as understood in its strict meaning, namely, as the Communion which is prescribed by divine as well as by ecclesiastical law when one falls into danger of death.[87] Communion received out of devotion *in periculo mortis* could also be administered

[83] Conran, *The Interdict,* p. 97; Hyland, *Excommunication,* p. 96.

[84] Canon 2261, § 3.

[85] Kilker, *Extreme Unction,* The Catholic University of America Canon Law Studies, n. 32 (Washington, D. C.: The Catholic University of America, 1926), p. 167.

[86] Conran, *The Interdict,* p. 99; Hyland, *Excommunication,* p. 94.

[87] Canon 864, § 1.

under the provisions of canon 2261, § 3. The law here makes provision for the administration of all the sacraments, with no exceptions made regarding any particular sacrament or the number of times it may be administered. The Holy Eucharist could be administered repeatedly during the continuance of the *periculum mortis,* as long as no other minister is present.

When it is stated here that under certain conditions it is lawful for one who has incurred a penalty to administer Holy Communion,[88] there is advertence simply to the fact that the minister is no longer restricted by the penal legislation of the Church. Whenever the Code permits an excommunicated, suspended, or personally interdicted cleric in some given situation to disregard the observance of his incurred penalty, he is not violating the restrictions normally attendant on the inflicted penalty, and consequently he does not thereby incur any irregularity.[89] But if the priest were at the same time in the state of mortal sin, he could not lawfully administer Holy Communion before he repented of the sin and also received absolution in the sacrament of penance, or at least elicited an act of perfect contrition.[90]

The Church has made these exceptions in its penal legislation for the welfare of the faithful, in order that they need not suffer through the malice of those to whom has been entrusted the administration of its spiritual goods. The faithful thus need have no scruples in asking for the services of such penalized ministers. However, if other priests are present, these should be asked for the administration of the sacrament of the Holy Eucharist, otherwise the censured priest may be needlessly exposed to the danger of committing sacrilege.[91]

ARTICLE 3. THE OBLIGATION TO ADMINISTER HOLY COMMUNION

The faithful are obliged by the Code to receive Holy Communion during the paschal season and especially also when they are in

[88] Canons 2232; 2261, §§ 2 and 3.

[89] Rainer, *Suspension of Clerics,* p. 190.

[90] Van Hove, *De Eucharistia,* p. 155; Iorio, *Theologia Moralis,* III, n. 123; Cerato, *Censures Vigentes Ipso Facto a Codice Iuris Canonicae Exerptae* (2. ed., Patavii, 1921), n. 37.

[91] Conran, *The Interdict,* p. 98.

danger of death.[92] Those who have the care of souls are obliged in justice to administer Holy Communion to their subjects, not only when the reception of Holy Communion lends itself to the fulfilling of a precept, but also whenever it is reasonably requested by the faithful.[93] This obligation is in and of itself a serious one. However, a pastor could be excused from serious fault if only rarely he refused to give Communion to his subjects when they are not under precept to receive It. If no serious scandal arises, then the pastor's sin of omission would not have to be accounted as a serious sin for the very reason that it has not occasioned any grave injury or harm.[94]

A pastor would be excused from all strict obligation of administering Holy Communion if the request for his services were unreasonable. For example, if the people could easily wait a few minutes and receive Holy Communion during Mass, or at a regularly scheduled period of distribution, then the pastor would be justified in putting them off until that time. Again, if the pastor were necessarily occupied or sick, he would lawfully decline the requests of his subjects.[95] But even though the pastor be justified in refusing or in delaying the administration of Holy Communion, he must exercise circumspect caution in order to forestall all emergence of scandal. The faithful are easily scandalized in these matters, even to the extent that they would refrain from further seeking all devotional reception of the sacraments.[96]

The Code obliges all who have the care of souls to diligently see that the dying receive Holy Viaticum.[97] This obligation is certainly a grave one, for the dying need the priest at this most critical time of their lives. The pastor is not obliged in all cases to fulfill this obligation personally, since in his stead he may care for his

---

[92] Canons 859, § 1; 864.

[93] Cappello, *De Sacramentis,* I, n. 381; Coronata, *De Sacramentis,* I, 273; Iorio, *Theologia Moralis,* III, n. 121; Van Hove, *De Eucharistia,* p. 163; Lehmkuhl, *Theologia Moralis,* II, n. 184; St. Alphonsus, *Theologia Moralis,* Lib. VI, n. 233.

[94] Van Hove, *De Eucharistia,* p. 163.

[95] *Loc. cit.*

[96] Iorio, *Theologia Moralis,* III, n. 122.

[97] Canon 865.

parishioners through the help and service of some other priest.[98] Likewise it is not incontrovertible that the pastor has an obligation to administer Holy Viaticum when there is a definite danger to his own life. This follows from the fact that Holy Viaticum is not absolutely necessary for salvation.[99]

Coronata does not indeed oppose this opinion, but he contends that the reason usually given by the older authors, namely, the danger of contracting a contagious disease, can hardly, short of scandal to the faithful, be of the same avail in our own day when powerful antiseptics and other disease prevention methods are so readily at hand. Nevertheless, the principle as such stands, namely, that in grave danger to himself the pastor is excused from all serious obligations to administer Holy Viaticum.[100]

Because of the enormous advantages which yield to the dying through the sacrament of the Holy Eucharist, a pastor would certainly be obliged to put himself to unusual inconveniences in order to forestall such dangers which, if present, could bar his service to the dying. The employment of preventive measures to forestall contagion is not too much to expect of the one who has an obligation to care for the spiritual needs of his parish. He is certainly obliged to put himself to the inconveniences which in reverse proportion do not transcend the benefits which will be accorded to the sick through the graces of Holy Viaticum.

Laymen have the right to receive from the clergy the spiritual benefits and graces that are necessary for salvation.[101] All the members of the Church have a right to all the means of sanctification that are possessed, and the obligation of dispensing these treasures is imposed on the priests who have the care of souls. The administration of the sacraments is a pre-eminent duty of the pastor.[102] The pastor's obligation will be grave indeed when the need is correspondingly grave on the part of the recipient. This is the situation when any one of his subjects is in danger of

---

[98] Woywod, *A Practical Commentary,* I, n. 764.

[99] Van Hove, *De Eucharistia,* p. 163; Coronata, *De Sacramentis,* I, n. 294; St. Alphonsus, *Theologia Moralis,* Lib. VI, n. 233.

[100] Coronata, *De Sacramentis,* I, 273.

[101] Canon 692.

[102] Canons 462; 467.

death.[103] Certainly the obligation is grave whenever there is question of relieving the grave or extreme spiritual necessity of the dying person.

Inasmuch as the pastor has the obligation of succoring those who are in grave need of his help, Suarez (1548-1617) insisted that the obligation of the pastor to administer Holy Viaticum continues as a serious obligation even at the risk of his own life.[104] But such an all-inclusive demand seems too stringent. For, when the pastor is at hand to administer to one in a dying condition, his first obligation is that of administering the sacrament of penance, or, should the person be unconscious, the sacrament of extreme unction. With this done, the person is no longer in any extreme spiritual necessity, and hence it appears that the pastor would not at the risk of his own life need to administer the sacrament of the Holy Eucharist.

As Noldin (1838-1922)[105] and Cappello[106] have pointed out, the sacraments of baptism and penance, along with the sacrament of extreme unction if the person is destitute of his senses, are the only sacraments that are necessary for salvation. These alone would demand that the pastor expose himself to certain peril in order to administer them to those who are within his care. After the dying person has received these sacraments there is no obligation incumbent on the pastor to risk his own life to administer Holy Viaticum.

Priests who have not had the care of souls assigned to them are obliged less strictly than the pastor. In those cases in which the pastor is obliged in justice to administer the sacraments, other priests are held by reason of the virtue of charity. But every priest, if his service is needed, is under a grave obligation to give Holy Viaticum to a person who is in danger of death, for although Viaticum is not necessary as an absolute means for salvation, nevertheless It is of surprising usefulness for the perseverance in grace

---

[103] Fanfani, *De Iure Parochorum* (Romae: Marietti, 1924), n. 229.

[104] *Tertia Pars Summae Theologicae,* Suppl. ad III, q. 32, a. 3.

[105] *Theologia Moralis,* III, n. 34.

[106] *De Sacramentis,* I, n. 54.

at the last hour. Yet, the sustaining of a serious hardship would excuse such a priest from this obligation.[107]

Apart from the obligation of administering Holy Viaticum, there exists for priests who are not by ecclesiastical appointment engaged in the care of souls but a light obligation of administering the Holy Eucharist. This obligation would become grave if the refusal of the priest to give Holy Communion would certainly cause scandal, or among the people would arouse surprise or shock to such an extent that an aversion to the sacraments or even a hatred of the Church could result.[108]

This is not a far-fetched contingency. It is easy to imagine the amazement of the faithful if on the occasion of some solemnity they were refused the opportunity to receive Holy Communion when a priest is available and could very well administer It to them. A large group gathered to receive Holy Communion on the occasion of the First Friday, or the First Saturday, would certainly be scandalized if, when their pastor was impeded from giving them Communion for some reason, some other priest deliberately refused to minister to them. In a case such as this the very situation would beget a grave obligation for any priest present to distribute Holy Communion.

Cappello states that a priest who is without the care of souls would be under a grave obligation to administer Holy Communion at Easter time for the fulfillment of the paschal precept, if no pastor or rector held appointment at a certain church.[109]

SCHOLION: THE MINISTER OF FIRST HOLY COMMUNION

The Code places a further obligation on the pastor. The obligation is not explicitly that of administering Communion by his own hand, but rather the obligation of seeing that Holy Communion is received. Canon 854, § 5, makes it a duty of the pastor to see

---

[107] Cappello, *De Sacramentis,* I, n. 384; Coronata, *De Sacramentis,* I, 273; Van Hove, *De Eucharistia,* p. 163; Noldin, *Theologia Moralis,* III, n. 35; Aertnys- Damen, *Theologia Moralis,* II, n. 26.

[108] Van Hove, *De Eucharistia,* p. 163.

[109] *De Sacramentis,* I, n. 384.

that children make their first Holy Communion as soon as they can be sufficiently disposed to do so.[110]

This appears to be an added obligation independent of that which is placed on the pastor by the ruling of canon 860, which obliges the pastor along with the parents, the guardians, the teachers and the confessors to take care that children satisfy the precept of Paschal Communion. In canon 854, § 5, the word *"quamprimum"* seems to have no connection with the paschal precept; it simply implies that Communion be received "without any notable delay." The law desires children to be ready to communicate immediately after attaining the use of reason, and canon 854, § 5, places on the pastor the duty of making sure that children receive their first Holy Communion soon after becoming qualified to do so. The pastor has a further and independent obligation in regard to the fulfillment of the paschal precept by the children of his parish.[111]

The Code does not give the pastor any exclusive prerogative in the administration of the first Holy Communion. But, since he has the duty of seeing that no child receives Communion without the proper dispositions, and at the same time has the additional duty of taking care that all the children, once they are sufficiently disposed, receive the Eucharist,[112] Cappello claims that the pastor has the right to administer the first Holy Communion.[113]

It is true that in certain circumstances the pastor may have the power to give or to refuse the child permission to communicate. He has a general power of vigilance, so that in virtue of his pastoral office he must warn parents of their obligation to induce their children, if they are properly qualified, to receive Holy Communion especially during the paschal season.[114]

On the other hand, he may be obliged to veto the decision of

---

[110] Canon 854, § 5. Parocho autem est officium . . . curandi ut usum rationis assecuti et sufficienter dispositi quamprimum hoc divino cibo reficiantur.

[111] Crotty, *The Recipient of First Holy Communion,* The Catholic University of American Canon Law Studies, n. 247 (Washington, D. C.: The Catholic University of America Press, 1947), pp. 81, 82.

[112] Canon 854, § 5.

[113] *De Sacramentis,* I, nn. 500, 501.

[114] Canons 854, § 5; 860.

fitness made by the parents. And, theoretically at least, the pastor has the power to veto the decision of the confessor regarding the fitness of the child, although in practice it could prove very imprudent for him to do so.[115] It also must be admitted that the pastor is within his right of exercising vigilance when he makes inquiry as to which children are to be admitted to Holy Communion, even though the parents or the confessor are under no obligation to make this known to him.[116]

Certainly the law gives the pastor wide authority in the matter of admitting children to their first Holy Communion. The confessor and the parents by no means enjoy an exclusive competence in this regard. Consequently it seems fitting that the pastor, as the spiritual father of the little ones and as the one who is obliged to vigilance by reason of his pastoral office, should be the minister of the first Holy Communion. But, fitting as it may seem, this function can in no wise be set forth as an exclusive pastoral right.

It is clear now in view of the recent Instruction of the Sacred Congregation of the Sacraments on daily Communion, as also in the light of the precautions which must be taken against possible and likely abuses, that the practice of having general or solemn first Communions can no longer be regarded as commendable.[117] This makes it quite obvious that the administration of first Holy Communion can hardly be regarded as an exclusive right of the pastor. The child could lawfully be admitted to its first Communion in a strange place, or also under circumstances which leave the pastor uninformed prior to the child's reception of its first Holy Communion. But subsequent to such a fact the parents or guardians should bring notice of it to the pastor, for normally it is only in such a way that he will learn with certainty that there no longer rests on him the obligation which he has towards all the children who are still to receive their first Holy Communion.

---

[115] Canon 854, § 5.

[116] Crotty, *The Recipient of First Holy Communion,* p. 91.

[117] S. C. de Sacramentis, 8 Dec. 1938—Bouscaren, *The Canon Law Digest* (2 vols., Milwaukee: Bruce, 1934-1943), II, 208.

CHAPTER IV

The Extraordinary Minister of Holy Communion

ARTICLE 1. THE RIGHT OF THE DEACON BY REASON OF HIS ORDINATION

Canon 845, § 2, states that the extraordinary minister of Holy Communion has been a part of the deacon's office since the very first days of the Church. In ancient times when the faithful received Holy Communion under both species, the ministry of the deacon was quite useful and necessary. After the Latin Church discontinued the administration of Holy Communion under both species the deacon was allowed to administer the Eucharist only under specific circumstances of necessity. The deacon retains the right to exercise this function today, but only under the conditions set down in canon 845, § 2.[1]

The deacon is constituted the extraordinary minister of Holy Communion through his ordination. In the ordination rite of the *Roman Pontifical* the deacons are told to minister at the altar, to baptize,, and to preach. Later the ordaining bishop in his admonition to the deacons exhorts them to be pure, chaste and clean, as befits ministers of Christ and dispensers of the mysteries of God, and again: "Et quia comministri et cooperatores estis Corporis et Sanguinis Domini, estate ab omni illecebra carnis alieni, sicut ait Scriptura: 'Mundamini, qui fertis vasa Domini.!' "[2]

Thus the deacon by his ordination becomes an aid and instrument of the priest in the priest's ministry at the altar. When the ordination rite was drawn up, "ministering at the altar" meant more than it could possibly mean at the present time, for the deacon

[1] "Extraordinarius Minister est diaconus, de Ordinarii loci vel parochi licentia, gravi de causa concedenda, quae in casu necessitatis legitime praesumitur."

[2] *Pontificale Romanum, Summorum Pontificum iussu editum, a Benedicto XIV et Leo XIII Pont. Max. recognitum et castigatum* (*Mechliniae, 1895*), *Pars Tertia, tit., De ordinatione diaconi.*

broke the consecrated loaves, passed the Cup, and brought Communion to the sick as part and parcel of his usual duties.[3] Certainly, today as always, the dispensing of the Holy Eucharist is among the functions whose exercise is conceded to the deacon by these words. As St. Thomas stated, by ordination the deacon is constituted *"propinquus ordini sacerdotali,"* or the immediate minister of the priest, whose pre-eminent right and duty it is to consecrate and distribute the Holy Eucharist.[4] It is beyond the powers of the deacon to share in the consecration, but he can exercise his supplementary role in the administration of the Holy Eucharist to the faithful.[5]

Thus it is that the deacon is constituted the extraordinary minister of Holy Communion. His ministry is called extraordinary not only in the sense that he is the occasional minister, but principally in the sense that he is the auxiliary or secondary minister of this sacrament. When the deacon distributes Holy Communion, he acts only as an instrument or helper of the priest, for it is the priest who is legitimately established by Christ through his priestly power to distribute the Holy Eucharist, and the priest must be the primary minister for the dispensing of Holy Communion to the faithful. This the Code establishes by naming the priest the ordinary minister of Holy Communion.[6] In this respect the administration of Holy Communion does not pertain to the deacon as a principal function which flows from his very office, but only in so far as he ministers to the bishops and to the priests. The deacon's ministry must by its very nature always be of an auxiliary and supplementary nature.

As is indicated by Augustine[7] and Coronata,[8] the power to administer Holy Communion as the deacon receives it in the sacrament of Orders is made subordinate to the jurisdictional powers of the local ordinary and of the pastor in order to show forth the hierarchical order. Since the pastor, who must be a priest, is the

---

[3] Fortescue *The Mass*, pp. 364-370.

[4] *Summa*, Pars III, q. 82, art. 3, ad 1.

[5] Cappello, *De Sacramentis*, I, n. 303.

[6] Canon 845, § 1.

[7] *Commentary*, IV, 213, 214.

[8] *De Sacramentis*, I, 270.

legitimate head of the flock assigned to him, it is becoming that the deacon, who is his inferior, should depend on him for permission to exercise this power. These statements are both quite true, but they do not imply the sole, or even the fundamental, reason for the dependence of the deacon upon the power of the priest in the administration of Holy Communion. A simple priest, one without any pastoral authority, likewise is subordinate to the pastor in the administration of Communion.

The dependent rôle of the deacon does not simply connote an artificial or arbitrary subjection to authority as created by centuries of customary usage. Both Augustine and Coronata seem to attach a disproportionate stress to the Church's early practice and discipline in this matter.[9] Rather, the rôle of the deacon in the administration of Holy Communion is by its very nature subsidiary and dependent on the power of the priesthood. This is further indicated from the fact that the authority of the pastor over the deacon is of a different nature than that which he exercises over any priest who may need his permission in order to distribute Communion. The secondary and supplementary rôle of the deacon is well illustrated in the comparison as drawn by the Salmanticenses with reference to the priest and the deacon. For the administration of Holy Communion the priest looked at most to one of his equals for permission; the deacon looked to the priest as a superior who could engage his inferior as a subordinate minister.

> Nam sacerdos ex sua ordinatione habet potestatem ad absolute ministrandum Eucharistiam; eget tamen assignatione ovium quibus ministret: sed diaconus, licet ex ordinatione sua sit subjectum idoneum ut ad hujusmodi ministerium eligatur, semper tamen respicit actum ministrandi ut dependetem a consensu alterius. Praeterea, sacerdos simplex, quamvis ex commissione ministret, nihilominus non ministrat ut famulus, minister, aut instrumentum alterium sacerdotis; sed utitur sua dispensandi potestate sibi in sua consecratione collata: sed diaconus in ipsa consecratione accipit, quod sit minister sacerdotis, et quod possit ab eo ad istud ministerium

[9] *Loc. cit.*

> eligi; unde, cum actu dispensat Eucharistiam, agit formaliter ut sacerdotis minister.[10]

The Council of Trent insisted that from the very manner of Christ's institution of it the sacrament of the Holy Eucharist falls under the authority and the power of the priest.[11] Yet within this framework there remains a place for the administration of Holy Communion by the deacon. With the proper authorization he can lawfully make use of the power conferred on him through the sacrament of Holy Orders.

The Council of Trent had stated that the manner of dispensing the Holy Eucharist has been left to the decision of the Church in accordance with the variety of circumstantial exigencies as they arose.[12] Suarez subsequently pointed out that the Eucharist in Its nature of Holy Communion could be differentiated from the Eucharist in its nature of a sacrament. From the viewpoint of the divine law it was not necessary that the consecrating agent be also the one who dispenses the sacrament. The consecration and the administration of the Holy Eucharist were distinct and separable actions. The use of this sacrament for the purpose of Holy Communion was certainly not an element that was essential to the sacrament's existence, for the giving of Holy Communion did not pertain inherently to the essence which gives to the Holy Eucharist Its reality of existence as a sacrament. Hence the Church, always with adequate safeguards for the reverence and veneration which are due, could authorize the deacon, as the aid and minister of the priest, to dispense the Eucharist in such measure as the utility of the faithful called for Its distribution.[13]

---

[10] *Cursus Theologia Moralis* (6 tom. in 3, Venetiis, 1728), *De Eucharistia,* disp. XII, sub. 4, § 2, n. 24.

[11] Sess. XIII, *de Eucharistia,* c. 8; sess. XXIII, *de ordine,* c. 1.

[12] Sess. XXI, *de Communione,* c. 2. "Praeterea declarat, hanc potestatem perpetuo in Ecclesia fuisse, ut in sacramentorum dispensatione, salva illorum substantia, ea statueret vel mutaret quae suscipientium utilitati seu ipsorum sacramentorum venerationi pro rerum, temporum et locorum varietate magis expedire iudicaret."

[13] Suarez, *Tertia Pars Summae Theologicae,* Disp. LXXII, Sect. I, n. 6—*Opera Omnia,* XXI, 577.

Suarez moreover contended that there was nothing incongruous in the act by which the deacon became authorized for the distribution of Holy Communion. There was no strict requirement for the possession of any supernatural power in the administration of the Eucharist. If that were so, then no human person could administer the sacrament. The Holy Eucharist Itself was certainly supernatural, but it sufficed that in the act of distributing It the deacon exercise that function by way of commission from the priest, who in his character participated in the powers of Christ.[14]

ARTICLE 2. AUTHORIZATION FOR THE LAWFUL ADMINISTRATION

Section 1. A Grave Cause

In order that a deacon may lawfully use his power to administer Holy Communion to the faithful, there is required, along with the existence of a grave cause for it, a commission from the local ordinary or the pastor. What precisely is the nature of this cause? Authors for the most part answer this question by way of illustrating what they consider as a grave cause. That is much simpler than attempting to explain the nature of a grave cause in accordance with the meaning of the law in canon 845, § 2.[15]

This question is a rather involved one, particularly in view of the fact that for a deacon's solemn administration of the sacrament of baptism the Code requires but a just cause.[16] The Code states that the deacon is the extraordinary minister of both functions, and that for the lawful exercise of either he needs permission and a justifying reason. Because of the parity of these ministries as allowed to the deacon, and in view of the generally similar language in which they are described in the Code, it could indeed be argued that in canon 845, § 2, the words *"gravi de causa"*

---

[14] *Loc. cit.*

[15] "Extraordinarius [minister] est diaconus, de Ordinarii loci vel parochi licentia, gravi de causa concedenda, quae in casu necessitatis legitime praesumitur."

[16] Canon 741—Extraordinarius baptismi sollemnis minister est diaconus; qui tamen sua potestate ne utatur sine loci Ordinarii vel parochi licentia, iusta de causa concedenda, quae, ubi necessitas urgeat, legitime praesumitur.

exact no more than the words *"iusta de causa"* demand in canon 741.[17]

It seems, however, that the Code has changed the age-old parity that may have existed between the two functions: It is known from Cardinal Gasparri's *Schema* that, in the drafting of the law for the distribution of Holy Communion by the deacon, the words *"iusta de causa"* did receive consideration, inasmuch as they then occupied the place of the words *"gravi de causa,"* which latter phrase was nevertheless adopted in the Code.[18] In this *Schema* one finds in canon 121, § 2, the identical law of canon 845, § 2, with the exception of that the words *"iusta de causa"* are used instead of the words *"gravi de causa."* It was thus not through any inadvertence on the part of the lawmaker that these two extraordinary ministries of the deacon were authorized in a different manner. Rather, it is evident that the lawmaker in a very positive way accepted the stricter reading in place of the less strict reading with reference to the possible authorization of the deacon for the distributing of Holy Communion. The less strict reading patently abided its acceptance by the lawgiver, but was in fact exchanged by him for the stricter reading. In view of this fact it can hardly be said that the Code in canons 741 and 845, § 2, indeed uses two different words but nevertheless adopts the same meaning for both.

If the pre-Code law on the administration of solemn baptism by the deacon is examined, it will be seen that a degree of necessity, at times even more extreme than that which was postulated for the lawful administration of Holy Communion by the deacon, was demanded. After the first five centuries, with the increase in the number of priests and the gradual disappearance of the diaconate as a functional order, there was rare mention, up until the time of Gratian, of the fact that the deacon retained any right to baptize solemnly. For the greater part, his competence in this

---

[17] Donovan, "When May Deacons Give Communion"—*The Homiletic and Pastoral Review* (New York, 1900—), XLII (1942), 823-826 (henceforth cited *HPR*).

[18] *Schema Codicis Iuris Canonici* (Romae, 1913), Lib. III. Canon 121, § 2.

regard seemed to be relegated to the rôle of assisting the priest in the administration of baptism.[19]

Even in the time of Gratian the necessity which was postulated if the deacon was to act lawfully even with the permission of the pastor was of equal gravity with that which would have allowed any lay person to baptize privately.[20] Particular legislation and the doctrine of the decretalists mitigated the severity of this law to the extent that no longer was an extreme necessity postulated for any necessity in the broad sense of the term was deemed sufficient in warrant of the pastor's authorization of the deacon to baptize solemnly.[21]

The Code no longer postulates even this necessity in its enactment that *"iusta de causa"* the deacon may be authorized to baptize solemnly. It should be noted that it is not a just cause, but rather a grave cause, that may duly be equated with the necessity which Gratian demanded in the law which reflects the common source of canon 741 and canon 845, § 2.[22] It is the presence of such a grave cause that is now set forth as a necessary requirement for the lawful administration of Holy Communion by the deacon, though it is no longer required for the lawful administration of solemn baptism. This change in canon 741 from the older law is a further indication that the strict parity no longer exists in the deacon's exercise of these two extraordinary functions.

Consequently, as is indicated by Van Hove, for the proper authorization of the deacon to administer Holy Communion more is required than the presence of simply a just cause.[23] A just cause may be either grave or light, depending on the nature of the law to which it pertains, and on the subjective circumstances of person and place; a grave cause is one which by its nature is more serious in its import. A just cause will be more or less grave according as there exists a greater or a lesser degree of a particular law's

---

[19] Waldron, *The Minister of Baptism,* The Catholic University of America Canon Law Studies, n. 170 (Washington, D. C.: The Catholic University of America Press, 1942), p. 35.

[20] Waldron, *op. cit.*, p. 51.

[21] Schmalzgrueber, Lib. III, tit. 42, n. 43.

[22] C. 13, D. XCIII.

[23] *De Eucharistia,* p. 154.

subordination to the common good, and according as there obtains a greater or a lesser universal necessity for the observance of the law.[24] When a grave excusing cause is postulated for a deviation from the law, there is implied this greater universal necessity for the observance of the law, or also the greater degree of subordination which invests the law in its relation to the common good. A just cause may be determined in many instances from the subjective dispositions of the subject, but a grave cause must be invested with an objective seriousness which connotes for it the likelihood of a universal applicability. The presence of a grave cause points to an extant condition of need which would make a deviation from the law the more reasonable thing for any and all individuals despite the greater universal need for the observance of the law.[25]

One must therefore look for an objective element in whatever is to constitute a grave cause which, in connection with at least a presumed permission or authorization, will suffice to allow a deacon to distribute Holy Communion. In this respect the pre-Code law proved very helpful, for it furnished just such a norm. The pre-Code law for many centuries was constant in its insistence on the presence of a necessity, along with the permission of the priest.[26] But this necessity was generally interpreted not in the sense of an extreme necessity, which as such could have furnished a reason for the deacon to exercise his ministry solely for the administration of Holy Viaticum. St. Alphonsus, after making a detailed study of the question, came to the conclusion that it was not an extreme necessity, such as the danger of being deprived of the Holy Eucharist at the hour of death, but rather a grave necessity or a grave cause that proved sufficient for the lawful authorization of a deacon to distribute Holy Communion.[27] This opinion was generally concurred in by the pre-Code commentators. For the deacon's lawful administration

---

[24] Michiels, *Normae Generales Iuris Canonici* (2 vols., Lublin: Universitas Catholica, 1929), II, 507.

[25] Coronata, *De Sacramentis*, I, 270, footnote 8.

[26] Gasparri, *De Eucharistia*, II, n. 1079.

[27] *Theologia Moralis*, Lib. VI, n. 237.

of Holy Communion nothing more was postulated than what they called a grave necessity in connection with the non-availability of a priest who could conveniently care for the legitimate need of the faithful.[28]

Inasmuch as the pre-Code law so generally interpreted the postulated necessity in the sense of a grave cause, Woywod remarked that the Code only seemingly but not actually changed the former law when it required *a grave reason* instead of *a necessity* for the administration of Holy Communion by the deacon.[29] For, so he added, if one consults the commentators of the earlier law, it becomes quite evident that they interpreted this necessity in the very sense of a grave reason. Coronata likewise notes that the difference between the earlier law and the law in the present Code is a verbal rather than a real one.[30]

The earlier law continues to have juridical force in so far as it can be said to be embodied in the Code. The former law as then understood serves as an interpretative norm of the law incorporated in the present Code whenever the new and old law coincide.[31] In regard to the administration of Holy Communion by the deacon, the entire matter of the earlier law is now regulated in canon 845, § 2. Though the language is different, albeit the terminology is not entirely new, the law appears to be the same. Whenever it is doubtful whether the newer law lacks harmony with the older law, the latter is to be upheld in its application.[32] So also, when it is doubtful whether a praescription of the canon changes the older law, the latter is to be favored as a more seasoned rule of interpretation.[33] As Coronata[34] and Woywod[35]

[28] Cf. Gasparri, Gury, Ballerini-Palmieri, Schmalzgrueber Genicot-Salsmans, Lehmkuhl, etc., *supra*, pp. 23-26; 50-56.

[29] *A Practical Commentary,* I, n. 743.

[30] *De Sacramentis,* I, 270, footnote 5.

[31] Canon 6, 2° and 3°.

[32] Canon 6, 4°.—In dubio num aliquod canonum praescriptum cum veteri iure discrepet, a veteri iure non est recendendum.

[33] Neuberger, *Canon 6, or the Relation of the Codex Iuris Canonici to the Preceding Legislation,* The Catholic University of America Canon Law Studies, n. 44 (Washington, D. C.: The Catholic University of America, 1927), pp. 84, 85.

[34] *De Sacramentis,* I, 270, footnote 5.

[35] *A Practical Commentary,* I, n. 743.

indicate, the law of the Code is similar enough to the older law to make it at least doubtful that there is a change. Hence, the acknowledged meaning of the older law can be accepted as a norm of interpretation for the present law, and the nature of the justifying reason which under the older law was called a necessity will help to determine the nature of a grave cause which in the present Code demands for the lawful authorization of the deacon to administer Holy Communion.

Certainly the Code does not demand a most grave reason before the deacon can be permitted to administer Holy Communion. Extreme spiritual necessity is not required before the deacon can lawfully be accorded the needed authorization.[36] Rather, a simply grave cause will be sufficient. If again one turn to the older law, one will note that two conditions were considered essential for the constituting of a grave cause: first, the utility of the faithful; secondly, the non-availability of a priest to administer to them. When these conditions were fulfilled, it was lawful to authorize the deacon to administer Holy Communion.[37]

In accordance with this principle one should look for these elements as present in every case if it is to justify the authorization of the deacon to distribute Communion. From this it appears that not sufficient justification is present if a deacon were allowed to distribute Communion solely for the reason of exercising his Orders, or simply out of devotion, or exclusively for the sake of gaining greater facility in the administration of the Holy Eucharist.[38] The principle is indeed sufficiently flexible to forestall all potential hardship on the part of the faithful. From this approach one may indeed conceive of the gravity of the cause in a broad sense. The cause exists as a grave cause when-

---

[36] Vermeersch-Creusen, *Epitome,* II, n. 112; Van Hove, *De Eucharisita,* p. 154; Coronata, *De Sacramentis,* I, 271; Noldin, *Theologia Moralis,* III, n. 125.

[37] Suarez, *Tertia Pars Summae Theologicae,* Disp. LXXII, Sect. I, n. 8—*Opera Omnia,* XXI, 578; Gasparri, *De Eucharistia,* II, n. 1079; Lehmkuhl, *Theologia Moralis,* II, n. 180; and the various authors cited by them.

[38] Regatillo, *Ius Sacramentarium,* I, n. 308.

ever a real physical or moral necessity underlies the deacon's act of distributing Holy Communion.[39]

All authors agree that the deacon could give Viaticum to a dying person if no priest were available to do so. Other justifying reasons are mentioned by the authors. The deacon may distribute Communion when the faithful come to receive, even if only out of devotion, but the priest is absent, or sick, or impeded for some reason.[40] He likewise may do so if great numbers desire to receive Communion when no additional priests are on hand to help with the distribution, for otherwise the distribution of Holy Communion would be drawn out for an unduly long time.[41] Furthermore, he can allowably do so if the priest is busy in some parochial work, such as the preaching of a sermon, the hearing of confessions, etc., and considerable inconvenience results for the faithful in their having to await the services of the priest.[42] Coronata also considers the priest's necessary proximate preparation of a sermon as a factor which proves sufficient to denote that the priest is not available for the distribution of Communion.[43]

Contrary to what Augustine stated,[44] it is not necessary that there be a large number of the faithful who would be inconvenienced through being deprived of Communion if there is to be a grave cause for the deacon to become authorized to minister to them. Today, with the Church's insistence on frequent Communion, and with the general increase of frequent and even daily Communion on the part of the faithful, the necessitated deferring or postponing of the reception of Holy Com-

---

[39] Cappello, *De Sacramentis,* I, n. 304.

[40] Cappello, *De Sacramentis,* I, n. 303; Coronata, *De Sacramentis,* I, 270; Vermeersch-Creusen, *Epitome,* II, n. 112; Iorio, *Theologia Moralis,* III, n. 119; Durieux, *The Eucharist, Law and Practice* (trans. by Oliver Dolphin, Fairbault, Minn., 1926), p. 160.

[41] Regatillo, *Ius Sacramentarium,* I, n. 308; Coronata, *loc. cit.;* Vermeersch-Creusen, *loc. cit.*

[42] Regatillo, *loc. cit.;* Noldin, *Theologia Moralis,* III, n. 125; Coronata, *loc cit.;* Cappello, *loc. cit.;* Jone, *Moral Theology,* n. 498; Iorio, *loc. cit.;* Vermeersch-Creusen, *loc. cit.*

[43] *De Sacramentis,* I, 270.

[44] *Commentary,* IV, 214.

munion on the part of a few persons, or even a single one, could constitute the grave cause which is postulated in the law.[45]

The mere convenience which the service of the deacon could offer to the parish priest would not constitute a grave cause, and hence, if that were the sole reason, the deacon could not be authorized to distribute Holy Communion. But if the aid of the deacon were extremely useful for the better arrangement of the parish schedule and the consequent accommodation and welfare of the faithful, then a deacon could be authorized to administer Communion as long as there were no additional priests to care for this need.

In the presence of an excommunicated priest who under command of the Church must be utterly shunned (*excommunicatus vitandus*), or of a priest whose excommunication, suspension, or personal interdict is attended with a declaratory or condemnatory sentence, there is certainly present a grave cause which serves as a justifying reason to call upon the services of a deacon.[46]

Priests who have simply contracted an excommunication, or have become suspended or personally interdicted apart from any attendant declaratory or condemnatory sentence, can lawfully administer the sacrament of Holy Eucharist as often as the faithful legitimately ask it of them.[47] However, Cappello holds as more probable the doctrime that the deacon could be called on to distribute Communion in the presence of such priests, provided that the censure or canonical penalty was of a public character.[48] The reason why Cappello makes a distinction between a secretly and a publicly excommunicated priest is hard to see, unless he feels that in the former situation all risk of scandal is foreclosed, whereas in the latter situation such a risk may be imminent. Canon 2261 does not make such a distinction. Since canon 2261, § 3, does not make mention even of the notoriously excommunicated priest, he evidently must find classification under § 2 of canon 2261, which would allow him

[45] Iorio, *Theologia Moralis,* III, n. 125.
[46] Cappello, *De Sacramentis,* I, n. 303.
[47] Canon 2261, § 2.
[48] *De Sacramentis,* I, n. 303.

to administer the sacraments when asked to do so. Consequently, in the presence of a priest who is simply excommunicated or suspended or under personal interdict apart from any attendant sentence, there would not be a grave cause justifying the authorization of the deacon to administer Holy Communion unless scandal were imminent.

Section 2. Proper Permission

Canon 845, § 2, demands the permission of the pastoral authority in addition to a justifying reason for the lawful administration of Holy Communion by the deacon.[49] The word "pastor" is to be undestood in a flexible sense. It denotes everyone who exercises a pastoral care and accordingly distributes Holy Communion *iure propria.*[50] Included, then, are local ordinaries,[51] clerical religious superiors,[52] pastors,[53] all who in this matter are placed on a par with pastors,[54] the rectors of seminaries,[55] the ordinary confessors of nuns,[56] the chaplains who are assigned for any group which is withdrawn from the jurisdiction of the local pastor,[57] and the chaplains of lay religious.[58] Coronata[59] and Regatillo[60] allow also the rector of a church to authorize the deacon to distribute Holy Communion. The rector's faculty to distribute Communion is indeed given to him by the law itself. However, the administration of Holy Communion is one of the

---

[49] "Extraordinarius [minister] est diaconus, de Ordinarii loci vel parochi licentia, gravi de causa concedenda, quae in casu necessitatis legitime praesumitur."

[50] Vermeersch-Creusen, *Epitome,* II, n. 112; Cappello, *De Sacramentis,* I, n. 303; Coronata, *De Sacramentis,* I, 271; Regatillo, *Ius Sacramentarium,* I, n. 308.

[51] Canon 198, § 1.

[52] Canon 514, § 1.

[53] Canon 467, § 1.

[54] Canon 452, § 2.

[55] Canon 1368.

[56] Canon 514, § 2.

[57] Canon 464, § 2.

[58] Canons 464, § 2, and 514, § 3.

[59] *De Sacramentis,* I, 271.

[60] *Ius Sacramentarium,* I, n. 308.

principal means of sanctification in the Church, and is therefore a pastoral function. Consequently the pastor of the territory in which the church or the public oratory is located has the right to grant the requisite permission which enables a deacon to assist in this pastoral work.[61]

In the presence of the pastor or of the local ordinary the deacon must have an express permission.[62] Such an express permission is required as evincing the due subordination and proper subjection of the deacon to the pastoral authority. However, the Code itself states that this permission may be presumed in a case of necessity.[63] Therefore, if in a case of necessity the pastor cannot be reached, the permission may be considered as granted by force of the common law itself. This holds true also if it were possible to have recourse to the bishop when the pastor is not available. Under such circumstances there is no need to attempt to reach the local ordinary, for the permission may be presumed from the interpretative will of the pastor in accordance with the norm of this canon.[64] Permission is also to be considered as granted by a higher authority and as lawfully presumed whenever the pastor would unreasonably or unjustly refuse the requested permission.[65]

The last phrase of the canon, *"quae in casu necessitatis legitime praesumitur,"* certainly means that the deacon may presume permission to administer Holy Viaticum to a person in danger of death who otherwise would die without the Holy Eucharist. Without doubt under such a necessity would also be included the administration of the Paschal Communion to such as would have no opportunity to receive it on some other day. But this

---

[61] Cappello, *De Sacramentis,* I, n. 303; Vermeersch-Creusen, *Epitome,* II, n. 112; Iorio, *Theologia Moralis,* III, n. 119; Durieux, *The Eucharist, Law and Practice,* p. 161.

[62] Coronata, *De Sacramentis,* I, 271; Cappello, *De Sacramentis,* I, n. 303.

[63] Canon 845, § 2.—Extraordinarius [minister] est diaconus, de Ordinarii loci vel parochi licentia, gravi de causa concedenda, quae in casu necessitatis legitime praesumitur.

[64] Blat, *Commentarium Textus Codicis Iuris Canonici* (5 vols. in 7, Lib. III, pars I [*De Sacramentis*], Romae, 1924), Lib. III, Pars I, n. 162 (hereafter cited *De Sacramentis*).

[65] Blat, *loc. cit.*; Cappello, *De Sacramentis,* I, n. 303.

necessity need not be restricted to such extreme cases. As Vermeersch noted, necessity in this instance is to be taken to mean that there is present a grave reason for the administration of Holy Communion, and that unless the deacon would administer Communion, It could not be distributed.[66]

The deacon would reasonably presume permission to administer Holy Communion whenever a grave cause presented itself and the pastor could not be reached for the purpose of obtaining from him permission.[67] This holds true even if those who desired to receive Communion sought to do so, not for the fulfillment of some precept, but simply out of devotion.[68]

The permission which the law demands in addition to the grave cause for the lawful dispensation of the Holy Eucharist by the deacon may be granted habitually. If the grave cause persists, there is no intrinsic reason why the deacon could not be given habitual permission to exercise this extraordinary function.[69] Cappello[70] and Regatillo[71] hold that apart from grave scandal or contempt it is more probable that a deacon does not sin gravely in administering Communion without a grave cause, or without the proper permission. Likewise they excuse the pastor and the local ordinary from grave fault if without a grave cause these authorize the deacon to distribute Holy Communion. These opinions seem tenable on at least the extrinsic authority of these authors.

However, the contrary opinion appears more probable, for in administering Holy Communion without the proper permission the deacon violates the right of the pastor in a notable matter. In addition, a deacon when acting without the needed authorization violates the rules of the hierarchic order, which demand that the deacon be subject to the jurisdictional power of the pastor and the local ordinary in the administration of the sacraments.[72]

---

[66] *Epitome,* II, n. 112.

[67] Cappello, *De Sacramentis,* I, n. 303.

[68] Regatillo, *Ius Sacramentarium,* I, n. 308.

[69] Iorio, *Theologia Moralis,* III, n. 119.

[70] *De Sacramentis,* I, n. 303.

[71] *Ius Sacramentarium,* I, n. 308.

[72] Vermeersch-Creusen, *Epitome,* II, n. 112; Iorio, *Theologia Moralis,* III, n. 119; Prümmer, *Manuale Theologiae Moralis* (3a. ed., 3 vols., Friburgi Brisgoviae: Herder, 1923), III, n. 217; Coronata, *De Sacramentis,* I, 272; Durieux, *The Eucharist, Law and Practice,* p. 161.

All authors concede that the deacon may be authorized to administer Holy Communion when there is doubt as to the gravity of the cause.

If the deacon administered Holy Communion unlawfully he would not become irregular, even though it be assumed that he thereby sinned gravely. Just on what score Cappello considers the contrary opinion as the more common opinion is difficult to discover. Even before the advent of the present Code the incurring of an irregularity through such an unlawful ministration was considered very doubtful.[73] Today the opinion that the irregularity is not incurred appears certain.[74]

When the deacon administers the Holy Eucharist unlawfully he does not incur the irregularity, for when in the distributing of Communion the deacon proceeds without the needed authorization he does indeed exercise a function which he is forbidden to exercise, but he does not perform an act whose potential exercise is not inherent in his ordination to the diaconate. It cannot be said that the deacon usurps the exercise of an order, for in virtue of his ordination he receives the power of administering the Holy Eucharist once It has been consecrated by the priest. He is by reason of his ordination constituted the extraordinary minister for the dispensing of the Holy Eucharist. Consequently the deacon does not, as one who lacks the needed Orders, exercise a function which is reserved to clerics in Sacred Orders,[75] for actually he has received this Order in his ordination to the diaconate. In reality, the case connotes rather a difficient jurisdictional commission than a lack of Sacred Orders when

---

[73] Gasparri, *De Eucharistia,* II, n. 1079; Ballerini-Palmieri, Tract. X, Sect. IV, n. 85.

[74] Cappello, *De Sacramentis,* I, n. 304; Aertnys-Damen, *Theologia Moralis,* II, n. 122; Noldin, *Theologia Moralis,* III, n. 498; Vermeersch-Creusen, *Epitome,* II, n. 112; Iorio, *Theologia Moralis,* III, n. 119; Regatillo, *Ius Sacramentarium,* I, n. 308; Coronata, *De Sacramentis,* I, 272; Van Hove, *De Eucharistia,* p. 155; Jone, *Moral Theology,* n. 498; Prummer, *Manuale Theologiae Moralis,* III, n. 217; et alii.

[75] Canon 985.—"Sunt irregulares ex delicto: 7°. Qui actum ordinis, clericis in ordine sacro constitutis reservatum, ponunt, vel eo ordine carentes, vel ab eius exercitio poena canonica sive personali, medicinali aut vindicativa, sive locali prohibiti.

the deacon administers Holy Communion without the proper authorization. The deacon who acts without authorization exercises a power that rightly belongs to him by reason of his ordination. The deformity of his act consists in the lact of his due subordination to the proper pastoral authority.[76]

Granted that there is present the measure of necessity which the law postulates, the deacon may lawfully administer Communion to himself. In extreme necessity, that is, in the event that no priest is at hand to administer Viaticum to the dying deacon, he may certainly communicate himself. But authors do not limit the deacon's right to give Communion to himself to the case of such extreme necessity. It is commonly held that the deacon may give Communion to himself in consideration of his legitimate devotion if no priest is available and if all occasion for scandal is precluded.[77]

In distributing Holy Communion the deacon observes the same ceremonies as the priest with the exception that the deacon wears the stole crossed on the right side after the manner of a deacon.[78] When the deacon distributes Communion in church, he performs all the usual ceremonies, inclusive of the final blessing of the people.[79]

By reason of canon 1274, § 2, there was never any question of the right of the deacon to bless the sick and the bystanders with the Blessed Sacrament after the administration of Viaticum.[80]

---

[76] Cappello, *De Sacramentis,* I, n. 304; Regatillo, *Ius Sacramentarium,* I, n. 308; Coronata, *De Sacramentis,* I, 272.

[77] Gasparri, *De Eucharistia,* II, n. 1081; Augustine, *Commentary,* IV, 215; Cappello, *De Sacramentis,* I, n. 307; Coronata, *De Sacramentis,* I, 273; Vermeersch-Creusen, *Epitome,* II, n. 113.

[78] Augustine, *Commentary,* IV, 214, 215; Cappello, *De Sacramentis,* I, nn. 388, 390; Coronata, *De Sacramentis,* I, 272; Noldin, *Theologia Moralis,* III, n. 125.

[79] *Rituale Romanum* (Editio II. Iuxta Typicam Vaticanam, Neo Eboraci: Benziger Brothers, 1945), Tit. IV, cap. II, n. 10; Pontificia Commissio Interpretationis (PCI), 13 iul. 1930—Bouscaren, *Canon Law Digest,* I, 404; *AAS,* XXII (1930), 365.

[80] ". . . minister vero benedictionis Eucharistiae est solus sacerdos, nec eam impertire diaconus potest, nisi in casu quo, ad normam can. 845, § 2, Viaticum ad infirmum detulerit."

When the deacon is without the possession of the Holy Eucharist after his administration of Holy Communion to the sick, he gives the blessing by hand in the customary manner.[81]

ARTICLE 3. THE OBLIGATION OF THE DEACON

The deacon as the auxiliary and extraordinary minister of Holy Communion has an obligation in charity to administer this sacrament. This obligation, which arises from the virtue of charity, is not a grave obligation except in cases of necessity.[82] Outside of the danger of death there would be a grave obligation for the deacon to administer the Paschal Communion to such as would have no opportunity to receive It on some other day.[83] In a similar manner, if on the occasion of a great solemnity many desired to receive Holy Communion when no priests were at hand, a grave obligation would be incumbent on the deacon as the extraordinary minister of Holy Communion to provide for the needs of the faithful.[84]

The deacon is under serious obligation to administer Holy Viaticum to a dying person who otherwise would not be able to receive It.[85] Although this sacrament is not absolutely necessary for salvation, the graces It confers are considered of such value that the Code places a serious obligation on all to receive It.[86] The obligation to administer Holy Viaticum is grave for the deacon when no priest is available, for out of charity one is bound to succor his neighbor when he is in great need, even at the cost of great effort.[87]

To what extent would the deacon be obligated in the face of danger to his own life to administer Holy Viaticum? The obligation of a simple priest to administer Viaticum is not a grave

[81] *Rituale Romanum,* Tit. IV, cap. IV, n. 28.

[82] Cappello, *De Sacramentis,* I, n. 384.

[83] Augustine, *Commentary,* IV, 214.

[84] Cappello, *De Sacramentis,* I, n. 384.

[85] St. Alphonsus, *Theologia Moralis,* Lib. VI, n. 237; Cappello, *De Sacramentis,* I, n. 384; Aertnys-Damen, *Theologia Moralis,* II, n. 122, Noldin, *Theologia Moralis,* III, n. 125.

[86] Canon 864, § 1.

[87] Genicot-Salsmans, *Institutiones Theologiae Moralis,* II, n. 120.

obligation when a certain and grave danger exists for his own life, despite the fact that under like circumstances he would be obliged to make an effort to give absolution to one who without the reception of the sacrament of penance would be in serious danger of losing his salvation.[88] A simple priest could with the administration of the sacrament of penance remove the spiritual necessity which weighs upon the dying man, and hence there would no longer exist for the priest a serious obligation to administer Holy Viaticum.

Under similar circumstances there does not rest upon the deacon any grave obligation to administer Holy Viaticum, namely, when there is an imminent great peril for his own life, even though the dying person is in such a condition of necessity that he can save himself only under the accompaniment of considerable difficulty. If the obligation is to exist as a grave obligation for the deacon, then it must be certain that his help is absolutely essential, that the peril of the dying person is positively certain, and that the hope of saving him exists as a duly warranted prospect.[89]

Inasmuch as Holy Viaticum is not necessary in the nature of an essential means for salvation, a man can never be said to be in extreme need of Holy Viaticum, since it is always possible for him to elicit an act of perfect contrition. In fact, if the dying person were in serious sin, he would be under the necessity of eliciting an act of perfect contrition before the deacon could administer Holy Viaticum to him.[90]

Authors state that under such circumstances the eliciting of an act of perfect contrition is a requirement not only of the ecclesiastical law, but of the divine law as well.[91] To say that the reception of the Blessed Sacrament is needed in order that the sinner may be able to elicit an act of perfect contrition is a rather gratuitous assertion. The very questionable warrant for such an assertion cannot be accepted as a foundation for the

---

[88] Coronata, *De Sacramentis,* I, 46; Noldin, *Theologia Moralis,* III, n. 35; Cappello, *De Sacramentis,* I, n. 56.

[89] Coronata, *loc. cit.;* Cappello, *De Sacramentis,* I, n. 54.

[90] Canon 856.

[91] Noldin, *Theologia Moralis,* III, n. 141; Cappello, *De Sacramentis,* I, n. 141; Coronata, *De Sacramentis,* I, 152.

claim that a certified grave obligation rests upon the deacon for the administration of Holy Viaticum even at the risk of serious peril to his own life.[92]

Corollary: The Administration of Holy Communion by Lower Clerics and by the Laity

The deacon alone is the extraordinary and secondary minister of Holy Communion.[93] It is only the deacon who in virtue of his ordination is made an auxiliary of the priest in the administration of the Holy Eucharist. There is no mention in the Code of the administration of the Holy Eucharist by clerics who are not at least deacons, or by lay people. Yet may there not be warrant for the possible administration of Holy Communion by lower Clerics, and even by the laity?

The common opinion today is that clerics with less than diaconal Orders, and also the laity, may administer Holy Viaticum to a dying person if no priest or deacon is available to minister to him.[94] As Cappello[95] and Noldin[96] have pointed out, it would be lawful for clerics and also for the laity to give Holy Viaticum to themselves under the same conditions of necessity as would make lawful their administration of Holy Viaticum to others.

The commission of the pastor or of the local ordinary is necessary for the lawful administration of Holy Communion by the deacon. *A fortiori,* lower clerics and the laity cannot lawfully administer Holy Viaticum without the authorization of the lawful pastoral authority. In the absense of a priest or of a deacon

[92] Ballerini-Palmieri (*Opus Theologicum Morale,* II, n. 51) and Genicot-Salsmans (*Institutiones Theologiae Moralis,* I, n. 217) state that no one is so unlearned that with the aid of God's grace he could not elicit an act of perfect contrition.

[93] Canon 845, § 2.

[94] Aertnys-Damen, *Theologia Moralis,* II, n. 122; Cappello, *De Sacramentis,* I, n. 305; Iorio, *Theologia Moralis,* III, n. 120; Coronata, *De Sacramentis,* I, 271; Jone, *Moral Theology,* n. 498; Noldin, *Theologia Moralis,* III, n. 125; Augustine, *Commentary,* IV, 214; Vermeersch-Creusen, *Epitome,* II, n. 113; Regatillo, *Ius Sacramentarium,* I, n. 309.

[95] *De Sacramentis,* I, n. 308.

[96] *Theologia Moralis,* III, n. 125.

to administer Holy Viaticum, given the extreme necessity which warrants the ministry on the part of the lower clerics or of the laity, these may act with a presumed permission when there is no possibility of reaching the pastor or the local ordinary.[97]

If the question is one of general policy, and not of immediate extreme necessity, then no one in authority below the local ordinary is qualified to commission lower clerics or the laity to administer the Holy Eucharist. At such times it pertains to the local ordinary to make the judgment regarding the verification of the conditions which are required for the creating of a necessity that calls for the aid of the laity or of the minor clerics in the administration of Holy Viaticum. Such a situation could obtain in what Iorio calls a general necessity,[98] as, for example, in times of persecution, plague, war, or other general disaster. The current practice is for the local ordinary in times of general necessity to apply to the Holy See which will authorize him to permit lower clerics and laymen of good repute to administer the Holy Eucharist. However, such an indult does not appear to be absolutely necessary.[99]

Certainly if the delay in having recourse to the Holy See might cause grave harm, lower clerics and laymen could be authorized by the local ordinary to secretly carry Holy Viaticum to the dying.[100] It must always be maintained as a fundamental principle that in such times of genearl necessity the manner of the administration of Holy Viaticum is not to be left to the discretion of the lower clerics or of the laity, but the instructions and orders of the local ordinary must be carefully observed.[101]

In the exercise of this exceptional ministry a due order of precedence is to be followed. The laity could exercise this function only when no clerics would be available, and clerics could under-

---

[97] Coronata, *De Sacramentis,* I, 271; Cappello, *De Sacramentis,* I, n. 305; Iorio, *La Communione agl 'Infermi* (Roma: F. Pustet, 1931), p. 58.

[98] *La Communione Agl 'Infermi,* p. 56.

[99] Cappello, *De Sacramentis,* I, n. 305; Durieux, *The Eucharist, Law and Practice,* p. 161; Iorio, *Theologia Moralis,* III, n. 120.

[100] Iorio, *La Communione agl 'Infermi,* p. 58.

[101] Vermeersch-Creusen, *Epitome,* II, n. 113.

take this ministry only when other clerics of higher rank in Orders would not be availablc.[102]

It is necessary in all cases that scandal and irreverence to the Holy Eucharist be obviated. Scandal is not apt to arise when due respect and proper reverence are shown in the carrying and administering of Holy Communion. In all cases wherein authorization for this exceptional ministry is expressly granted by the pastor or by the local ordinary, scandal may easily be obviated by means of a word of explanation and instruction.

In support of their belief that in a case of necessity Holy Viaticum may be administered by lower clerics and by the laity, modern authors restate the reasoning of the older authors, principally that of Suarez and of St. Alphonsus.

Suarez treated of a very fundamental point. By divine law the priest was indeed the minister of the Holy Eucharist, but by divine law it was not forbidden that others be made to share in this function. The sacraments were intended for the sanctification of the faithful, and hence, as long as scandal was duly obviated and proper reverence was shown, a sacrament could be utilized even when the priest was impeded or absent.

As Suarez stated, this was especially true if the sacrament itself could be differentiated from the use of the sacrament. The Council of Trent had declared that the Church could change whatever pertained to the dispensing of the sacraments, provided that the essence of the sacraments was maintained inviolate (*salva substantia sacramentorum*).[103] Suarez showed that in the Holy Eucharist the consecration and the administration of the sacrament were distinct and separable actions. Once consecrated, the Eucharist could then be sacramentally called into use either by the one who had consecrated It or by someone else. Whatever looked to the dispensing of the Eucharist certainly did not concern Its substance. There was, consequently, no intrinsic reason why under certain conditions this sacrament could not be administered even by a lay person.[104]

---

[102] Cappello, *De Sacramentis,* I, n. 308

[103] Sess. XXI, *de Communione,* c. 2.

[104] Suarez, *Tertia Pars Summae Theologiae,* Disp. LXXII, Sect. I, n. 6; Sect. III, n. 3;—*Opera Omnia,* XXI, 577; XXI, 587.

St. Alphonsus, with a view to furnishing a detailed reply, took up the several objections offered by those who stood opposed to the idea of a permissable lay administration of the Holy Eucharist. His arguments and reasoning have been used by authors down to the present day.[105] He explained that the lay administration of the Holy Eucharist did not imply any outrage or affront for the sacrament, since in every case wherein a lay administration was deemed allowable there was always sought the needed guarantee of due and proper reverence. The prohibition in the *Decretum* of Gratian,[106] so St. Alphonsus stated, was predicated on the assumption of ordinary circumstances, which barred the priest from commissioning a layman when the priest himself remained available; such a prohibiting law did not forbid the layman to give Viaticum if a priest or a deacon did not remain available.

He answered the objection that Viaticum was not necessary for salvation by stating that a precept of receiving Communion at the hour of death did exist, and that on the other hand there did not exist any explicit divine or ecclesiastical law which in the face of very exceptional conditions forbade a lay person to administer this sacrament. He admitted that the practice which he defended did not constitute the current common practice, but he adverted also to the fact that in an earlier age of the Church it was a quite common practice for lay people to communicate themselves. Lastly, he pointed out that the verified conditions which warrant the lay administration of Holy Communion occur in fact so rarely that the force of any established custom or practice in this regard seems hardly applicable.[107]

Despite the clarity of these arguments, some modern authors, including Merkelbach[108] and Van Hove,[109] see no valid reason to abandon what they call the modern practice. This modern practice, as they see it, strictly demands that, even in extreme necessities, only the priest or a deacon may administer Holy

---

[105] Cf. Cappello, *De Sacramentis,* I, n. 305.
[106] C. 29, D. II, *de cons.*
[107] *Theologia Moralis,* Lib. VI, n. 237.
[108] *Theologia Moralis,* III, n. 338.
[109] *De Eucharistia,* p. 155.

Viaticum. On this particular point the comment of St. Alphonsus is quite appropriate:

> . . . immo notum est quod olim fideles laici Eucharistiam in suas domos deferebant, et seipsos propriis manibus communicabant: et hoc quidem propter necessitatem permittebatur. Cur autem, eadem necessitate occurrente, aliquando permitti non poterit?[110]

This practical attitude appears to be precisely the mind and the practice of the Church. Suarez mentioned that Pope Sixtus V (1585-1590) allowed the Holy Eucharist to be given to Mary, Queen of Scots, (+1587), a short time before her death, in order that It might be kept until the time of her execution, at which time she could administer the Holy Viaticum to herself with her own hands.[111]

Noldin stated that during the persecution in France the women of Paris were authorized to carry Holy Communion to the priests who were in prison.[112]

On July 21, 1841, the Sacred Congregation for the Propagation of the Faith, in response to a question proposed by the Vicar apostolic of Tonkin, French Indo-China, stated that, as long as the Blessed Sacrament was not exposed to irreverence or indignity, confessors of the faith condemned to death were to be allowed to take the Holy Eucharist in their hands and secretly to give themselves Communion, lest their priests also be apprehended.[113]

---

[110] *Theologia Moralis,* Lib. VI, n. 237.

[111] *Tertia Pars Summae Theologiae,* Disp. LXXII, Sect. III, n. 3—*Opera Omnia,* XXI, 587.

[112] *Theologia Moralis,* III, n. 125.

[113] S.C. de Prop. Fide (C.P. pro Sin.-Tunkin. Occident.) 21 iul. 1841, ad 3: "An permitti potest in hoc persecutionis tempore ut fidei confessores ad mortem propter fidem damnati, et quibus in carcere defertur SS. Eucharistiae Sacramentum occulte, possint illud manibus accipere et sese occulte communicare, ne sacerdos illos more ordinario communicans cognoscatur et prehendatur; vel satiusne est in illo casu ab illis confessoribus communicandis abstinere, maximo cum illorum animae detrimento?" R. ad 3°. "Affirmative

From the extraordinary faculties granted to the ordinaries and the people of Mexico on December 23, 1927, it is evident that the policy of the Holy See in regard to the administration of the Holy Eucharist by lower clerics and by the laity has not changed. In view of the conditions created by the Mexican persecution, the faithful were allowed to receive the Holy Eucharist at any hour of the day or night, even without fasting, and they were allowed to communicate themselves.[114]

In addition, the ordinaries were given wide permission to enlist the services of lower clerics and of the laity in the administration of Viaticum. As cited by Bouscaren, this faculty reads as follows:

> Ordinaries are likewise permitted, whenever no suitable and ready priest, deacon, subdeacon, or cleric can be had to administer Holy Viaticum to the sick or dying, to make use of a pious layman who has a common good reputation for moral character, who may carry the Sacred Species in a vessel, which is blessed or to be blessed; and the sick person may receive the Sacred Species with his own hands. If the latter is unwilling or unable so to receive the Sacred Species, They are to be administered by the man who carried Them, who shall thereafter wash or purify his hands.[115]

Bouscaren likewise mentions an indult of the Commission for Russia under date of January 20, 1930, which empowered the ordinaries of Russia to permit pious laymen to carry Holy Communion to Catholics in prison.[116]

These recent indults of the Holy See indicate that the mind of the Church today is to enlist the services of the laity and of the minor clerics, not only in extreme necessity, but whenever their services will promote the common spiritual welfare of the faithful. They permitted the lay administration of the Eucharist not

---

quoad primam partem, dummodo nullo irreverentiae aut conculcationis periculo tantum Sacramentum exponatur."—*Fontes,* n. 4789; *Collectanea,* n. 928.

[114] Bouscaren, *Canon Law Digest,* II, 26.

[115] Bouscaren, *Canon Law Digest,* II, 28.

[116] *Canon Law Digest,* II, 207.

only to the dying but also in other emergencies. Certainly, when there is no other way to avoid profanation of the Holy Eucharist, lower clerics and the laity may give Communion to themselves or to others.[117]

Authors also hold that, when in certain sicknesses the administration of Viaticum requires a special skill, the priest may allow the sister infirmarian to administer It with the use of a spoon.[118] As Coronata remarks, such a contingency may well arise in certain types of cancer of the mouth or of the throat.[119]

According to canon 985, n. 7, clerics in minor orders or laymen who exercise an act of orders reserved to clerics in major orders become irregular, According to many commentators this abuse of Sacred Orders does not cause irregularity unless it is exercised solemnly, that is, with the distinctive insignia of the major order and in a function which is exclusively reserved to one in major orders.[120] These authors base this opinion on the former law, from which the Code does not appear to differ. Consequently, all clerics who are not at least deacons, and also laymen, incur an irregularity when they solemnly administer Holy Communion unlawfully.[121]

Although the private and secret administration of Holy Communion to oneself on the part of a minor cleric or of a lay person is an unlawful act, Cappello holds that more probably it does not cause an irregularity.[122] Cappello does not give his reason for holding this opinion, but most likely it is because he does not consider such an action as the performance of an act in the manner in which it is customarily performed by a minister with the proper Orders, and therefore not the solemn and official usurpation of an Order which has not been received.

---

[117] Aertnys-Damen, *Theologia Moralis,* II, n. 122.

[118] Noldin, *Theologia Moralis,* III, n. 125; Jone, *Moral Theology,* n. 498.

[119] *De Sacramentis,* I, 271, footnote 2.

[120] Vermeersch-Creusen, *Epitome,* II, n. 257; Noldin, *Theologia Moralis,* III, n. 497; Woywod, *A Practical Commentary,* I, n. 941.

[121] Merkelbach, *Theologia Moralis,* III, n. 338; Noldin, *Theologia Moralis,* III, n. 125.

[122] *De Sacramentis,* I, n. 306.

CHAPTER V

The Minister of Holy Communion to the Sick

ARTICLE 1. PRIVATE AND PUBLIC CARRYING OF THE HOLY EUCHARIST

The Code distinguishes between Holy Communion brought to the sick either publicly or privately. Holy Communion is brought publicly when all the solemnities of the *Rituale Romanum,* tit. IV, c. 4, *de communione infirmorum,* nn. 10-27, are observed. The priest, vested in surplice, stole, and cope, and proceeding under a canopy or unbrella, is to be accompanied by acolytes and a number of the faithful carrying a tinkling bell and lighted candles. When Holy Communion is brought to the sick according to n. 29 of the same title and chapter, It is said to be brought privately and secretly. In this case the Holy Eucharist is carried to the sick by a priest dressed in street clothes, and all external solemnity is omitted. Cappello also calls private the carrying of the Holy Eucharist to the sick with all solemnity indeed, but within the very house where the Blessed Sacrament is reserved, as in a convent or a hospital.[1]

Canon 847[2] and the *Rituale Romanum*[3] indicate that as a general rule when the Holy Eucharist is to be brought to the sick It is to be brought publicly and with solemnity. In the past, special faculties were issued to countries in which there was danger of sacrilegious irreverence to the Blessed Sacrament, or excessive difficulty in carrying Holy Communion publicly and solemnly to the sick.[4] On other occasions the Holy See always insisted on the existence of a just and reasonable cause for the

---

[1] *De Sacramentis,* I, n. 300.

[2] "Ad infirmos publice sacra communio deferatur, nisi iusta et rationabilis causa aliud suadeat."

[3] Tit. IV, c. 4, n. 6: "Privatim vero seu occulte ad infirmos sacra communio ne deferatur, nisi iusta et rationabilis causa aliud suadeat."

[4] S.R.C., *Molinen.,* 12 sept. 1857, ad 19—*DA,* n. 3059; *Vicariatus Apostolici de Dania,* 10 febr. 1871, ad 1—*DA,* n. 3234.

substitution of the private bringing of Holy Communion to the sick instead of the solemn public method.[5] The Code follows this constant attitude of the Holy See, and directs that Holy Communion be carried to the sick publicly unless a just and reasonable cause is present to render such a mode inadvisable.[6]

The Code demands not a grave cause but a just and reasonable cause for the lawful bringing of Holy Communion to the sick privately. The mind of the Church is that Communion of the sick should not be made difficult. A just cause is one that proportionately counterbalances the law, a cause that would make a deviation from the law the more reasonable thing, the thing intended by the legislator. A cause is reasonable when it is in accordance with prudence, equity, and other practical considerations of the time and place. In this whole matter of a just and reasonable cause for the private administration of Holy Communion to the sick, a controlling presumption that must be kept in mind is the Church's desire for frequent, even daily Communion.[7]

Among the just and reasonable causes for not carrying the Holy Eucharist publicly to the sick are the following: the fear of some hostile manifestation or of scandal in heretical countries or in irreligious communities; the danger of public irreverence in non-Catholic places, especially in cities; the opposition of the sick person because of his timidity and his fear of uncharitable comment; the opposition of the relatives of the sick person, who are afraid of incurring the enmity of the civil authorities, or the criticism of their neighbors, or the ill will of their customers; the inconveniences which the frequent carrying of the Holy Eucharist publicly into the same house might occasion; the difficulty of publicly carrying Holy Communion to many sick persons.[8]

---

[5] S.R.C., *Gandaven.*, 16 dec. 1826—*DA*, n. 2650; *Bisinianen.*, 23 maii 1846—*DA*, n. 2908; *Mantuana*, 6 febr. 1875—*DA*, n. 3337; *Templen.*, 12 ian. 1878, ad 7—*DA*, n. 3438; S.C. de Sacramentis, *Romana et Aliarum*, 23 dec. 1912—*Fontes*, n. 2107; S.C. de Prop. Fide, 11 sept. 1779, n. 3—*Fontes*, n. 4581.

[6] Canon 847.

[7] S.C.C., decr., *"Sacra Tridentina Synodus,"* 20 dec. 1905—*Fontes*, n. 2103.

[8] Vermeersch-Creusen, *Epitome*, II, n. 114; Coronata, *De Sacramentis*, I, 277; Van Hove, *De Eucharistia*, p. 166.

In the modern large city the difficulties involved in taking Holy Communion publicly and solemnly to the sick will easily give sufficient cause for the private administration. There is not much chance of publicly showing the reverence and veneration due the Blessed Sacrament, and the danger of irreverence is always present. This fact in addition to the practical impossibility of the necessary frequent and even daily bringing of Holy Communion publicly to the sick certainly presents a just and reasonable cause for the private carrying of Holy Communion to the sick. For these reasons the practice in the city of Rome itself is that of the private and secret carrying of Communion to the sick.[9]

In the present discipline of the Church the frequent administration of Holy Communion to the sick is certainly to be preferred to the observance of the solemnities of the public carrying of the Holy Eucharist. The Church desires that the faithful, and especially those who are sick, should communicate as often as possible, and in many instances the responsible minister can achieve this only by bringing the Holy Eucharist to them privately.[10]

Cappello holds that the just and reasonable cause for the private bringing of Communion to the sick need only be a light cause. Consequently he maintains that Holy Communion may be brought privately, not only when there is need of forestalling the danger of irreverence, but even when it would afford a greater convenience to the sick person, or to his family, or to the minister himself.[11]

Next, a very practical question must be considered. May the local ordinary alone specify the conditions which would justify the carrying of the Holy Eucharist to the sick? In other words, who is qualified to make the judgment as to the sufficiency of the cause which would enable a priest to bring Holy Communion privately to the sick?

---

[9] Wernz-Vidal, *Ius Canonicum ad Codicis Normam Exactum* (7 tom. in 8 vols., Tom. IV, Vol. 1, 1934, Romae: Apud Aedes Universitatis Gregorianae), Tom. IV, Vol. 1, n. 105, footnote (hereafter cited *Ius Canonicum*).

[10] Regatillo, *Ius Sacramentarium,* I, n. 310.

[11] *De Sacramentis,* I, n. 390.

Authors for the most part maintain that it is not within the exclusive power of the local ordinary, or even of the pastor, to decide whether in a particular case Communion should be taken privately to the sick. They state that in accordance with canon 849, § 1, any priest who has the right to give Communion may decide this matter, as long as he keeps in mind the laws of the Church, which aim at reconciling the respect due to the Holy Eucharist with the spiritual advantages of Communion for the faithful.[12] These authors hold this view in the face of a contrary response from the Sacred Congregation of the Sacraments, given on January 5, 1928.[13]

Despite this response of the Sacred Congregation, authors hold that by reason of Canon 849, § 1, the judgment concerning the weight and reasonableness of the cause pertains not only to the local ordinary but to any priest capable of carrying the Holy Eucharist to the sick. As indicated by Vidal (1868-1939), if there is question of introducing into some place a general practice of the private bringing of Holy Communion to the sick, there is required a common cause, and the judge of the existence of such a common and general cause will be the local ordinary alone.[14]

For the introduction or the continuation of such a general practice there need not be explicit pronouncement of the local ordinary as to the existence of a just and reasonable cause. It is sufficient that the ordinary give his tacit approbation to an

---

[12] Regatillo, *Ius Sacramentarium,* I, n. 310; Cappello, *De Sacramentis,* I, n. 393; Vermeersch-Creusen, *Epitome,* II, n. 114; Coronata, *De Sacramentis,* I, 279; Van Hove, *De Eucharistia,* p. 166; Durieux, *The Eucharist, Law and Practice,* p. 160; Wernz-Vidal, *Ius Canonicum,* Tom. IV, Vol. 1, n. 105.

[13] Dubium.: "An iudex causae iustae et rationalibus, prout ex Codicis I. C. can. 847 requiritur, ut Sacra Communio privatim ad infirmos deferatur, sit quilibet sacerdos ministrans vel tantum Ordinarius loci?" R. "Negative ad primam partem; affirmative ad secundam, addita tamen *mente,* quae sequens est: Si ex communi experientia et opinione nullum in dioecesi aut in aliquo particulari loco adsit inconveniens pro privata delatione Sacrae Communionis ad infirmos, ab Ordinario cavendum est ne per regulas nimis praefinitas aut generales praecipientes publicam delationem, vel per reservationem sibi factam dandi veniam in singulis casibus deferendi privatim Sacramentum Eucharistiae, praepediatur infirmis solatium Communionis etiam quotidianae." —*AAS,* XX (1928), 81.

[14] Wernz-Vidal, *Ius Canonicum,* Tom. IV, Vol. 1, n. 105.

existing practice. Therefore if the local ordinary makes no contrary regulations, his acquiescence may be interpreted as an approval of the private carrying of the Holy Eucharist to the sick.[15]

The local ordinary has the right and duty to check abuses which might diminish in the faithful the respect due to the Holy Eucharist. He would act wisely therefore by specifying in general the reasons which in his diocese appear to him to be sufficient to justify an exception to the law of the Church which demands that the Holy Eucharist be carried publicly to the sick.[16] Although the ordinary alone can determine a general policy of the private administration of Communion to the sick, and although in a place where the public bringing of Communion is carried out he may propose accurate norms for the private carrying of the Holy Eucharist to the sick, yet he is not to be the sole judge of the sufficiency of a cause in a particular case.[17]

For as Vidal goes on to say, in a particular case as touched by the rule of canon 849, § 1, there must be applied the same juridic principle that is applied in other cases of a similar nature. This principle is that, when the law places no limitations, it pertains to the one to whom is given the unqualified power to place an action to verify the existence of the circumstances and conditions under which this power may be used. Consequently in a place where the general practice points to the public carrying of Holy Communion to the sick, as is contemplated under canon 849, § 1, this canon gives to every priest the right to bring Holy Communion privately to the sick, and by that very fact qualifies the priest to make the judgment as to the existence of a sufficient cause for the lawful exercise of this function.[18]

Cappello states that the priest who is to bring Communion to the sick is the one to judge the existence of a just and reasonable cause, since canon 849, § 1, in no way limits his right. This faculty is conceded to the priest by the Code itself, and therefore is not to be taken away or restricted by any authority below

[15] Coronata, *De Sacramentis,* I, 279.

[16] Durieux, *The Eucharist, Law and Practice,* p. 159.

[17] Van Hove, *De Eucharistia,* p. 166.

[18] *Ius Canonicum,* Tom. IV, Vol. 1, n. 105, footnote.

the supreme lawgiver. The Code requires no permission of the local ordinary, and therefore such a permission may not be demanded.[19]

Cappello further insists that the response of the Sacred Congregation of the Sacraments of January 5, 1928, cannot take away the faculty which under canon 849, § 1, is extended to any priest capable of carrying the Blessed Sacrament to the sick, nor can it furnish an authentic interpretation of canon 847, since the competency for this pertains exclusively to the Pontifical Commission for the Interpretation of the Code.[20] Cappello maintains that the competence of the Sacred Congregation is that of settling controversies and of removing abuses by giving practical rules and by advising the observance of ecclesiastical discipline, but that it cannot restrict the genuine sense of canon 847.[21]

According to Regatillo, it was the fact that the response of the Sacred Congregation of the Sacraments on January 5, 1928, was not in accordance with the Code, and for that reason would probably have caused wonderment, that prompted the *ex officio* added annotations of Iorio, the Secretary of the Sacred Congregation.[22] This explanation of the decision mitigated the severity of its application by warning the local ordinaries that they should not impede the frequent administration of Holy Communion to the sick by insisting on the solemn carrying of the Holy Eucharist. Interpreted widely in the light of these annotations, this decision does little to restrict the right of any priest as conceded to him under canon 849, § 1.[23]

This point Iorio himself stated three years later in his book, *La Communione agl' Infermi* (Roma, 1931), when he taught that it is the mind of the Sacred Congregation and the living desire of the Church that Holy Communion be given frequently, even daily,

---

[19] *De Sacramentis,* I, n. 392.

[20] Motu proprio *Cum Iuris Canonici,* 15 sept. 1917—*AAS,* IX (1917), pars II, appendix II.

[21] *Loc. cit.*

[22] Regatillo, *Ius Sacramentarium,* I, n. 308.

[23] Vermeersch-Creusen, *Epitome,* II, n. 114; Beste, *Introductio in Codicem,* p. 494.

to the sick, and since it would not be possible to carry the Holy Eucharist in the solemn and public manner so frequently, it is necessary to cede to each priest the right under canon 849 to bring Communion to the sick privately.[24]

The decree of the Sacred Congregation of the Sacraments of December 23, 1912,[25] whence canon 847 is taken, indicates in a general manner what is a sufficient cause for the private carrying of Holy Communion to the sick, namely, that Communion is sought by many sick people, or by some oftentimes. This situation nearly always exists in large parishes. Consequently, unless Holy Communion could be brought to the sick publicly every day or very frequently, the mind of the Sacred Congregation is that any priest may privately take the Holy Eucharist to the sick without any need of recourse to the local ordinary for a verification of the sufficiency of the cause at hand.

Similarly the local ordinary may not forbid the private administration of Holy Communion to the sick by means of a synodal law or of a general decree. The faculty in question is conceded to the priest by the law itself, so that the ordinary neither can reserve to himself the right to judge regarding the existence of the cause, nor may he demand that he give a previous permission for every exercise of this faculty.[26] The decree of the Sacred Congregation of the Sacraments of December 23, 1912,[27] which is a source of canon 847, authorized ordinaries to give permission for the private carrying of Holy Communion to the sick. This authorization of the local ordinary is not mentioned in the Code, hence the priest needs no further permission than that which is given him by the law itself.

Cappello states that it is within the province of the local ordinary to forbid the private administration of Holy Communion to the sick in a particular case.[28] This is certainly true if abuses of any kind have arisen, or if manifestly Holy Communion were being

---

[24] Nn. 109, 111.

[25] *Fontes*, n. 2107.

[26] Coronata, *De Sacramentis*, I, 278-279; Cappello, *De Sacramentis*, I, n. 393.

[27] *Fontes*, n. 2107.

[28] *De Sacramentis*, I, n. 393.

brought privately to the sick without a just cause. However, when a just and reasonable cause exists, or when the general custom of the place points to the private carrying of Communion to the sick, the local ordinary may not deprive the priest of the right which he enjoys by reason of canon 849, § 1.[29]

In this country it is the universal custom to bring Holy Communion to the sick privately.[30] The private administration of Holy Communion to the sick in the United States was regretfully sanctioned by the II Plenary Council of Baltimore (1866).[31]

When Holy Communion is taken privately to the sick, the reverence and respect due to so great a Sacrament must be zealously safeguarded through the observance of the regulations enacted by the Holy See.[32] The norms of reverence and decency for the private carrying of the Holy Eucharist to the sick are taken from the decree of the Sacred Congregation of the Sacraments,[33] which quotes from the Constitution *Inter omnigenas* of Pope Benedict XIV.[34] These rules demand that the priest must always wear the stole under his outer garb. The pyx must be placed in a burse suspended from his neck and carried on his breast. The decree further adds that the priest should be accompanied by at least a layman, if a cleric cannot be had. The *Rituale Romanum* prescribes the same, with the addition: "*Cum autem ad infirmi cubiculum pervenerit, sacerdos superpelliceum quoque induat cum stola, si illud antea non induerit.*"[35]

As Coronata mentions, there may arise circumstances in the private carrying of Holy Communion to the sick when it would be virtually impossible to carry out the full prescriptions of the law.[36] In an urgent necessity the priests may administer Holy

---

[29] Coronata, *De Sacramentis,* I, 278.

[30] Beste, *Introductio in Codicem,* p. 494; Woywod, *A Practical Commentary,* I, n. 745.

[31] *Concilii Plenarii Baltimorensis Secundi Acta et Decreta* (2. ed., Baltimore, 1880), n. 264 (hereafter cited *Acta et Decreta*).

[32] Canon 849, § 2.

[33] *Romana et aliarum,* 23 dec. 1912, ad III—*Fontes,* n. 2107.

[34] 2 febr. 1744—*Fontes,* n. 339, § 23 of this Constitution is based on the regulations prescribed by the Council of Albanum (1703) (the present Elbasan in Albania)—Mansi, XXV, 1398, 1399.

[35] Tit. IV, c. 4, *de communione infirmorum,* n. 29.

[36] *De Sacramentis,* I, 279.

Viaticum without any sacred vestments.[37] The Holy See has stated that if there would be grave danger of irreverence or of the priest's apprehension or molestation, he need not wear even the stole in carrying the Holy Eucharist to the sick.[38] However, the II Plenary Council of Baltimore warned that the priests in the United States were always to wear the stole in the taking of the Holy Eucharist to the sick.[39]

In the private bringing of Holy Communion to the sick the *Roman Ritual* prescribes that the priest be accompanied by a cleric, or, if no clerics are available, by a layman.[40] Vermeersch (+ 1936) lamented that this rublic was widely neglected even in the city of Rome.[41]

Certainly the greatest consideration and respect must be given the Holy Eucharist as the Most Excellent Sacrament. This means also that consummate reverence be shown in Its administration to the sick. Yet even in the administration of this sacrament it must be admitted that not all the prescriptions of the *Rituale Romanum* bind with the same degree of gravity. Whether one admit with most of the authors[42] that some rubrics are preceptive and bind under pain of sin while others are of counsel only, or whether one hold that all rubrics have indeed the force of law, but bind either lightly or gravely, according to their varying nature,[43] it must be granted that those rubrics which are less intimately connected with the actual consecrating or administering of the sacrament require a proportionately lesser inconvenience in lawful warrant either of their total omission or of an excuse from their full observance. Now, manifestly the presence of an associate when the priest privately brings Holy Communion to the sick is in no way intrinsically related to the administration of the Holy

---

[37] St. Alphonsus, *Theologia Moralis,* Lib. VI, n. 241; Iorio, *Theologia Moralis,* III, n. 133.

[38] S.C. de Prop. Fide, 20 sept. 1739—*Fontes,* n. 4511.

[39] *Acta et Decreta,* n. 264.

[40] Tit. IV, c. 4, *de communione infirmorum,* n. 29.

[41] *Epitome,* II, n. 114.

[42] Cf. Cappello, *De Sacramentis,* I, nn. 50, 390; Noldin, *Theologia Moralis,* III, n. 30; Aertnys-Damen, *Theologia Moralis,* II, n. 16.

[43] Coronata, *De Sacramentis,* I, 56; Pruemmer, *Manuale Theologiae Moralis,* III, n. 70.

Eucharist. Consequently even less than a grave cause could excuse one from the obligation of taking an associate when bringing Holy Communion to the sick. Van Hove maintained that any reasonable cause provides a sufficient excuse from this obligation.[44]

In this country the almost universal practice of taking Holy Communion to the sick without an associate could well be justified on the degree of inconvenience that would be incurred if such a practice were carried out. The usual manner of taking Communion is that of using an automobile, and thus the reverence and the security as demanded by the Holy See are adequately provided for. There is less emotional recoil and consequently also a lesser danger of irreverence among the non-Catholic population of the United States when they see the priest making his Communion calls alone than when they note that he is accompanied by someone, and, *a fortiori,* by another cleric. This fact along with the difficulty and the inconvenience involved in seeking a worthy and at the same time available companion appears to offer a sufficient excuse from this obligation.

In carrying the Holy Eucharist privately to the sick the priest may wear a hat or a cap. On the other hand, when the Blessed Sacrament is carried publicly and solemnly to the sick the priest should go with his head uncovered,[45] unless for reasons of health or because of the severe cold or stormy conditions he would need to wear a hat. In an urgent case the priest could presume permission, but if such climatic conditions are usual in a given territory the priest should apply through his local ordinary to the Holy See for the necessary permission. In practice it would be better that Holy Communion be taken to the sick privately under such circumstances.[46]

Authors likewise find it difficult to justify the use of any means of transportation in the public carrying of the Blessed Sacrament to the sick. However, all admit that particular circumstances of distance, or the arduousness of the journey, or the danger of delay,

[44] *De Eucharistia,* p. 167.

[45] S.R.C., *Toletana,* 31 aug. 1872, ad II—*DA,* n. 3276.

[46] Coronata, *De Sacramentis,* I, 280; Cappello, *De Sacramentis,* I, n. 394; Iorio, *Theologia Moralis,* III, n. 133; Regatillo, *Ius Sacramentarium,* I, n. 310.

may justify the use of any mode of transportation useful or necessary for making the trip. Special precautions must be taken with a view to insuring a proper reverence to the Holy Eucharist. Again, it is advisable that Holy Communion be taken privately and secretly to the sick when it is not feasible to make the journey on foot.[47]

The *Rituale Romanum* states that the priest, after bringing Holy Communion privately to the sick, is to put on the surplice and stole upon entering the sick room if he has not been wearing them.[48] It is assumed that the priest is wearing the cassock. The Sacred Congregation of Rites in 1871 decreed that, whenever possible, the wearing of the cassock and the stole was not to be omitted in the actual administration of the Holy Eucharist.[49] Evidently it is the mind of the Church that when the priest brings the Holy Eucharist privately to the sick he should, upon reaching the room of the sick, put on the cassock, the surplice, and the stole for the actual administration of Holy Communion.

This rubric as not actually touching the essence of the sacrament would not oblige under all circumstances. Grave inconvenience would be a sufficient excusing cause. Most certainly, if there is danger to the priest from the enemies of the faith, or if the danger is imminent, the priest would not be required to put on the cassock and the surplice.[50]

The administration of Holy Communion in public and sectarian institutions may likewise afford an emergency case in which there would be no obligation to put on the cassock and the surplice. In many instances of this kind wherein the priest is merely tolerated, the presence of a priest in cassock and surplice is quite apt to do harm to religion by arousing resentment and prejudice, or even

---

[47] Cappello, *loc. cit.;* Coronata, *loc. cit.*

[48] Tit. IV, c. 4, *de communione infirmorum,* n. 29.

[49] *Vicariatus Apostolici de Dania,* 4 febr. 1871, ad I, n. 4: "Nam in hisce casibus [quando agitur de iis qui longo tempore in carceribus acatholicis detinentur] saltem sufficeret, si Sacerdos in ipso cubiculo infirmi aut carcerati veste talari et Stola se induat?" R. "Id omittendam non esse, quotiescumque fieri potest."—*DA,* n. 3234.

[50] Woywod, *A Practical Commentary,* I, n. 745; Iorio, *Theologia Moralis,* III, n. 133.

by provoking irreverence to the Blessed Sacrament. On the other hand, his ministration to the sick would go unnoticed and unmolested if he ministered without wearing the cassock and surplice.

However, it is quite a different matter when the administration of Holy Communion in the Catholic home is concerned. It is hard to conceive how the putting on of the cassock and the surplice in the actual administration of Communion under such conditions would offer the grave inconvenience which has to be present if there is to be an excuse from this regulation. If in large parishes it would be necessary to make a great number of Communion calls daily, then the controlling mind of the Church would militate in favor of the reception of frequent Communion by the faithful even apart from the priest's wearing of the cassock and the surplice, if the delay caused by putting on and off the cassock and surplice would be the reason for the failure of some of the sick to have the opportunity of receiving the Holy Eucharist. But sheer sloth and laziness on the part of the minister would never constitute a sufficient reason for his neglect to wear the cassock and surplice.

May custom be alleged in support of the practice of administering Holy Communion to the sick without the cassock and the surplice? Some authors will not admit the validity of customs against liturgical laws. They maintain that nothing qualifies as a custom against the *Rituale Romanum* except when Rome itself on the presentation of a local bishop makes an exception for a given locality. However, Guilfoyle argues that the practice of the Sacred Congregation of Rites indicates that there may arise customs against the liturgy. One cannot point to any law which prohibits, reprobates, or abrogates all customs against the liturgy. Rather the practice of the Sacred Congregation in condemning or tolerating customs reflects simply an application of the regular principles of customary law to liturgical matters.[51]

Even though one be ready to grant in this matter the possible force of custom along with the consequent application of the prin-

---

[51] Guilfoyle, *Custom,* The Catholic University of America Canon Law Studies, n. 105 (Washington, D. C.: The Catholic University of America, 1937), pp. 121, 122; Vermeersch-Creusen, *Epitome,* I, 143.

ciples of customary law, it appears very doubtful if there is a legitimate custom in the United States for the administration of Holy Communion to the sick apart from the priest's use of a cassock and surplice. Even if one conceded the reasonableness of such a custom at the time of its inception, such a custom would have been abrogated by the II Plenary Council of Baltimore (1866), which stated that the prescriptions of the Roman Ritual were to be observed, in so far as it was possible, in the administration of Holy Communion to the sick.[52] Furthermore, even if it were established that the custom which existed at the time of the II Plenary Council of Baltimore (1866) was immemorial in its character, the reasons given for the law along with the exhortation to show great reverence in the administration of the Holy Eucharist, as indicated in n. 264, would have proved sufficient for the abrogation of even such a custom.[53]

The Code[54] acknowledged the rubrics of the *Rituale Romanum* for the administration of the sacraments, and in consequence thereof any ordinary custom which opposed the rubrics was abrogated by canon 5.[55] From 1866 to 1918 there was no room for the establishment of an immemorial or centenary custom.

If there does not exist any custom which has the force of law, does there perhaps exist the possibility of introducing a usage which may eventually obtain the force of law? Canon 27, § 1, requires that the practice which is opposed to the law be a reasonable practice.[56] The practice of administering Holy Communion in present day Catholic homes apart from the use of the cassock and surplice does not appear to be proper sacramental etiquette. Precisely for the reason that the inconvenience is small, such a practice shows a lack of respect and devotion to the Holy Eucha-

---

[52] *Acta et Decreta*, n. 264.

[53] Cf. Gulifoyle, *Custom*, p. 68.

[54] Canon 733, § 1.

[55] "Vigentes in praesens contra horum statuta canonum consuetudines sive universales sive particulares . . . suppressae habeantur, nisi expresse Codex aliud caveat."

[56] "Iuri divino sive naturali sive positivo nulla consuetudo potest aliquatenus derogare; sed neque iuri ecclesiactico praeiudicum effert, nisi fuerit rationabilis et legitime per annos quadraginta continuos et completos praescripta."

rist. It is certainly not consonant with the mind of the Church as expressed by the Sacred Congregation of Rites.[57]

Woywod, writing in the *Homiletic and Pastoral Review* in 1921 stated: "To call this neglect a legitimate custom is not in harmony with sound principles. There can be no custom that will excuse from proper marks of respect to Our Lord in the Holy Eucharist."[58] When Donovan in 1944 wrote in the same periodical he presented the same view. He maintained that in this matter there is no room for legitimate custom, since such a practice is not reasonable on the simple score that it indicates a lack of becoming reverence to the Holy Eucharist.[59] It must be held, therefore, that the only justification for the administration of Holy Communion to the sick apart from the use of the cassock and surplice can be sought solely in the existence of that measure of inconvenience which is truly grave.

ARTICLE 2. THE MINISTER OF HOLY COMMUNION TO THE SICK OUTSIDE THE DANGER OF DEATH

The public carrying of Holy Communion to the sick is a reserved parochial function.[60] The local pastor alone has the right to take the Holy Eucharist publicly to the sick within his parish, even when the sick are not members of his parish.[61a]

It is only in a case of necessity, or with the permission, at least presumed, of the pastor or the local ordinary, that another priest may publicly take Communion to the sick.[61] This permission may safely be presumed if the pastor is absent or is himself prevented for any reason from taking Communion to the sick

[57] *Vicariatus Apostolici de Dania,* 4 febr. 1871—*DA,* n. 3234.

[58] "The New Code and the Administration of the Blessed Sacrament," *HPR,* XXI (1921), 1012-1020.

[59] "Careless Custodians of the Sacraments," *HPR,* XLV (1944), 183-186.

[60] Canon 462, 2°.—Functiones parocho reservatae sunt, nisi aliud iure caveatur: Sanctissimam Eucharistiam publice ad infirmos in propria paroecia deferre.

[61a] Can, 848, § 1.

[61] Canon 848, § 2.—Ceteri sacerdotes id possunt [sacram communionem publicae ad infirmos deferre] in casu tantum necessitatis aut de licentia saltem praesumpta eiusdem parochi vel Ordinarii.

person. The non-availability of the pastor to publicly take Holy Communion personally to the sick would constitute the necessity which is indicated by canon 848, § 2, as sufficient to warrant the public administration of the Holy Eucharist by another priest. For by necessity here is not meant an extreme emergency, or the immediate danger of death. Rather, by necessity in this canon is signified any grave inconvenience that would be forthcoming to the pastor or to the sick person should another priest not take upon himself the carrying of Communion to the sick person.[62]

If the pastor should unreasonably refuse to grant permission to another priest to take Communion publicly to the sick, such a priest may reasonably presume the permission of the local ordinary and proceed with a safe conscience to bring Holy Communion publicly to the sick person.[63]

When there is a just and reasonable cause, any priest may carry Holy Communion to the sick privately with at least the presumed permission of the priest who has charge of the Blessed Sacrament in the church from which It is taken.[64] This does not imply that the Blessed Sacrament must be taken from the parish church, nor is any permission needed from either the local or the proper pastor for the administration of Communion privately to their sick parishioners. The Code wishes to encourage frequent Communion for the sick; consequently, when Communion is privately brought to the sick the permission of the pastor is in no way necessary. The permission of the pastor is not required by law, nor may the local ordinary impose the obligation of asking for this permission. Every priest has the right of taking Communion privately to the sick by reason of canon 849, § 1, and neither the local ordinary nor the pastor may restrict or take away this faculty.[65]

---

[62] Coronata, *De Sacramentis,* I, 278; Cappello, *De Sacramentis,* I, n. 300.

[63] Vermeersch-Creusen, *Epitome,* II, n. 114; Coronata, *De Sacramentis,* I, 278.

[64] Canon 849, § 1.—Communionem privatim ad infirmos quilibet sacerdos deferre potest, de venia saltem praesumpta sacerdotis, cui custodia sanctissimi Sacramenti commissa est.

[65] Vermeersch-Creusen, *Epitome,* II, n. 114; Durieux, *The Eucharist, Law and Practice,* p. 159.

As indicated in the annotations officially published by the secretary of the Sacred Congregation of the Sacraments in the reply concerning the private bringing of the Holy Eucharist to the sick, the exclusive right of the pastor under canon 848, § 1, ceases, and the right of every priest under canon 849, § 1, arises, whether there is a just and reasonable cause for the carrying of Holy Communion privately to the sick.[66] From this it follows that a pastor may, without any need of further authorization, privately take Communion of devotion to his own parishioners who are sick in hospitals or asylums outside their own parish. He would take the Holy Eucharist from his own church on his own authority, and when taking Communion privately to the sick residing in another parish he is in no way considered to trespass on the rights and prerogatives of the local pastor.

When the Holy Eucharist is brought privately to the sick, the only permission required by the law is the permission, at least presumed, of the priest who has the legitimate custody of the Blessed Sacrament in the church from which It is taken. As Vermeersch pointed out, the administration of Communion to the sick privately and secretly without any external solemnity is similar in the sight of the law to the administration of Hoiy Communion in church. Thus, just as canon 846, § 2, demands at least the presumed permission of the rector of the church for the administration of Holy Communion outside of Mass in that church, so the private carrying of Communion to the sick demands only at least the presumed permission of the pastor, the rector, or the chaplain who is responsible for the custody of the Holy Eucharist in the church from which It is carried to the sick.[67]

Holy Communion is to be administered to the sick according to the prescriptions of the *Rituale Romanum,* tit. IV, c. 4, *de communione infirmorum.* However, the Sacred Congregation of Rites in an Instruction given on January 9, 1929, approved a modification of these ceremonies for the administration of Holy Communion to several sick persons who are in the same house or

---

[66] *"Romana et aliarum,"* 5 ian. 1928—*AAS,* XX (1928), 81; Bouscaren, *Canon Law Digest,* I, 406.

[67] *Epitome,* II, n. 114.

hospital but in different rooms. The priest or deacon who administers the Sacrament shall, in the first room only, recite in the plural number all the prayers that are usually to be said before the Communion of the sick. In each of the other rooms he shall say only the prayers, *Misereatur tui. . . ; Indulgentiam. . . ; Ecce Agnus Dei. . . ;* once the *Domnine non sum dignus. . . ; Accipe frater (soror) . . .* or *Corpus Domini Nostri Jesu Christi. . . .* In the last room he shall add the *Dominus vobiscum* with its response, and the prayer *Domine Sancte . . .* to be said in the plural number. Then, if any particle is left over, the priest or the deacon shall give the blessing with the Blessed Sacrament, and on his return to the church or the chapel he shall finish the rest of the usual prayers.[68]

Should there be several sick persons in the same room, the prayers *Misereatur, Indulgentiam, Domine Sancte,* and the blessing are to be recited in the plural number, as is indicated in the *Rituale.*[69]

ARTICLE 3. THE MINISTER OF HOLY VIATICUM

In danger of death, whatever may be its cause, all of the faithful are bound under serious obligation to receive Holy Communion.[70] Authors indicate that the Code here calls attention to a divine precept.[71]

The danger of death which is sufficient for the administration of Holy Viaticum may arise either from an intrinsic cause, such as the probability of death from wounds, sickness, or old age, or it may arise from an extrinsic cause, such as the danger of death from war, or storm, or an impending serious operation. Even children who have not as yet received their first Holy Communion are bound by this precept if they reverently can

---

[68] *AAS,* XXI (1929), 43; Bouscaren, *Canon Law Digest,* I, 408.

[69] Tit. IV, c. 4, *de communione infirmorum,* nn. 17, 22, 27.

[70] Canon 864, § 1.

[71] Coronata, *De Sacramentis,* I, 321; Cappello, *De Sacramentis,* I, n. 432; Vermeersch-Creusen, *Epitome,* II, n. 114; Woywod, *A Practical Commentary,* I, n. 764; Gasparri, *De Eucharistia,* II, n. 1149.

adore the Body of Christ inasmuch as they can discern between It and ordinary bread.[72]

Moral certitude that death will soon follow is not required as a necessary condition for the administration of Holy Communion by the way of Viaticum. The subject need not be *in articulo mortis*. Rather, it sufficies that the person stand a chance of losing his life even if his chances of surviving are more likely. Under such circumstances he is constituted a fit subject for the reception of Holy Viaticum.[73]

In interpreting canon 859, which enshrines the law regarding the lawful minister of Holy Viaticum, authors note a distinction between Holy Viaticum strictly so-called and Holy Viaticum in its broader connotation. Strictly considered, Viaticum is the Communion prescribed by divine as well as ecclesiastical precept whenever one falls into a serious danger of death.[74] In its broader meaning, Holy Viaticum signifies the Communion which one receives out of devotion while still seriously ill, especially a Communion received by a seriously sick person while not fasting, as is contemplated in canon 864, § 3.[75] The Holy Viaticum which is referred to under canon 850 as a reserved function is simply the Viaticum strictly so-called; hence the administration by a priest who is not the local pastor, of other Communions to a sick person, even to one who is not fasting, is not forbidden by this law.

Also, since there is no obligation to receive the Viaticum of precept immediately as soon as the danger of death arises, it follows that it is not forbidden to administer Communion to seriously sick persons even before they have fulfilled their precept, as long as it is prudently forseen that there is sufficient time for the fulfillment of the precept at the hand of the proper minister. It is contrary to the mind of the Church to make exceedingly difficult the reception of the sacraments by the faithful, especially when they are seriously sick. Therefore, since the law

---

[72] Canon 854, § 2.

[73] D'Annibale, *Summula Theologiae Moralis,* I, n. 38.

[74] Canon 864, § 1.

[75] "Perdurante mortis periculo, sanctum Viaticum, secundum prudens confessarii consilium, pluries, distinctis diebus, administrari et licet et decet."

of canon 850, as one which restricts the free exercise of another minister's rights, is to be interpreted strictly in accordance with canon 19,[76] it follows that the administration of Holy Viaticum in the strict sense alone is reserved. Consequently, the administration of Holy Communion to the seriously sick before or after the administration of the Viaticum of precept is not an act against which canon 850 sets up any prohibition.[77]

Canon 850 provides that, with the exceptions noted, the administration of Holy Viaticum, whether public or private is the exclusive right of the pastor within whose territory the one who is in danger of death actually resides.[78] This is a repetition of canon 462, n. 3, where the administration of Holy Viaticum is enumerated among the functions reserved to the pastor.[79] It is the local pastor who possesses this right whether the dying person be one of his parishioners or a stranger.

No other priest may lawfully administer Holy Viaticum unless he has the permission, at least presumed, of the local pastor or of the local ordinary, or in some case of necessity.[80] If there is an urgent necessity for the administration of Viaticum, and the local pastor is not available or refuses to administer It when the need arises, then any priest, or even a deacon in the absence of a priest, not only may but should take Holy Viaticum to the one who is in danger of death.[81]

The proper pastor does not have the right to administer Holy Viaticum to one of his parishioners who is in danger of death

---

[76] "Leges quae poenam statuunt, aut liberum iurium exercitium coarctant, aut exceptionem a lege continent, stractae subsunt interpretationi."

[77] Vermeersch-Creusen, *Epitome,* II, n. 114; Cappello, *De Sacramentis,* I, n. 300; Regatillo, *Ius Sacramentarium,* I, n. 313; Coronata, *De Sacramentis,* I, 276, 323; Bouscaren-Ellis, *Canon Law,* (Milwaukee: The Bruce Publishing Company, 1946), p. 204.

[78] "Sacram communionem per modum Viatici sive publice sive privatim ad infirmos deferre, pertinet ad parochum ad normam can. 848, salvo praescripto can. 397, n. 3 et can. 514, §§ 1-3."

[79] "Functiones parocho reservatae sunt, nisi aliud iure caveatur: 3°. Sanctissimam Eucharistiam publice aut privatim tanquam Viaticum ad infirmos deferre . . . salvo praescripto can. 397, n. 3, 514, 848, § 2, 938, § 2."

[80] Vermeersch-Creusen, *Epitome,* II, n. 114; Regatillo, *Ius Sacramentarium,* I, n. 313; Noldin, *Theologia Moralis,* III, n. 126.

[81] Cappello, *De Sacramentis,* I, n. 301.

while actually staying outside the parish, unless he has the permission of the pastor within whose territory the person is staying. Such a permission may easily be presumed when one has positive reasons to know the local pastor does not object.[82] To disregard and trespass upon the rights of the local pastor in the administration of Holy Viaticum would be a violation of the pastor's right.[83] However, Cappello holds that such an act would not be seriously sinful unless a deliberate contempt were shown to the express will of the pastor.[84]

The law regarding the excommunication which formerly was incurred by regulars who administered Viaticum without permission[85] is no longer a part of the Code, and hence no longer exists as a binding norm.

Canon 850 allows several exceptions to the exclusive parochial right in the administration of Holy Viaticum. In the first instance, the administration of Holy Viaticum to the residential bishop is reserved to the dignitaries and the canons of the cathedral chapter according to their order of precedence.[86]

In all houses of clerical religious the local superior has the right and the duty of administering Holy Viaticum either personally or through a delegate. This right and duty extends for him not only to all the professed members and novices of the institute, but also to any other persons residing within the community day and night as servants, guests, students, or patients.[87] The words *"diu noctuque"* in this instance signify one entire day, or twenty-four hours, or at least an actual visit which is made at

[82] Woywod, *A Practical Commentary,* I, n. 745.

[83] Van Hove, *De Eucharistia,* p. 153; Durieux, *The Eucharist, Law and Practice,* p. 160.

[84] Cappello, *De Sacramentis,* I, n. 302.

[85] Const. *Apostolicae Sedis,* 12 oct. 1869, § II, n. 14—*Fontes,* n. 552.

[86] Canon 397, 3°.—Nisi aliud in statutis capitularibus caveatur, dignitatibus et canonicis secundum ordinem praecedentiae ius et officium est: 3°. Eidem [episcopo] decumbenti ministrare Sacramenta: defuncto iusta funebria persolvere.

[87] Canon 514, § 1.—In omni religione clericali ius et officium Superioribus est per se vel per alium aegrotis professis, novitiis, aliisve in religiosa domo diu noctuque degentibus causa famulatus aut educationis aut hospitii aut infirmae valetudinis, Eucharisticum Viaticum et extremam unctionem ministrandi.

the monastery with the intention of remaining for that length of time.[88] The religious house as contemplated in this canon embraces any and ever building within the confines of the monastery, and extends to any canonically erected religious house regardless of the number of religious who are living there.[89]

The Code Commission has stated that the superior in a clerical religious institute has the right to administer Holy Viaticum to the professed and novices of that institute even when they are in danger of death outside the religious house. However, the superior may not take Viaticum to them publicly without the permission of the local pastor.[90] Any other persons who habitually dwell in the religious house but become sick while away must receive Holy Viaticum from the pastor within whose territory they actually are staying.

Again, in a religious community of women professed with solemn vows, it is the right of the ordinary confessor or of his substitute to administer Holy Viaticum, rather than of the local pastor.[91] The right of the confessor extends to all classes of persons mentioned in § 1 of canon 514. Consequently, domestics or others who may reside in the convent day and night are to be given Holy Viaticum by the ordinary confessor.

The administration of Holy Viaticum in lay religious institutes pertains to the local pastor, but the local ordinary may entrust these lay religious to a chaplain and withdraw them from the jurisdiction of the local pastor.[92] In such cases the right to administer Holy Viaticum belongs to the chaplain.

In a similar manner the priest designated by the local ordinary to care for the spiritual welfare of a pious or charitable house

---

[88] Woywod, *A Practical Commentary,* I, n. 485; Coronata, *Institutiones Iuris Canonici* (2. ed., 5 vols., Taurini: Marietti, 1939-1946), I, 669, 670.

[89] Coronata, *loc. cit.*

[90] *PCI,* 16 iulii 1931—*AAS,* XXIII (1931), 353; Bouscaren, *Canon Law Digest,* I, 294.

[91] Canon 514, § 2.—In monialium domo idem ius et officium habet ordinarius confessarius vel qui eius vices gerit.

[92] Canon 514, § 3.—In alia religione laicali hoc ius et officium [Eucharisticum Viaticum et extremem unctionem ministranda] spectat ad parochum loci vel ad cappellanum quem Ordinarius parocho suffecerit ad normam can. 464, § 2.

has the right to administer Holy Viaticum within the house.[93] Thus, hospitals, asylums, orphanages, and other institutions destined for pious and charitable purposes may be entrusted to a chaplain, who thus may acquire the exclusive pastoral care of the institution. The mere appointment of a chaplain does not exempt these places from the pastoral care. It is necessary that the bishop make specific provision for such an exemption.[94] Once such a chaplaincy is established by the local ordinary it pertains to the chaplain, rather than to the local pastor, to administer Holy Viaticum to all within the institution.

Although not specifically excepted, either in canon 850, or in canon 462, n. 3, wherein the administration of Holy Viaticum is discussed as a parochial function, the lawful minister of Holy Viaticum to all persons residing in a seminary is the rector or his delegate. This is established by canon 1368, which exempts from the parochial jurisdiction all who are in the seminary, and sets up the rector with full pastoral rights in all matters save in the administration of the sacraments of matrimony and penance.[95]

The rights and duties of the rector extend to all who reside in the seminary. To establish this authority of the rector over others besides the seminarians, the Code makes no demand as to the duration of the stay in the seminary as it does when referring to a situation with reference to those residing in a religious house. It simply exempts from the pastoral jurisdiction *"omnes qui in Seminario sunt."*[96] Consequently it is the right and the duty of the seminary rector or his delegate to administer Holy Viaticum not only to all the seminarians but also to all others who are actually resident at the seminary.[97]

---

[93] Canon 464, § 2.—Potest Episcopus iusta et gravi de causa religiosas familias et pias domos, quae in paroeciae territorio sint et a iure non exemptae, a parochi cura subducere.

[94] Fanfani, *De Iure Parochorum,* n. 477.

[95] Canon 1368.—Exemptum a iurisdictione paroeciali Seminarium esto; et pro omnibus qui in Seminario sunt, parochi officium, excepta materia matrimoniali et firmo praescripto can. 891, obeat Seminarii rector eiusve delegatus, nisi in quibusdam Seminariis fuerit aliter a Sede Apostolica constitutum.

[96] Coronata, *Institutiones Iuris Canonici,* II, 300.

[97] Coronata, *loc. cit.;* Vermeersch-Creusen, *Epitome,* II, n. 702.

CHAPTER VI

The Administration of Holy Communion

ARTICLE 1. THE TIME FOR THE DISTRIBUTION OF HOLY COMMUNION

Section 1. The Day

The general principle that Holy Communion may be distributed on every day is set down by canon 867, § 1. This principle is immediately modified by the second and third paragraphs of canon 867, which concern the administration of Holy Communion on the last two days of Holy Week.[1] Outside of the limitations placed by this law, there are no other days on which Holy Communion may not be distributed lawfully. Consequently, the former regulations prohibiting the administration of Holy Communion in non-parochial churches on certain days, especially on Holy Thursday and Easter Sunday, are no longer in effect.[2]

Although canon 862 highly recommends that Holy Communion be distributed during Mass on Holy Thursday, it is certainly lawful to distribute Communion before Mass, and more probably also lawful even after Mass on that day.[3] If only a private Mass is celebrated and the solemn functions of Holy Thursday are not held, there is no prohibition against the administering of Holy Communion before, during, or even after the Mass.[4] How-

---

[1] Canon 867, § 1.—Omnibus diebus licet sanctissimam Eucharistiam distribuere. § 2. Feria tamen VI maioris hebdomadae solum licet sacrum Viaticum ad infirmos deferre. § 3. In Sabbato Sancto sacra communio nequit fidelibus ministrari nisi inter Missarum sollemnia vel continuo ac statim ab iis expletis.

[2] Coronata, *De Sacramentis,* I, 325.

[3] Cappello, *De Sacramentis,* I, n. 367; Regatillo, *Ius Sacramentarium,* I, n. 359; Vermeersch-Creusen, *Epitome,* II, n. 136; Coronata, *De Sacramentis,* I, 325.

[4] Cappello, *loc. cit.;* Iorio, *Theologia Moralis,* III, n. 127; Jone, *Moral Theology,* n. 515.

ever, a difficulty arises where the liturgical functions of the day are observed, for the Missal expressly states that some consecrated Hosts are to be reserved for the sick. This would seem to eliminate the possibility of having the Blessed Sacrament for administration to others. This, however, is not a direct prohibition which bars the Holy Eucharist's distribution from an altar other than the altar of respository.[5]

As Cappello[6] and Vermeersch[7] point out, canon 867, § 4, which states that Holy Communion can be distributed at the hours at which Mass can be celebrated,[8] cannot be adduced as forbidding the distribution of Holy Communion subsequent to the solemn services of Holy Thursday, on the score namely that the liturgical functions of the day have been brought to a close and that accordingly the distribution of Holy Communion cannot any longer be undertaken, for the same canon contains the modification, *"nisi aliud rationabilis causa suadeat."* These authors rightfully regard any reasonable request on the part of the faithful for Holy Communion on the anniversary day of the institution of the Holy Eucharist as a reasonable cause for the administration of Holy Communion.

On Good Friday, Holy Communion may be given only in the form of Holy Viaticum.[9] In the early days of the Church the faithful received Communion on this day as on any other, but the practice began to disappear in the ninth century, but even as late as 1679 the Sacred Congregation of the Council found it necessary to issue a decree in order to enforce the rubrics of the *Missale Romanum,* in which the prohibition had been made part of the written liturgical law.[10] The Code has confirmed this prohibition.

Some authors limit the meaning of Holy Viaticum as here

---

[5] Regatillo, *Ius Sacramentarium,* I, n. 359.

[6] *De Sacramentis,* I, n. 367.

[7] *Epitome,* II, n. 136.

[8] "Sacra communio iis tantum horis distribuatur, quibus Missae sacrificium offerri potest, nisi aliud rationabilis causa suadeat."

[9] Canon 867, § 2.

[10] S.C.C., decr. 12 febr. 1679—*Fontes,* n. 2848.

mentioned to simply that reception of Holy Viaticum which is made preceptive by both the divine and the ecclesiastical law.[11] But since the Code does not expressly state this restriction, there does not appear to be any jurisdically supported reason for excluding the possible administration of Holy Viaticum in the sense in which it is mentioned in canon 864, § 3, where the term refers to the Communion of devotion received by one in danger of death who has already received the Viaticum of precept. Under either of these assumptions Holy Viaticum can be administered on Good Friday.[12]

Apart from scandal or contempt, Cappello does not consider the violation of the law of canon 867, § 2, as one of serious import. Likewise he believes that the local ordinary could permit Holy Communion to be distributed on Good Friday to soldiers or others who were about to leave on a long journey, if they would have no other opportunity of receiving Communion for a long time.[13] In view of considering the fulfillment of the paschal precept to be of greater importance than the observance of the liturgical prohibition here in question, Regatillo deems it allowable to distribute Holy Communion on Good Friday for the fulfillment of the Easter precept to one who could conveniently fulfill his obligation only on Good Friday.[14] Although the statement of Regatillo may stand in principle, it is rather difficult to imagine an actual case of a person when not in danger of death who could not find equal convenience for the fulfillment of his Easter precept on one of the many other days that are available besides Good Friday.

Canon 867, § 3, states that Holy Communion cannot be given to the faithful on Holy Saturday except in the Mass of the day, or *"continuo et statim ab iis expletis."* The Mass here mentioned means especially the solemn or conventual Mass, but it also comprises the Mass sung according to the norm of the *Memoriale*

---

[11] Durieux, *The Eucharist, Law and Practice,* p. 205; Vermeersch-Creusen, *Epitome,* II, n. 136; Davis, *Moral and Pastoral Theology* (4. ed., 4 vols., London: Sheed and Ward, 1943), III, 230.

[12] Coronata, *De Sacramentis,* I, 325.

[13] *De Sacramentis,* I, n. 368.

[14] *Ius Sacramentarium,* I, n. 357.

Rituum Benedicti XIII.[15] Thus the law prescribes that on Holy Saturday Holy Communion can be administered to the faithful only in churches where the solemn functions take place, and only during the solemn functions or within a very short time after them, so that one can still think of a moral union between the Mass and the administration of Holy Communion.[16]

Some authors present a very liberal opinion which holds that for a just cause Communion may be distributed on Holy Saturday at any time after Mass, and even if Mass was not celebrated in the church.[17] Vermeersch, though he seemed to adhere to the stricter opinion, may be adduced as an authority for the more liberal interpretation. He wrote that the prohibition should not be considered a grave one, and that consequently any just cause would warrant a priest in giving Holy Communion apart from the Mass on Holy Saturday.[18]

Regatillo[19] and Cappello[20] do not see canon 867, § 3, as containing any true and strict prohibition, or at most a very slight one, so that any just cause, even the mere devotion of the faithful piously seeking Holy Communion would be a sufficient cause for the administration of Holy Communion any time after the services of Holy Saturday. This appears to be a very gratuitous assertion on the part of these authors. This law contains a very definite prohibition, since it is drawn up in a negative fashion and states that Holy Communion may not be distributed on Holy Saturday except under specific circumstances of time. The act of administering Holy Communion is prohibited *"nisi inter Missarum sollemnia vel continuo ac statim ab iis expletis."*

Regatillo apparently understands the phrase *"continuo ac statim ab iis expletis"* as signifying the time from which Holy Com-

---

[15] Iorio, *Theologia Moralis,* III, n. 127.

[16] Noldin, *Theologiae Moralis Summa,* III, n. 129; Davis, *Moral and Pastoral Theology,* III, 231; Augustine, *Commentary,* IV, 246; Durieux, *The Eucharist, Law and Practice,* p. 205; Vermeersch-Creusen, *Epitome,* II, n. 136.

[17] Regatillo, *Ius Sacramentarium,* I, n. 358; Cappello, *De Sacramentis,* I, n. 369.

[18] *Epitome,* II, n. 136.

[19] *Loc. cit.*

[20] *Loc. cit.*

munion may freely be distributed, for the reason that it is only after the consecration of Holy Saturday that the Holy Eucharist is again available for administration to the faithful.[21] In other words, according to Regatillo, the purpose of canon 867, § 3, is solely to warn against the reception of Holy Communion before Mass on Holy Saturday. Such a prohibition is hardly necessary, since the liturgical law demands an empty tabernacle before the Mass on Holy Saturday. The liturgical law does not contemplate even the possibility of the administration of Holy Communion before Mass on Holy Saturday. Canon 867, § 3, is quite unnecessary and useless if its purpose is solely to call attention to the absence of the Blessed Sacrament in the tabernacle before Mass on Holy Saturday and to the equally obvious fact that Holy Communion could be received after the consecration of the Holy Eucharist in that Mass.

This canon simply states that Holy Communion may not be distributed on Holy Saturday except during Mass and immediately after the Mass is finished.[22] It is hard to see in what sense "*continuo ac statim ab iis expletis*" could be understood to designate a *terminus a quo* for the distribution of Holy Communion. It is more consonant with sound juridical reasoning to take the wording of the law at its face value. If the words of the law mean anything at all, the phrase designates that the distribution of Holy Communion is allowed immediately after the completion of the Mass. "*Continuo*" in itself implies that there is no interval of any kind between the Mass and the distribution of Holy Communion. The adverb "*statim*" emphasizes the fact that Holy Communion is allowed at once, or immediately after the conclusion of the Mass. Any other rendering of the phrase does violence to the meaning of the words. Therefore instead of stating that the Holy Eucharist consecrated in the Mass of Holy Saturday is to be given in Communion on that day, and that Holy Communion is not to be distributed before the Mass, canon 867, § 3, forbids

---

[21] *Loc. cit.*

[22] Canon 867, § 3.—In Sabbato Sancto sacra communio nequit fidelibus ministrari nisi inter Missarum sollemnia vel continuo ac statim ab iis expletis.

the distribution of Holy Communion on Holy Saturday except during the Mass or immediately after the Mass is concluded.

Regatillo states that canon 867, § 3, does not refer to churches where the liturgy of Holy Week is not carried out, and therefore Holy Communion may be distributed in such churches and oratories on Holy Saturday.[23] There is nothing in the law to warrant this assumption. The fact that Regatillo can point to certain violations of the liturgical law in Rome would certainly not establish his assertion. If the purpose of the law is to warn against the administration of Holy Communion when the Holy Eucharist is not available as Regatillo implies, it is easy to see why he would not apply canon 867, § 3, to places where the liturgical functions are not carried out, for obviously the Blessed Sacrament is actually available in these places. However, it is quite unreasonable to think that the purpose of canon 867, § 3, is to labor the obvious to the extent that Regatillo implies. Therefore his assertion that this canon does not prohibit the administration of Holy Communion on Holy Saturday in churches or oratories in which the Holy Week liturgy is not observed can hardly be accepted.

A just cause in itself is surely not reason enough, apart from a dispensation, to do the exact opposite of what the law demands. Canon 867, § 3, in very clear fashion prohibits the administration of Holy Communion on Holy Saturday except during Mass or immediately thereafter. A just cause could well furnish a sufficient reason for a dispensation from the law, but it is difficult to see how a just cause for the reception of Holy Communion long after the Mass has been offered could in itself effect a cancellation of the law which allows the reception only at Mass or immedately thereafter.

Authors however point to custom as a factor which would allow Holy Communion to be distributed contrary to the common law on the last days of Holy Week.[24] These authors cite dioceses, parishes,

---

[23] *Loc. cit.*

[24] Cappello, *De Sacramentis,* I, n. 372; Prümmer, *Manuale Theologiae Moralis,* III, n. 221; Coronata, *De Sacramentis,* I, 325; Regatillo, *Ius Sacramentarium,* I, n. 357.

and communities of religious with customs approved by the Holy See which countenance the administration of Holy Communion on Good Friday. In view of the importance of the Holy Eucharist as a means of sanctification in the Church, and in view also of the mind and the desire of the Church which highly recommends the frequent and even the daily reception of Holy Communion, these authors hold as certainly reasonable any custom which would extend the right to administer Holy Communion. On the other hand, any restrictive custom which would limit the days on which Holy Communion could be distributed could hardly become a legitimate usage, since it is unreasonable in that it is opposed to the purpose, mind and desire of the Church.[25]

Section 2. The Hour

Holy Viaticum may be administered at any hour of the day or night.[26] The spiritual welfare of the dying is a prime consideration in the Church, and is not to be jeopardized by any circumstances that bear any relation to the factor of time. Even though a doctor might indicate that Holy Viaticum could be delayed until the day hours, the minister may proceed to take Viaticum to the dying during the night. No restrictions exist and no special reasons are required by the law as long as the person is in the danger of death.[27]

The ordinary and usual hours for the distribution of Holy Communion are the hours when the celebration of Mass is permitted.[28] Since the Communion is part of the Sacrifice of the Mass, it was normal that the Church should desire that the reception of Holy Communion be associated with the Mass. The Council of Trent had indicated the increased benefits that the faithful derive from the reception of Holy Communion at Mass.[29] But a reasonable request outside of Mass must not be refused.[30]

---

[25] Cappello, *loc. cit.*

[26] Canon 867, § 5.

[27] Cappello, *De Sacramentis,* I, n. 373.

[28] Canon 867, § 4.—Sacra communio iis tantum horis distribuatur quibus Missae sacrificium offerri potest, nisi aliud rationabilis causa suadeat.

[29] Sess. XXII, *de sacrificio missae,* c. 6.

[30] Canon 846, §§ 1 and 2; S.R.C., Ianuen., 7 dec. 1844—*DAG,* n. 4984.

Canon 867, § 4, provides that Holy Communion may be administered only at the times when the Sacrifice of the Mass can be offered, unless a reasonable excuse would permit otherwise. Canon 821, § 1, regulates the hours at which Mass may be celebrated.[31] Consequently, the distribution of Holy Communion should normally not be earlier than one hour before dawn or later than one hour after midday. However, at the Christmas Midnight Mass, or on other occasions when by indult Mass is celebrated in the afternoon or evening, Holy Communion may be distributed unless the local ordinary in a particular case and for a just cause has forbidden it.[32]

Any reasonable cause will justify the administration of Holy Communion at an hour when Mass may not be offered. In view of the association of this function with the time for the saying of Mass, any privilege of anticipating the time for the celebration of Mass would be extended to the administration of Holy Communion.[33] A reasonable excuse would need only be a light excuse, and could arise on the part of the minister or from the needs of the recipients.

Causes that would justify the administration of Holy Communion outside the usual time would be the physical or moral impossibility of receiving at the regular time in view of necessary work, because of the absence of the minister, or for the reason that some journey has to be undertaken; the much greater convenience, or the increase of devotion resulting from the reception of Holy Communion would also suffice to warrant the priest in administering It outside the regular time.[34] As Vermeersch[35] and Coronata[36] point out, the mere fact that someone has observed the natural fast as required for the lawful reception of Holy Communion beyond the time at which Mass may be offered would

---

[31] "Missae celebrandae initium ne fiat citius quam una hora ante auroram vel serius quam una hora post meridiem."

[32] Cf. *PCI,* 16 mart. 1936—*AAS,* XXVIII (1936), 178. The question of the administration of Holy Communion at Midnight Mass was taken up at length in Chapter III, Art. 2, Section 3. Cf. *supra,* pp. 96-106.

[33] Vermeersch-Creusen, *Epitome,* II, n. 136.

[34] Cappello, *De Sacramentis,* I, n. 373.

[35] *Epitome,* II, n. 136.

[36] *De Sacramentis,* I, 327.

in itself certainly be a sufficient reason for the administering of Holy Communion to him.

The law demands a reasonable cause for any deviation from the prescribed time for the distribution of Holy Communion. Therefore the earlier before dawn or the later in the afternoon that Communion would be distributed, the more serious would have to be the excusing cause. However, some authors hold that it would not be more than a slight offense to give Holy Communion outside the prescribed time even if there were no reasonable cause.[87]

ARTICLE 2. THE PLACE FOR THE DISTRIBUTION OF HOLY COMMUNION

Canon 869 states that unless the local ordinary should forbid it, Holy Communion may be distributed in any place where Mass can lawfully be celebrated, even in a private oratory. This canon treats of two questions, the lawful place for the distribution of Holy Communion and the right of the local ordinary to prohibit the distribution of Communion under certain conditions. Canon 869 does not refer exclusively to the administration of Holy Communion in private oratories, nor exclusively to the administration of Holy Communion outside of Mass.

Canon 846, § 1, states that subject to the prohibitory authority of the local ordinary, as warranted in canon 869, every priest may distribute Holy Communion during his Mass and, if he celebrates Mass privately, also directly before and immediately after his Mass. Canon 869 states further that Holy Communion may be distributed not only when the priest celebrates Mass, but also wherever he could say Mass. Canon 846, § 1, declares when every priest is authorized by law to administer Holy Communion; canon 869 establshes the lawful place for the distribution of the Holy Eucharist.

Canon 869 is found in that Article of the Code which concerns the time and place for the distribution of Holy Communion.[88]

---

[87] Cappello, *De Sacramentis,* I, n. 373; Durieux, *The Eucharist, Law and Practice,* p. 206.

[88] Liber III, Tit. III, Cap. II, Art. III.

There is no reason to believe that this canon is to be restricted in meaning exclusively to the administration of Communion in private oratories. It is true that the sources which are listed in the footnote of the Code for this canon refer only to the private oratory.[39] But this does not imply that canon 869 refers to the distribution of Holy Communion solely in a private oratory. Rather, the particular mention that is given to a private oratory indicates that this law is relatively new and exceptional in that also a private oratory is now acknowledged as a place for the lawful distribution of Holy Communion.

Unlike the status that obtained in the legislation, there is now no longer any need for the minister to possess an indult in order to be authorized to give Holy Communion in a private oratory. As late as 1906 the Sacred Congregation of Rites had allowed Holy Communion to be distributed in a private oratory solely to those persons who were mentioned in the indult that authorized the privilege of the private oratory.[40] But on May 8, 1907, Pope Pius X stated that the indult of a private oratory included also the permission to give Holy Communion to all who were present at the Mass celebrated therein, provided that the rights of the pastor in the administration of Easter Communion were preserved whole and intact.[41]

The Code indeed recommends but does not command that the faithful satisfy the Easter precept in their parish church.[42] Accordingly no restriction is placed on the administration of Holy Communion in a private oratory. The very fact that the private oratory is made equal to other oratories and churches as a lawful place for the distribution of Holy Communion explains why specific mention is made of the private oratory in canon 869.

Canon 869 does not refer exclusively to the administration of Holy Communion outside of Mass, as Coronata seems to imply.[43]

---

[39] S.C.C., decr. 12 febr. 1679—*Fontes*, n. 2848; S.R.C., *Urbis et Orbis*, 8 maii 1907—*Fontes*, n. 6357.

[40] *ASS*, XL (1907), 173.

[41] S.R.C., *Urbis et Orbis*, 8 maii 1907—*Fontes*, n. 6357; *DA*, n. 4201; *ASS*, XL (1907), 589.

[42] Canon 859, § 3.

[43] *De Sacramentis*, I, 328.

In the first place, the fundamental law for the distribution of Holy Communion in a private oratory is the decree which Pius X issued through the Sacred Congregation of Rites in 1907, and this pertained specifically to the administration of Communion to those who attended Mass in a private oratory.[44] Canon 846, § 1, deals with the authorization of a priest to administer Holy Communion during Mass, or directly before or immediately after a private Mass, subject to the precept of canon 869.[45] This linking up of canon 869 with the law of canon 846 which is concerned with the distribution of Holy Communion at Mass, or in close relation to the Mass, shows that canon 869 should not be thought to refer exclusively to the administration of Holy Communion *extra Missam.* Rather, canon 869 refers to the administration of Holy Communion in general.

But the clearest argument to show that canon 869 does not refer exclusively to the administration of Holy Communion *extra Missam,* or exclusively to the administration of the Eucharist in a private oratory, is drawn from the response which the Code Commission gave to the query concerning the distribution of Holy Communion at Midnight Mass.[46] When asked whether it was allowed to distribute Holy Communion in parochial churches at Midnight Mass the response was: "Affirmative, nisi loci Ordinarius, iustus de causis, in casibus particularibus, id prohibuerit ad norman can. 869." The Commission was concerned with Holy Communion at Mass, not *extra Missam;* it was concerned with the distribution of Communion in parochial churches, and not with the distribution of Communion in private oratories. Yet it ordered that the local ordinary was to proceed in accordance with the norm of canon 869 in the event that he prohibited the distribution of Holy Communion in a particular case. Evidently, then, the scope of canon 869 is not to be restricted to the administration of Holy Communion in a private oratory or outside of Mass.

---

[44] *Urbis et Orbis,* 8 maii 1907—*Fontes,* n. 6357; *DA,* n. 4201.

[45] Canon 846, § 1.—Quilibet sacerdos intra Missam et, si privatim celebrat, etiam proxime ante et statim post, sacram communionem ministrare potest, salvo praescripto can. 869.

[46] 16 mart. 1936—*AAS.* XXVIII (1936), 178; Bouscaren, *The Canon Law Digest,* II, 217.

Canon 869 states that the local ordinary may forbid the administration of Holy Communion only in a particular case and for a just cause. The local ordinary has this power fundamentally because he is the guardian of faith and morals in his territory, and he must be vigilant to see that abuses and errors, especially in the administration of the sacraments, are repudiated and corrected without delay.[47] Any regulation which would forbid the administration of Holy Communion would have to be in the form of a particular precept; a diocesan statute or law, or also a general precept, would have no legal force. A just cause could be constituted solely through a serious reason, for there is question here of a right which is given by the common law and is not to be arbitrarily interfered with. The prohibition would cease as soon as its cause would no longer exist.[48]

Since Holy Communion may be distributed wherever it is lawful to say Mass, it follows that when Mass is celebrated on a portable altar, even in a private home, Holy Communion may be distributed to all present. Whenever Mass is celebrated outside of a church or oratory either with the authorization of the local ordinary in accord with canon 822, § 4, or by way of special indult obtained from the Holy See, Holy Communion may be distributed to all there present.[49]

On January 5, 1928, a response of the Sacred Congregation of the Sacraments explained a further application of canon 869 to the question of the distribution of Holy Communion outside of Mass.[50] This response stated that under certain circumstances

---

[47] Canon 336, § 2.

[48] Coronata, *De Sacramentis,* I, 273; Cappello, *De Sacramentis,* I, n. 374

[49] Regatillo, *Ius Sacramentarium,* I, n. 361; Cappello, *De Sacramentis,* I, n. 377.

[50] "I. An fideles in montanis pagis habitantes, quoties ad infirmos sacra Eucharistia deferatur, possint sacra synaxi refici in loco sacro, vel etiam, cum agatur de re tam sacra, in loco decenti et honesto qui in itinere extet, non valentes ea die ecclesiam petere? II. Num sacra communio et Confessionis sacramentum administrari possint iis qui in domo infirmi versantur? III. An administrari debeant in enunciatis circumstantiis iis, qui aetate sunt provecti vel morbo laborant?" "Ad I. Affirmative, ad normam can. 869, iuncto canone 822, § 4, seu dummodo Ordinarius loci id concedat ad normam citatae praescriptionis, scilicet pro singulis casibus et per modum actus. Ad.

the faithful may be given Communion in a church or an oratory which the priest would pass as he carries Viaticum or Holy Communion to the sick for, according to canon 869, Holy Communion may be distributed wherever it is permitted to say Mass; in addition, since the local ordinary for a just and reasonable cause in an extraordinary case, and not habitually but *per modum actus,* may permit Mass to be said in any decent place except in a bed room,[51] he may in a similar manner permit Holy Communion to be distributed in any such decent place. Mass need not actually be celebrated in this place in order that Holy Communion may be distributed; all that is necessary is that Mass could be celebrated therein. Since the faculty to designate any decent place for the administration of Holy Communion under the foregoing circumstances is within the ordinary powers of the local ordinary, he may delegate it.[52]

The annotations of the Secretary of the Sacred Congregation of the Sacraments as pertaining to this response were officially published.[53] In these remarks, Iorio, the Secretary, stated that the pious desire of those who are prevented from going to church and who wish to receive Holy Communion on a certain day may be satisfied in any oratory which the priest would pass as he goes to the sick, since canon 869 states that Holy Communion may be distributed wherever it is allowed to say Mass. If an oratory is not available, then Holy Communion may be distributed in any decent and honorable place, such as the hall of a house or any place capable of being arranged to resemble an oratory in which the celebration of Mass could be permitted. With these conditions verified, the local ordinary could allow the distribution of Holy Communion. The permission of the local ordinary is necessary, for

II et III. Quoad communionem, provisum in primo; quoad Confessionem: affirmative, servatis servandis ad norman cc. 910, §§ 1 et 2, et 909, §§ 1 et 2."—*AAS,* XX (1928), 79; Bouscaren, *The Canon Law Digest,* I, 391.

[51] Canon 822, § 4.—Loci Ordinarius aut, si agatur de domo religionis exemptae, Superior maior, licentiam celebrandi extra ecclesiam et oratorium super petram sacram et decenti loco, nunquam autem in cubiculo, concedere potest iusta tantum ac rationabili de causa, in aliquo extraordinario casu et per modum actus.

[52] Canon 199, § 1.

[53] *AAS,* XX (1928), 79.

the place must be designated as suitable and licit for the celebration of Mass and the consequent distribution of Holy Communion. The Secretary of the Congregation then explained that this faculty, as in the case of all ordinary powers when delegation is not expressly prohibited, may be delegated by reason of canon 119, § 1. However, he warned the local ordinary that, in view of the gravity of the matter and the narrow limits within which this power may be exercised, this faculty should not be delegated except to very prudent men who will not abuse it.

The following conclusions can be drawn from this response. The faithful who are not able to attend Mass in that they live at a great distance from the church or for some other reason, such as the necessity of caring for the sick, may be given Holy Communion in an oratory or in their own homes. In the event that an oratory lies along his route when a priest takes Holy Communion to the sick, then by reason of canon 869, which allows the distribution of Communion there inasmuch as Mass could be celebrated in that oratory, the priest may distribute Holy Communion to the faithful, and no previous permission of the local ordinary is required. For this case the response does not make any mention of the need of any previous permission. That such permission is not needed becomes obvious from the reasoning of the Secretary of the Sacred Congregation. Canon 869 offers sufficient authorization for the distribution of Holy Communion in the oratory.[54]

If an oratory is not available, Holy Communion may with the previous permission of the local ordinary or his delegate be distributed in one of the homes. This authorization must be made within the norms of canon 822, § 4, which postulates individual action in an extraordinary case at the suggestion of a cause that is at least both just and reasonable.[55]

Holy Communion should not be given in a bedroom, except to the sick. However, when in an exceptional case the one who cares for the sick person cannot possibly leave him to go to an oratory or to some other becoming place, *epikeia* can warrant the

---

[54] Cappello, *De Sacramentis,* I, n. 375.

[55] Coronata, *De Sacramentis,* I, 328; Iorio, *Theologia Moralis,* III, n. 134.

distribution of Communion to the attendant in the bedroom of the sick person.[56]

Beste[57] emphasizes the fact that the priest must be taking Communion to the sick if he is rightfully to make use of the faculty explained in the response of the Sacred Congregation. He implies that Holy Communion could not be taken to the faithful who could not go to Mass over a long period of time, unless there was some one sick among them. It is true that normally a priest would not make a long journey in bringing Holy Communion except for the sake of administering Holy Viaticum or Communion to the sick, and certainly in an isolated district, as it is contemplaed in the response of the Sacred Congregation, there might be at least one sick person in warrant of the use of this faculty.

However, is it necessary that Communion be carried to the sick by the priest before he may use the faculty here explained? In other words, does this response confer a privilege on the priest who would take Holy Communion to the sick, or is it rather an explanation of the full ramifications of canon 869, which determines the lawful place for the distribution of Holy Communion?

The response of the Sacred Congregation of the Sacraments indicated two facts, first, the just cause for the taking of Holy Communion to the faithful who are not sick, and secondly, the lawful place for the administration of Holy Communion to them. The cause was grave, for the people were of an isolated mountainous district who evidently were unable to attend Mass over a period of time and thus could not receive the sacrament of Holy Eucharist. When the sick cannot go to church for the purpose of there receiving Holy Communion, the law insists and allows that their pastor bring Holy Communion to them. Yet the sick are not bound, either by divine or ecclesiastical precept, to any purely devotional reception of Holy Communion. It appears that the Church is ready to allow the same service for the faithful who are so unfortunate as not to be able to go to Mass over a long period of time for the purpose of there receiving Holy Communion.

---

[56] Iorio, *loc. cit.;* Vermeersch-Creusen, *Epitome,* II, n. 137.

[57] *Introductio in Codicem,* p. 496.

The response of the Sacred Congregation of the Sacraments took advantage of the occasion of a sick-call to point out the connection between canon 869, which states that the place for celebrating Mass and distributing Holy Communion is one and the same, and canon 822, which points to the lawful place for the celebration of Mass. In the reasoning as set forth in the officially published *Annotationes* the bringing of Holy Communion to the sick is not set as an essential preliminary for the faculty of bringing Holy Communion also to those who, though they are not sick, are yet unable to make their way to a church for the reception of Holy Communion. The presence of a sick person was made the occasion, but not the condition or the cause, that made it allowable for Holy Communion to be distributed to the rest of the faithful who could not approach a church. It does not seem reasonable that their spiritual welfare should be contingent on the physical misfortune of one of their number.

When Communion is distributed during Mass, the celebrating priest is not allowed to give Holy Communion to people who are so far away that in order to reach them he must go out of sight of the altar.[58] The Church does not want the continuity of the Mass to be broken without necessity. It will normally be very simple to give Communion later to those who at the time of distribution during Mass were outside of the church, or oratory, and thus there will not result any interruption of the ceremonies of the Mass. It is lawful to distribute Holy Communion within a church even though as a result of its architectural design the building pillars or walls actually obstruct the priest's view of the altar in his act of distributing Holy Communion.[59]

Authors consider it allowable for a priest to give Communion during Mass to the sick who in rooms near the chapel can hear the priest while he is celebrating Mass, even though they cannot see him at the altar. Thus a person could be given Communion

---

[58] Canon 868.—Sacerdoti celebranti non licet Eucharistiam intra Missam distribuere fidelibus adeo distantibus ut ipse altare e conspectu amittat.

[59] Regatillo, *Ius Sacramentarium*, I, n. 361; Vermeersch-Creusen, *Epitome*, II, n. 138.

in the sacristy. The same can be said for a sick person in a room adjoining a private oratory.[60] The Sacred Congregation of Rites on February 7, 1874, allowed the practice of taking Holy Communion during Mass to all the sick who in rooms near enough to the sanctuary could hear the priest's voice while he celebrated Mass. The Sacred Congregation demanded that the *umbella* be used whenever the Holy Eucharist was carried to another room for the purpose of administering Communion.[61] But it was postulated that the rooms be on the same floor level as the chapel, for the same Sacred Congregation had at an earlier time forbidden the practice of bringing Communion during Mass to anyone on a different story of the building.[62]

Holy Communion should not be distributed either during or outside of Mass at an altar on which the Blessed Sacrament is exposed.[63] An indult from the Holy See or a grave cause would make it permissible. When there is but one altar in the church, or if the altar of exposition, e.g., the high altar, is also the sole altar that contains a tabernacle, so that from a side altar Holy Communion could not be given to a large number without great inconvenience and distraction, it would undoubtedly be lawful to distribute Holy Communion from the altar of exposition.[64]

The extent and effect of a local interdict on the administration of Holy Communion may vary. Hence the decree of interdict must be carefully read if one is properly to determine its full import. In general, the distribution of Holy Communion is one of the sacred functions which is prohibited in an interdicted place. Nevertheless the law makes several exceptions. Holy Communion may always be administered to the dying, but all pomp and solemnity should be foregone.[65] On Christmas, Easter, Pentecost,

---

[60] Regatillo, *loc. cit.;* Vermeersch-Creusen, *loc. cit.;* Coronata, *De Sacramentis,* I. 237; Davis, *Moral and Pastoral Theology,* III, 231.

[61] Ad dubium II—*DA,* n. 3322.

[62] *Ianuen.,* 7 dec. 1844—*DA,* 2885.

[63] S.R.C., Societas Iesu, 11 maii 1878, ad 1—*DA,* n. 3448; *Marianopolitana,* 17 apr. 1919—*AAS,* XI (1919), 246.

[64] Regatillo, *Ius Sacramentarium,* I, n. 362; Mueller-Ellis, *Handbook of Ceremonies* (10. English edition, St. Louis: B. Herder, 1940), p. 216.

[65] Canon 2270, § 1.

Corpus Christi and the feast of the Assumption of the Blessed Virgin, local interdicts do not affect the distribution of Holy Communion.[66]

If the administration of Holy Communion is not expressly forbidden, then Holy Communion may be distributed in interdicted capitular and parochial churches, as also in any interdicted church which is the only church in a town, unless the decree of interdict demands that another church be used meanwhile.[67] No solemnities may be observed, and Holy Viaticum is to be taken to the dying privately.

When a particular altar or chapel in a church is under interdict, then Holy Communion may not be distributed there, for the interdict proscribes the conducting of all sacred offices.[68]

ARTICLE 3. THE MANNER IN WHICH HOLY COMMUNION IS TO BE ADMINISTERED

In the administration of the sacraments the liturgical rites and ceremonies prescribed in the approved liturgical books of the Church must be accurately observed.[69] For the administration of Holy Communion during the Mass there must be observed the rubrics that are found in the *Missale Romanum, Ritus servandus in celebratione missae*, c. X, *de oratione dominica et aliis usque ad factam communionem*, n. 6. When a priest distributes Holy Communion in church outside of Mass, he must follow the prescriptions set down in the *Rituale Romanum*, tit. IV, c. 2, *ordo administrandi sacram communionem*. When Holy Communion is distributed outside the church, the rubrics of the *Rituale Romanum*, tit. IV, c. 4, *de communione infirmorum*, are to be followed.

Canon 852 states that Holy Communion is to be given only under the species of bread. This law pertains solely to priests of the Latin rite; it does not equally apply to priests of the Oriental rites.[70] The Council of Constance (1414-1418) justified the prac-

---

[66] Canon 2270, § 2.

[67] Canon 2271, 2°; canon 2272, § 3, 1° and 2°.

[68] Canon 2271, § 1.

[69] Canon 733, § 1.

[70] Cf. canon 1

tice of Communion under the species of bread alone, and condemned those who taught that Communion under both species was necessary.[71] The Council of Trent imposed the reception of Holy Communion under the species of bread alone.[72] This law was framed for the purpose of preventing abuses and of precluding the danger of irreverence as well as for the purpose of counteracting the disbelief and the heresy of those who contended that the whole Christ was not contained under the separate elements of the consecrated species, and that the Church was therefore wrong in proclaiming the full presence of Christ under either of the separate species.[73]

This is an ecclesiastical law of serious import.[74] Yet, since it is an ecclesiastical and not also a divine law, the Church may allow divergent practices, as in fact it has done with respect to many of the Oriental rites. On their reunion with Rome the Eastern Churches which wished to retain the practice of administering Holy Communion under both species were permitted to do so.[75]

In a rare case, for example, when a consecrated Host to be given to a dying person is not at hand, but the consecrated wine has not yet been consumed in the Mass, it is thought that Holy Viaticum may be administered under the species of the consecrated wine. The reason alleged is that the reception of Viaticum is of divine precept, whereas the reception under the species of consecrated bread is only of ecclesiastical precept, so that in danger of death the faithful would be held to the divine law rather than to the ecclesiastical law.[76]

All danger of scandal and irreverence must of course be definitely precluded, and it is postulated also that there be absolutely no consecrated Host available. If a person had difficulty in swallowing the consecrated Host, it does not follow that Holy Viaticum

[71] Sess. XIII—Denzinger, *Enchiridion,* n. 626.

[72] Sess. XXI, *de communione,* cc. 1, 2, can. 1, 2.

[73] Cappello, *De Sacramentis,* I, n. 385.

[74] Coronata, *De Sacramentis,* I, 282; Cappello, *loc. cit.;* Vermeersch-Creusen, *Epitome,* II, n. 115; Augustine, *Commentary,* IV, 224.

[75] Benedictus XIV, const. *Etsi pastoralis,* 26 maii 1742 § VI, n. XV—*Fontes,* n. 328.

[76] Coronata, *De Sacramentis,* I, 282; Cappello, *De Sacramentis,* I, n. 385; Davis, *Moral and Pastoral Theology,* III, 199.

could be administered under the species of the consecrated wine, for a small particle of the Host could be placed in a spoon partly filled with water, and thus Holy Viaticum under the species of the consecrated bread could readily be administered.[77]

It is not lawful to administer a large Host or several small Hosts in simple satisfaction of the misguided devotion of a communicant. Several small Hosts may be given for a grave reason, such as the necessity of a speedy consumption of the Sacred Species. In an emergency a priest may detach smaller parts of the large Host used in the Mass, or he may break the small Hosts into several parts, in order to distribute them to communicants who would be gravely inconvenienced if they could not receive Communion at that time. The danger of any irreverence and the likelihood of any scandal must always be effectively counteracted.[78]

Holy Communion must be administered in that form of bread which is proper to the rite of the ministering priest.[79] This law binds all priests of every rite, Oriental as well as Latin. All are to distribute Holy Communion consecrated in either the leavened or the unleavened bread, according as their own proper rite will direct them to do. There is to be no unnecessary commingling of rites. Pope Benedict XIV (1740-1758) forbade all commixture of rites in his Encyclical Letter *Allatae sunt*.[80] In accord with this principle he ruled that every priest was to distribute the Holy Eucharist in his own proper rite.[81] The law now demands that there be used that form of bread which is proper to the rite of the ministering priest.

Canon 851, § 2, of the Code formulates an exception to the ruling which is contained in canon 851, § 1. This exception was first introduced by Pope Pius X in his Constitution *Tradita ab antiquis* of September 14, 1912.[82] Paragraph two of canon 851 is taken almost word for word from this Constitution of Pius X.

---

[77] Davis, *loc. cit.*

[78] Coronata, *De Sacramentis*, I, 282.

[79] Canon 851, § 1.

[80] 26 iul. 1755, § 23—*Fontes*, n. 434.

[81] Const. *Etsi pastoralis*, 25 maii 1742, § VI, n. XI—*Fontes*, n. 328; ep. encycl., *Allatae sunt*, 26 iul. 1755, § 23—*Fontes*, n. 434.

[82] N. II—*Fontes*, n. 698.

The same law is contained in the decree *Cum Episcopo*[83] and also in the decree *Cum data fuerit,* both of which were issued for the Greek-Ruthenians in the United States.[84] With certain conditions verified, canon 851, § 2, concedes to priests the right to administer Holy Communion in a form of bread different from the form of bread used in their own rite.[85]

The distinctive and important factor stressed in canon 851, § 2, relative to the administration of Holy Communion is not the rite in which the Holy Eucharist was consecrated but rather the type of bread that was used in the consecration. With reference to the distribution of Holy Communion, the differentiation lies solely in whether leavened or unleavened bread was used for the consecration in any particular rite. The law of canon 851, § 2, makes no distinction between priests of the different Oriental rites who use leavened bread, or between Latin priests and priests of the Oriental rites who use unleavened bread. Consequently Oriental priests of various Oriental rites are not forbidden to administer the Holy Eucharist consecrated in some Oriental rite other than their own, as long as in all of the rites in question the consecration was effected in the leavened bread. Likewise, a priest of an Oriental rite who uses unleavened bread, as do the priests of the Latin rite, is not forbidden by canon 851, § 2, to administer Holy Communion consecrated in the Latin rite, nor is a priest of the Latin rite forbidden to administer Holy Eucharist consecrated in such an Oriental rite. This applies to the Armenians and the Maronites, who use unleavened bread in their liturgy as the Latins do.[86]

With reference to the Holy Eucharist consecrated in another rite and under a form of bread different from that which is used in his own rite, a priest may indeed administer It, but only when

[83] S.C. de Prop. Fide pro negotiis ritus orientalis, decr. 18 aug. 1914, art. 23—*AAS,* VI (1914), 462

[84] S.C. pro Ecclesia Orientali, decr., 1 mart. 1929, art. 32—*AAS,* XXI (1929), 158; Bouscaren, *The Canon Law Digest,* 1, 14.

[85] Canon 851, § 2.—Ubi vero necessitas urgeat nec sacerdos diversi ritus adsit, licet sacerdoti orientali qui fermentato utitur, ministrare Eucharistiam in azymo, vicissim latino aut orientali qui utitur azymo, ministrare in fermentato; at suum quisque ritum ministrandi servare debet.

[86] Benedictus XIV, ep. encycl., *Allatae sunt,* 26 iul 1755 § 23—*Fontes,* n. 434.

there are verified the three conditions which canon 851, § 2, postulates. In order that a priest may avail himself of the concession granted by this law it is necessary that there be a case of necessity, that there be no priest of the proper rite available, and that the priest who distributes Holy Communion observe the rubrics of his own rite in the actual administration of the sacrament. This implies that a Latin priest who in a case of necessity administers the Holy Eucharist under both species will use the customary formula: *"Corpus Domini nostri Iesu Christi custodiat animam tuam in vitam aeternam. Amen."* He will not use any other improvised formula, such as, *"Corpus et Sanguis Domini nostri Iesu Christi custodiant animam tuam in vitam aeternam. Amen."*

The only problem in the application of canon 851, § 2, is to discover what is meant by the *necessity* which makes it lawful for a priest to administer Holy Communion in a form of bread not proper to his own rite. If a priest in a case of necessity for the purpose of administering Holy Viaticum to the dying can consecrate in a form of bread that is not proper to his own rite,[87] then he certainly also can distribute Holy Communion which was consecrated in a form of bread that is not proper to his own rite. But the law of canon 851, § 2, does not postulate a case of extreme necessity, or the danger that a person die without Holy Viaticum, as a condition for a priest's lawful administration of Holy Communion consecrated in a form of bread that is not proper to his own rite.[88]

It must be remembered that canon 851, § 2, is explicitly constituted as an exception to the law of canon 851, § 1, which demands that every priest administer the Holy Eucharist in the form of bread that is proper to his own rite. It is constituted as the concession of a faculty that derogates the former law which forbade any and all commixture of rites. This concession was first made

---

[87] Cappello, *De Sacramentis,* I, n. 261; Coronata, *De Sacramentis,* I, 171; Prümmer, *Manuale Theologiae Moralis,* III, n. 171; Henry, *The Mass and Holy Communion: Interritual Law,* The Catholic University of America Canon Law Studies, n. 235 (Washington, D. C.: The Catholic University of America Press, 1946), pp. 58-60.

[88] Woywod, *A Practical Commentary,* I, n. 748; Henry, *The Mass and Holy Communion: Interritual Law,* p. 84.

by Pope Pius X, who so enthusiastically recommended and encouraged the frequent and even daily reception of the Holy Eucharist.[89]

It is interesting to note that in his Constitution *Tradita ab antiquis,* which is the source of the law of canon 851, § 2, Pope Pius also explicitly conceded to the faithful of any rite the permission out of simple devotion to receive the Holy Eucharist consecrated in any rite. These two faculties were contained in successive sections in this papal Constitution.[90] From these two documents it is quite evident that Pope Pius X intended that the sacrament of the Holy Eucharist should be frequently received and made easily available to the faithful. This definitely leads one to think that the case of necessity as demanded by canon 851, § 2, should not be taken in a rigidly restrictive sense.

Rather, according to the mind of the Church, which desires the frequent and even daily reception of Holy Communion, the necessity referred to in canon 851, § 2, seems better interpreted in the same sense in which the term necessity is used in canon 845, § 2,[91] with reference namely to the distribution of Holy Communion by the deacon. Not an extreme necessity, but a necessity which implies the existence of a grave reason, seems postulated as sufficient for the use of the faculty conceded by the law. This appears more properly to accord with the canonical principle that the laws of the Church which cede spiritual favors to the faithful are to be interpreted benignly in their benefit.[92] Therefore it appears safe to hold that, if a person would otherwise have to forego receiving Holy Communion, even out of devotion, then a priest may administer the Holy Eucharist, even though It was consecrated in another rite under a form of bread that is not proper to the rite of the ministering priest.[93]

---

[89] S.C.C., *Sacra Tridentina Synodus,* 20 dec. 1905, n. 6—*Fontes,* n. 2103.

[90] *Tradita ab antiquis,* 14 sept. 1912, nn. II, III—*Fontes,* n. 698.

[91] *Supra,* pp. 140, 141.

[92] Cappello, *De Sacramentis,* I, n. 367.

[93] Coronata, *De Sacramentis,* I, 281; Vermeersch-Creusen, *Epitome,* II, n. 115; Blat, *De Sacramentis,* Lib. III, Pars I, n. 168; Duskie, *The Canonical Status of Orientals in the United States,* The Catholic University of America Canon Law Studies, n. 48 (Washington, D. C.: The Catholic University of America, 1928), p. 118.

A priest may certainly administer the Holy Eucharist though It was consecrated in a form of bread other than the one he uses in his own rite, when a long interval of time has elapsed since the person has last received the Holy Eucharist. A priest could do the same if a person were to take a long journey during which it would be impossible for him to receive Communion, or if a person needed to receive Holy Communion in order that he might fulfill his Easter precept.[94]

However, such a serious reason is not required. The "necessity" postulated in canon 852, § 2, seems to demand nothing more than a grave reason for the administration of Holy Communion when a minister of the proper rite is not available. Therefore, if a number of communicants, or even one, would not be able to satisfy the devout desire of receiving Holy Communion on any given day for the lack of an available priest of the proper rite, then another priest could distribute the Holy Eucharist to them, even though the Holy Eucharist was consecrated in another rite and in a form of bread not proper to the rite of the ministering priest.[95]

---

[94] Woywod, *A Practical Commentary,* I, n. 748; Duskie, *loc. cit.*

[95] Coronata, *De Sacramentis,* I, 281.

CONCLUSIONS

The priest is the ordinary minister of Holy Communion not simply in the sense of the usual or customary minister, but rather also in the sense of the primary minister, who by reason of his authority over the Holy Eucharist has the essential and inherent right to administer Holy Communion.

The administration of Holy Communion is not an act of jurisdiction, but jurisdiction is the basis for the authority to administer Holy Communion lawfully, and also for the authority to delegate this faculty to others. Therefore there is required in the minister some pastoral power or jurisdiction with respect to the recipient, or he must have obtained the faculty from one who possesses such jurisdiction. However, the factor of jurisdiction as touching the administration of Holy Communion is not an element related to the validity of the administration; rather, it is an element calculated for the preservation of due order in the administration of this sacrament.

Curates or assistants in a parish (*vicarii cooperatores*) need no further authorization for the lawful administration of Holy Communion than that which is contained in the very act of their assignment to the parish. As priests assigned to a definite church for exercising the care of souls under the direction of the pastor, *vicarii cooperatores* are qualified by the law to distribute Holy Communion, and hence need no further permission.

The right to administer Holy Comunion whenever Mass is celebrated is a right conferred by the law and cannot be taken away arbitrarily by anyone. Only the local ordinary within the norms of canon 869, and neither the local pastor nor the rector of the church, may forbid a priest to administer Holy Communion at any time he celebrates Mass.

By his ordination the deacon is constituted the extraordinary minister of Holy Communion not in the sense that he is the occasional minister, but principally for the reason that he is the subsidiary and secondary minister of this sacrament.

Two conditions are essential for the constitution of the grave cause that is postulated in canon 845, § 2, for the lawful authorization of the deacon to administer Holy Communion: first, the utility of the faithful; secondly, the non-availability of a priest to administer to them.

In the law of the Code on the minister of Holy Communion the term "necessity" not only denotes a case of extreme emergency, but points also to the presence of any grave reason for the administration of Holy Communion.

When the deacon administers Holy Communion unlawfully he does not incur an irregularity, for while he indeed exercises a function which he is forbidden to exercise, yet he does not lack the needed power of Orders for the proper exercise of this function.

It is contrary to the mind and purpose of the Church to make difficult the reception of the sacraments by the faithful, especially when they are seriously sick. Consequently the private carrying by some priest other than the local pastor of Holy Communion to the seriously sick before or after the administration of the Viaticum of precept is not an act against which canon 850 sets up any prohibition.

In imminent danger of death and with no proper minister of the Sacrament available, a lay person could, if scandal were duly precluded, give Viaticum to himself or to another. In addition, the service of the laity may be enlisted by the proper ecclesiastical authority for the administration of Holy Communion not only in extreme necessity but whenever their services would be necessary to promote the common spiritual welfare of the faithful.

When it would not be possible to carry Holy Communion frequently, even daily, to the sick in a solemn and public manner, it is the right of every priest, under canon 849, to carry Holy Communion to the sick privately. Whenever there is a just and reasonable cause for the administration of Holy Communion privately, the exclusive right of the local pastor under canon 848, § 1, ceases, and the right of every priest under canon 849, § 1, arises. Therefore a proper pastor may, without any need of further authorization, privately take Communion of devotion to his own parishioners who are sick outside of their own parish.

In the private administration of Holy Communion to the sick those rubrics which are more intimately connected with the actual consecrating or administering of the Holy Eucharist require a proportionately greater reason in warrant of their partial or total omission. Any reasonable cause would excuse from the obligation of taking an associate when bringing Holy Communion privately to the sick. Only grave inconvenience would allow the administration of Holy Communion to the sick without the cassock and surplice.

The liberal views presented by some canonists with reference to canon 867, § 3, cannot be accepted. The law, which is drawn up in a negative fashion, contains a definite prohibition and therefore it forbids the administration of Holy Communion on Holy Saturday before the liturgical services and in churches or oratories in which the liturgical services are not carried out.

The law in canon 869 relates to the lawful place for the administration of Holy Comunion, and therefore is not solely enacted for the purpose of establishing the right to administer Communion in a private oratory. The right given to the local ordinary in canon 869 to prohibit the administration of Holy Communion in a particular case is not restricted exclusively to a prohibition of the dispensıng of the Eucharist in a private oratory, nor exclusively to the prohibition of the administration of Holy Comumnion outside of Mass.

Holy Communion may be distributed in any place in which it is lawful either by reason of the common law, or in consequence of an indult, or also by way of the special permission of the local ordinary to celebrate Mass, even though Mass is not actually celebrated in connection with the act of distribution.

The case of necessity postulated in canon 851, § 2, for the lawful administration of Holy Communion in a form of bread that is not proper to the rite of the ministering priest need not be an extreme necessity; rather, a necessity in the broad sense, or the presence of a grave reason for the administration of Holy Communion when a minister of the proper rite is not available, furnishes a sufficient warrant. A grave reason exists if the faithful would otherwise have to forego receiving devotional Holy Communion.

BIBLIOGRAPHY

Sources

Acta Apostolicae Sedis, Commentarium Officiale, Romae, 1909—

Acta Sancta Sedis, 41 vols., Romae, 1865-1908.

Bouscaren, T. Lincoln, *The Canon Law Digest,* 2 vols., Milwaukee: Bruce, 1934-1943.

Bruns, Hermann, *Canones Apostolorum et Conciliorum Saeculorum IV-VII,* 2 vols., Berolini, 1839.

Bullarum Diplomatum et Privilegiorum Sanctorum Pontificum Taurinensis Editio, 24 vols. et Appendix, Augustae Taurinorum, 1857-1872.

Bullarium Franciscanum, 4 vols., ed. J. H. Sbaralea, Romae, 1759-1768.

Codex Iuris Canonici Pii X Pontificis Maximi iussu digestus Benedicti Papae XV auctoritate promulgatus, Romae: Typis Polyglottis Vaticanis, 1917. Reimpressio, 1932.

Codicis Iuris Canonici Fontes, cura Emi Petri Card. Gasparri editi, 9 vols., Romae (later Civitate Vaticana): Typis Polyglottis Vaticanis, 1923-1939. (Vols. XII-IX, ed. cura Emi Iustiniani Serédi.)

Collectanea S. Congregationis de Propaganda Fide, 2 vols., Romae: Typographia Polyglotta, S. C. de Propaganda Fide, 1907.

Concilii Plenarii Baltimorensis Secundi Acta et Decreta, 2. ed., Baltimore, 1880.

Corpus Iuris Canonici, Editio Lipsiensis II (Richter-Friedberg), 2 vols., Lipsiae, 1879-1881.

Corpus Scriptorum Ecclesiasticorum Latinorum, 68 vols., Vindobonae: F. Tempsky, 1866—

Decreta Authentica Congregationis Sacrorum Rituum, 5 vols. et 2 Appendices, Romae: Ex Typographia Polyglotta, 1898-1927.

Decreta Authentica Congregationis Sacrorum Rituum ex actis eiusdem collecta, cura et studio Aloisii Gardellini, 3. ed., 5 vols. cum Supplementis usque ad annum 1888, Romae, 1856-1888.

Decretales D. Gregorii Papae IX, suae integritati, una cum glossis restituta, Romae, 1582.

Denzinger, H-Bannwart, C-Umberg, J., *Enchiridion Symbolorum Definitionum et Declarationum de Rebus* Fidei et Morum, ed. 21.-23., St. Louis, Herder and Co., 1937.

Die griechischen christlichen Schriftsteller der ersten drei Jahrhunderte, Eusebius Werke: 7 vols. in 10, ed. E. Schwartz, Leipsig, 1902-1926; Vol. II (*Historia Ecclesiastica*), pars I-pars III, 1903-1909.

Hardouin, Jean, *Acta Conciliorum et Epistolae Decretales ac Constitutiones Summorum Pontificum,* 12 vols., Parisiis, 1714-1715.

Hefele, Carolus-Leclercq, Henricus, *Histoire des Conciles,* 10 vols. in 19, Paris: Letouzey et Ané, 1907-1938.

Jaffé, Philippus, *Regesta Pontificum Romanorum ab condita Ecclesia ad annum post Christum natum MCXCVIII (1198),* 2 ed., cura G. Wattenbach, F. Kaltenbrunner (ad annum 590), P. Ewald (anno 590-882), S. Lowenfeld (anno 882-1198), 2 vols. in 1, Lipsiae, 1885-1888.

Mansi, J. D., *Sacrorum Conciliorum Nova et Amplissima Collectio,* 53 vols. in 60, Parisiis, 1901-1927.

Monumenta Germaniae Historica, 188 vols., incomplete, Hannoverae, 1826— *Leges in 4,* Sectio III (*Concilia*), Tom. I, ed. F. Maassen, 1893; Tom. II, ed. A. Werminghoff, 1906-1908.

Pallottini, S., *Collectio omnium conclusionum et resolutionum quae in causis propositis apud Sacram Congregationem Cardinalium S. Concilii Tridentini interpretum prodierunt ab eius institutione anno MDLXIV ad annum MDCCCLX distinctis titulis alphabetico ordine per materias digesta,* 18 vols., Romae, 1868-1895.

Pontificale Romanum Summorum Pontificum iussu editum, a Benedicto XIV et Leo XIII Pont. Max. recognitum et castigatum, Mechliniae, 1895.

Potthast, A., *Regesta Pontificum Romanorum inde ab anno post Christum natum MCXCVIII ad annum MCCCIV,* 2 vols., Berolini, 1874-1875.

Quasten, Johannes, *Monumenta Eucharistica et Liturgica Vetustissima,* Bonnae: Petrus Hanstein, 1935.

Rituale Romanum, Editio II. juxta Typicam Vaticanam, Neo Eboraci: Benziger Brothers, 1945.

Schema Codicis Iuris Canonici, ed. P. Gasparri, Romae, 1913.

Schroeder, H. J., *Canons and Decrees of the Council of Trent,* St. Louis: Herder, 1941.

Thesaurus Resolutionum Sacrae Congregationis Concilii, 167 vols., Romae, 1718-1908.

Thiel, Andreas, *Epistolae Romanorum Pontificum a Sancto Hilario (461-468) usque ad Sanctum Hormisdam (514-523),* Brunsbergae, 1868.

Wilkins, David, *Concilia Magnae Brittaniae et Hiberniae,* 4 vols., London, 1737.

Reference Works

Adone, Aloysius, *Synopsis Canonico Liturgica,* Neapoli, 1886.

Aertnys, J.-Damen, C. A., *Theologia Moralis,* 13. ed., 2 vols., Taurini-Romae: Marietti, 1939.

Alphonsus de Liguori, *Theologia Moralis,* ed. L. Gaude, 4 vols., Romae, 1905-1912.

Aquinas, St. Thomas, *Summa Theologica,* 6 vols., Taurini: Marietti, 1937.

Augustine, Charles, *A Commentary on the New Code of Canon Law,* 8 vols., Vol. IV, 6. ed., St. Louis, Herder and Co., 1931.

Ballerini, A.-Palmieri, D., *Opus Theologicum Morale,* 3. ed., 7 vols., Prati, 1898-1901.

Barbosa, A., *De Officio et Potestate Parochi Descriptio,* ed. U. Giraldi a S. Cajetano, Romae, 1774.

Benedictus XIV, *De Synodo Dioecesana,* 2 vols., Romae, 1806.

———, *Institutiones Ecclesiasticae,* 3 vols., Romae, 1784.

Bernardus Papiensis, *Summa Decretalium,* ed. E. A. T. Laspeyres, Ratisbonae, 1860.

Beste, Udalricus, *Introductio in Codicem,* 2. ed., Collegeville, Minn.: St. John's Abbey Press, 1944.

Blat, Albertus, *Commentarium Textus Codicis Iuris Canonici,* 5 vols. in 7, Vol. III, pars I (*De Sacramentis*), Romae: Ex Typographia Pontificia in Instituto Pii IX, 1924.

Bona, Ioannes, *Rerum Liturgicarum Libri Duo,* Romae, 1671.

Bouix, D., *Tractatus de Parocho,* 3. ed., Parisiis, 1880.

Brightman, F. E., *Eastern Liturgies,* Oxford, 1896.

Bouscaren, T.-Ellis, A., *Canon Law, A Text and Commentary,* Milwaukee: Bruce, 1946.

Cappello, F. M., *Tractatus Canonico-Moralis de Sacramentis,* 3 vols. in 6, Vol. I, 4. ed., Romae: Marietti, 1945.

Cerato, P., *Censures Vigentes Ipso Facto a Codice Iuris Canonici Exerptae,* 2. ed., Patavii, 1921.

Cicognani, Amleto, *Canon Law,* 2. ed., trans. by J. M. O'Hara and F. Brennan, Westminster, Md.: Newman Book Shop, Reprint, 1947.

Cocchi, Guidus, *Commentarium in Codicem Iuris Canonici,* 8 vols. in 5, Vol. VIII, 4. ed., Taurinorum Augustae: Marietti, 1938.

Conran, E. J., *The Interdict,* The Catholic University of America Canon Law Studies, n. 56, Washington, D. C.: The Catholic University of America, 1930.

Coronata, Matthaeus Conte a, *Institutiones Iuris Canonici,* 2. ed., 5 vols., Taurini: Marietti, 1939-1947.

———, *Tractatus Canonicus de Sacramentis,* 3 vols., Romas: Marietti, 1943-1946.

Crotty, M. M., *The Recipient of First Holy Communion,* The Catholic University of America Canon Law Studies, n. 247, Washington, D. C.: The Catholic University of America Press, 1947.

D'Annibale, J., *Summula Theologiae Moralis,* 3. ed., 3 vols., Romae, 1889-1892.

Davis, Henry, *Moral and Pastoral Theology,* 4. ed., 4 vols., London: Sheed and Ward, 1943.

De Augustinis, Aegidius, *De Re Sacramentaria,* 2 vols., Woodstock, Md., 1878.

De Luca, Ioannes B., *Theatrum Veritatis et Iustitiae,* 16 vols. in 4, Romae, 1706.

De Lugo, Ioannes Card., *Disputationes Scholasticae et Morales,* ed. nova accurante Furnials, 8 vols., Parisiis, 1868-1869.

Devoti, Ioannes, *Institutionum Canonicarum Libri Quatuor,* 3 vols., Venetiis, 1827.

Doronzo, Emmanuel, *Tractatus Dogmaticus de Eucharistia,* Tom. I, *De Sacramento,* Milwaukee: Bruce, 1947.

Durieux, P., *The Eucharist, Law and Practice,* trans. by Oliver Dolphin, Faribault, Minn., 1926.

Duskie, J. A., *The Canonical Status of Orientals in the United States,* The Catholic University of America Canon Law Studies, n. 48, Washington, D. C.: The Catholic University of America, 1928.

Duchesne, Louis, *Christian Worship: Its Origin and Evolution,* translated from the third French edition by M. L. McClure, London: Society for Promoting Christian Knowledge, 1903.

Fagnanus, Prosper, *Commentaria in Quinque Libros Decretalium,* 4 vols., Venetiis, 1697.

Fanfani, L., *De Iure Parochorum,* Romae: Marietti, 1924.

Feldhaus, A. H., *Oratories,* The Catholic University of America Canon Law Studies, n. 42, Washington, D. C.: The Catholic University of America, 1927.

Fortescue, Adrian, *The Mass: A Study of the Roman Liturgy,* ed. by H. Thurston, New York: Longmans, Green and Co., 1937.

Fournier, P.-LeBras, G., *Histoire des Collections Canoniques en Occident depuis les Fausses Décrétales jusqu'au Décret de Gratian,* 2 vols., Paris: Recueil Sirey, 1931-1932.

Funk, Francis X., *Didascalia et Constitutiones Apostolorum,* 2 vols., Paderbornae, 1905.

Gasparri, Petrus, *Tractatus Canonicus de Sanctissima Eucharistia,* 2 vols., Parisiis, 1897.

Genicot, E.-Salsmans, I., *Institutiones Theologiae Moralis,* 6. ed., 2 vols., Bruxellis, 1909.

Gonzalez-Tellez, Manuel, *Commentaria Perpetua in singulos textus quinque librorum Decretalium Gregorii IX,* 5 vols., Lugdini, 1749.

Guilfoyle, M., *Custom,* The Catholic University of America Canon Law Studies, n. 105, Washington, D. C.: The Catholic University of America, 1937.

Gury, J. P., *Compendium Theologiae Moralis,* ed. tertia ab H. Dumas emendata, 2 vols., Parisiis, 1881.

Henry, J. A., *The Mass and Holy Communion: Interritual Law,* The Catholic University of America Canon Law Studies, n. 235, Washington, D. C.: The Catholic University of America Press, 1946.

Hostiensis, Cardinalis (Henricus de Segusia), *Commentaria in Quinque Libros Decretalium,* 5 vols. in 3, Venetiis, 1581.

———, *Summa Aurea,* Venetiis, 1570.

Hyland, *Excommunication,* The Catholic University of America Canon Law Studies, n. 49, Washington, D. C.: The Catholic University of America, 1928.

Jone, H., *Moral Theology,* translated and adapted to the Code and customs of the United States of America by Urban Adelman, Westminster, Maryland: Newman Book Shop, 1945.

Jorio, D., *La Communione agl' Infermi,* Roma: Pustet, 1931.

———, *Theologia Moralis,* 3. ed., 3 vols., Neapoli: D'Auria, 1946-1947.

Kilker, A. J., *Extreme Unction,* The Catholic University of America Canon Law Studies, n. 32, Washington, D. C.: The Catholic University of America, 1926.

Laymann, P., *Theologia Moralis in quinque libros partita,* 5 vols. in 1, Venetiis, 1719.

Lega, Michael Card., *Praelectiones in Textum Iuris Canonici de Iudiciis Ecclesiasticis, De Iudiciis Criminalibus in genere et in specie, De Delictis et Poenis Praemisso Tractatu,* Libr. II, vol. IV, Romae, 1901.

Lehmkuhl, A., *Theologia Moralis,* 12. ed., 2 vols., Friburgi, Brisgoviae, 1914.

Leurenius, Petrus, *Forum Beneficiale sive Questiones et Responsa Canonica,* 2 vols., Venetiis, 1752.

Martène, E., *De Antiquis Ecclesiae Ritibus,* 4 vols., Rotomagi, 1700-1706.

Merkelbach, B. H., *Summa Theologiae Moralis,* 3. ed., 3 vols., Parisiis: Desclée, de Brouwer et Cie, 1939.

Michiels, G., *Normae Generales Iuris Canonici,* 2 vols., Lublin: Universitas Catholica, 1929.

Migne, J. P., *Patrologiae Cursus Completus, Series Latina,* 221 vols., Parisiis, 1844-1864.

———, *Series Graeca,* 161 vols., Parisiis, 1856-1866.

Mueller, J. B., Ellis, Adam C., *Handbook of Ceremonies,* 10. English edition, St. Louis: B. Herder, 1940.

Nueberger, N., *Canon 6, or the Relation of the Codex Iuris Canonici to the Preceding Legislation,* The Catholic University of America Canon Law Studies, n. 44, Washington, D. C.: The Catholic University of America, 1927.

Noldin, H.-Schmitt, A., *Summa Theologiae Moralis,* 26. ed., 3 vols., Ratisbonae: Pustet, 1940.

Panormitanus, Abbas (Nicholaus de Tudeschis), *Commentaria super quinque Libros Decretalium,* 5 vols., Lugdini, 1547.

Pennacchi, I., *Commentaria in Constitutionem Apostolicae Sedis,* 2 vols., Romae, 1883.

Pohle, J.-Preuss, A., *The Sacraments,* authorized English ed. based on the fifth German edition with some abridgements and additional references, 4 vols., St. Louis, 1917.

Prümmer, D., *Manuale Theologiae Moralis,* 3. ed., 3 vols., Friburgi Brisgoviae: Herder, 1923.

Rainer, E. G., *Suspension of Clerics,* The Catholic University of America Canon Law Studies, n. 111, Washington, D. C.: The Catholic University of America Press, 1937.

Regatillo, E., *Ius Sacramentarium,* 2 vols., Santander: Sal Terrae, 1945-1946.

Rufinus, *Summa Decretorum,* ed. H. Singer, Paderborn, 1902.

Sabetti, A.-Parrett, T., *Compendium Theologicae Moralis,* 27. ed., New York: Pustet, 1919.

Salmanticensium Collegium, *Cursus Theologia Moralis,* 6 tom. in 3. Venetiis, 1728.

Santi, F., *Praelectiones Iuris Canonici,* 2. ed., 5 vols. in 1, Ratisbonae, 1892.

Studies in Medieval History, edited by Geoffrey Barraclough, *Medieval Germany,* 911-1250, Vol. I (Introduction); Vol. II (Essays), Oxford: Blackwell and Mott, Ltd., 1938.

Schmalzgrueber, F., *Ius Ecclesiasticum Universum,* 5 vols. in 12, Romae, 1843-1845.

Schroeder, H. J., *Disciplinary Decrees of the General Councils, Text, Translation and Commentary,* St. Louis: Herder, 1941.

Suarez, F., *Opera Omnia,* ed. C. Berton, 28 vols., Parisiis, 1859-1878. Vol. XXI, 1866.

Thomassinus, L., *Vetus et Nova Ecclesiae Disciplina,* 3 vols., Parisiis, 1688.

Van Hove, *Commentarium Lovaniense in Codicem Iuris Canonici,* Vol. I, tom. 1, *Prolegomena ad Codicem Iuris Canonici,* 2. ed., Mechliniae et Romae: Dessain, 1945.

———, *Tractatus de Sanctissima Eucharistia,* 2. ed., Mechliniae: H. Dessain, 1941.

Van Espen, Z. Bernardus, *Ius Ecclesiasticum Universum,* 10 vols., Venetiis, 1769.

Vermeersch, A.-Creusen, J., *Epitome Iuris Canonici,* 6. ed., 3 vols., Mechliniae, Romae: H. Dessain, 1937-1946.

Waldron, J., *The Minister of Baptism,* The Catholic University of America Canon Law Studies, n. 170, Washington, D. C.: The Catholic University of America Press, 1942.

Wernz, F. X., *Ius Decretalium,* 2. ed., 6 vols., Romae et Prati, 1906-1913.

Wernz, F. X.-Vidal, P., *Ius Canonicum,* 7 vols. in 8, Romae: Universitas, Gregoriana, Tom. IV, Vol. 1, 1934.

Witasse, Carolus, *Tractatus Theologici,* 6 vols., Venetiis, 1783.

Woywod, S., *A Practical Commentary on the Code of Canon Law,* 5. revised ed., 2 vols., New York: J. Wagner, Inc., 1939.

Zubizaretta, V., *Theologia Dogmatico-Scholastica,* 3. ed., 4 vols., Bilbao: Elixpuru Hños., 1937-1939.

Articles

Browne, P., "Die Kommunion in der Pfarrkirche," *Zeitscrift für katholische Theologie,* LIII (1929), 477-516.

Donovan, J. P., "Careless Custodians of the Sacraments," *The Homiletic and Pastoral Review,* XLV (1944), 183-186.

———, "When May Deacons Give Communion," *The Homiletic and Pastorial Review,* XLII (1942), 823-826.

Woywod, S., "The New Code and the Administration of the Blessed Sacrament," *The Homiletic and Pastoral Review,* XXI (1921), 1012-1020.

PERIODICALS

Homiletic and Pastoral Review, The, New York, 1900—

Zeitschrift für katholische Theologie, Innsbruck, 1877—

ABBREVIATIONS

AAS—*Acta Apostolicae Sedis.*
ASS—*Acta Sanctae Sedis.*
Bruns—*Canones Apostolorum et Conciliorum saec.* IV-VII, ed. Bruns.
Bull. Rom.—*Bullarum Diplomatum et Privilegiorum Sanctorum Pontificum Taurinensis Editio.*
DA—*Decreta Authentica Congregationis Sacrorum Rituum.*
DAG—*Decreta Authentica Congregationis Sacrorum Rituum, cura et studio Aloisii Gardellini.*
Fontes—*Codicis Iuris Canonici Fontes cura . . . Gasparri editi.*
Hardouin—*Acta Conciliorum,* etc.
Mansi—*Sacrorum Conciliorum Nova et Amplissima Collectio.*
GCS—*Die Grieschischen christlichen Schriftsteller der ersten drei Jahrhunderte.*
HPR—*The Homiletic and Pastoral Review.*
MGH—*Monumenta Germaniae Historica.*
MPG—Migne, *Patrologia Graeca.*
MPL—Migne, *Patrologia Latina.*
PCI—Pontificia Commissio Interpretationis.
S.C.C.—Sacra Congregatio Concilii.
S.C. de Prop. Fide—Sacra Congregatio de Propaganda Fide.
S.R.C.—Sacrorum Rituum Congregatio.

BIOGRAPHICAL NOTE

Daniel Eugene Sheehan was born May 14, 1917, in Emerson, Nebraska. After graduating from Sacred Heart School in Emerson, he attended The Creighton University, Omaha, Nebraska, for two years. He completed his studies for the Holy Priesthood at St. Louis Preparatory and Kenrick Seminary in St. Louis, Missouri. He was ordained in Omaha on May 23, 1942. He was appointed to St. Cecilia's Cathedral parish, where he served until September, 1946, when he enrolled in the School of Canon Law of the Catholic University of America. He received the degree of the Baccalaureate in Canon Law in June, 1947, and the degree of Licentiate in Canon Law in June, 1948.

INDEX

CANON LAW STUDIES*

1. Freriks, Rev. Celestine A., C.PP.S., J.C.D., Religious Congregations in Their External Relations, 121 pp. 1916.
2. Galliher, Rev. Daniel M., O.P., J.C.D., Canonical Elections, 117 pp., 1917.
3. Borkowski, Rev. Aurelius L., O.F.M., J.C.D., De Confraternibus Ecclesiasticis, 136 pp., 1918.
4. Castillo, Rev. Cayo, J.C.D., Disertacion Historico-Canonica sobre la Potestad del Cabildo en Sede Vacante o Impedida del Vicario Capitular, 99 pp., 1919 (1918).
5. Kubelbeck, Rev. William J., S.T.B., J.C.D., The Sacred Penitentiaria and Its Relation to Faculties of Ordinaries and Priests, 129 pp., 1918.
6. Petrovits, Rev. Joseph, J.C., S.T.D., J.C.D., The New Church Law on Matrimony, X-461 pp., 1919.
7. Hickey, Rev. John J., S.T.B., J.C.D., Irregularities and Simple Impediments in the New Code of Canon Law, 100 pp., 1920.
8. Klekotka, Rev. Peter J., S.T.B., J.C.D., Diocesan Consultors, 179 pp., 1920.
9. Wanenmacher, Rev. Francis, J.C.D., The Evidence in Ecclesiastical Procedure Affecting the Marriage Bond, 1920 (Printed 1935).
10. Golden, Rev. Henry Francis, J.C.D., Parochial Benefices in the New Code, IV-119 pp., 1921 (Printed 1925).
11. Koudelka, Rev. Charles J., J.C.D., Pastors, Their Rights and Duties According to the New Code of Canon Law, 211 pp., 1921.
12. Melo, Rev. Antonius, O.F.M., J.C.D., De Exemptione Regularium, X-188 pp., 1921.
13. Schaaf, Rev. Valentine Theodore, O.F.M., S.T.B., J.C.D., The Cloister, X-180 pp., 1921.
14. Burke, Rev. Thomas Joseph, S.T.D., J.C.D., Competence in Ecclesiastical Tribunals, IV-117 pp., 1922.
15. Leech, Rev. George Leo, J.C.D., A Comparative Study of the Constitution "Apostolicae Sedis" and the "Codex Juris Canonici," 179 pp., 1922.
16. Motry, Rev. Hubert Louis, S.T.D., J.C.D., Diocesan Faculties According to the Code of Canon Law, II-167 pp., 1922.
17. Murphy, Rev. George Lawrence, J.C.D., Delinquencies and Penalties in the Administration and the Reception of the Sacraments, IV-121 pp., 1923.

*All published numbers are available from the Catholic University of America Press, 620 Michigan Avenue, N.E., Washington 17, D. C., except the following: Nos. 1-114 inclusive, 115, 118, 120, 122, 123, 136, 153, 162, 182 and 198. But the following numbers, now reissued, are obtainable from *The Jurist*, The Catholic University of America, Washington 17, D. C., namely: Nos. 5, 7, 11, 17, 18, 19, 26, 28, 30, 31, 34, 42, 44, 51, 52 and 61.

18. O'Reilly, Rev. John Anthony, S.T.B., J.C.D., Ecclesiastical Sepulture in the New Code of Canon Law, II-129 pp., 1923.
19. Michalicka, Rev. Wenceslas Cyrill, O.S.B., J.C.D., Judicial Procedure in Dismissal of Clerical Exempt Religious, 107 pp., 1923.
20. Dargin, Rev. Edward Vincent, S.T.B., J.C.D., Reserved Cases According to the Code of Canon Law, IV-103 pp., 1924.
21. Godfrey, Rev. John A., S.T.B., J.C.D., The Right of Patronage According to the Code of Canon Law, 153 pp., 1924.
22. Hagedorn, Rev. Francis Edward, J.C.D., General Legislation on Indulgences, II-154 pp., 1924.
23. King, Rev. James Ignatius, J.C.D., The Administration of the Sacraments to Dying Non-Catholics, V-141 pp., 1924.
24. Winslow, Rev. Francis Joseph, O.F.M., J.C.D., Vicars and Prefects Apostolic, IV-149 pp., 1924.
25. Correa, Rev. Jose Servelion, S.T.L., J.C.D., La Potestad Legislativa de la Iglesia Catolica, IV-127 pp., 1925.
26. Dugan, Rev. Henry Francis, A.M., J.C.D., The Judiciary Department of the Diocesan Curia, 87 pp., 1925.
27. Keller, Rev. Charles Frederick, S.T.B., J.C.D., Mass Stipends, 167 pp., 1925.
28. Paschang, Rev. John Linus, J.C.D., The Sacramentals According to the Code of Canon Law, 129 pp., 1925.
29. Piontek, Rev. Cyrillus, O.F.M., S.T.B., J.C.D., De Indulto Exclaustrationis necnon Saecularizationis, XIII-289 pp., 1925.
30. Kearney, Rev. Richard Joseph, S.T.B., J.C.D., Sponsors at Baptism According to the Code of Canon Law, IV-127 pp., 1925.
31. Bartlett, Rev. Chester Joseph, A.M., LL.B., J.C.D., The Tenure of Parochial Property in the United States of America, V-108 pp., 1926.
32. Kilker, Rev. Adrian Jerome, J.C.D., Extreme Unction, V-425 pp., 1926.
33. McCormick, Rev. Robert Emmett, J.C.D., Confessors of Religious, VIII-266 pp., 1926.
34. Miller, Rev. Newton Thomas, J.C.D., Founded Masses According to the Code of Canon Law, VII-93 pp., 1926.
35. Roelker, Rev. Edward G., S.T.D., J.C.D., Principles of Privilege According to the Code of Canon Law, XI-166 pp., 1926.
36. Bakalarczyk, Rev. Richardus, M.I.C., J.U.D., De Novitiatu, VIII-208 pp., 1927.
37. Pizzuti, Rev. Lawrence, O.F.M., J.U.L., De Parochis Religiosis, 1927. (Not Printed.)
38. Bliley, Rev. Nicholas Martin, O.S.B., J.C.D., Altars According to the Code of Canon Law, XIX-132 pp., 1927.
39. Brown, Mr. Brendan Francis, A.B., LL.M., J.U.D., The Canonical Juristic Personality with Special Reference to its Status in the United States of America, V-212 pp., 1927.

40. Cavanaugh, Rev. William Thomas, C.P., J.U.D., The Reservation of the Blessed Sacrament, VIII-101 pp., 1927.
41. Doheny, Rev. William J., C.S.C., A.B., J.C.D., Church Property: Modes of Acquisition, X-118 pp., 1927.
42. Feldhaus, Rev. Aloysius H., C.PP.S., J.C.D., Oratories, IV-141 pp., 1927.
43. Kelly, Rev. James Patrick, A.B., J.C.D., The Jurisdiction of the Simple Confessor, X-208 pp., 1927.
44. Neuberger, Rev. Nicholas J., J.C.D., Canon 6 or the Relation of the Codex Iuris Canonici to the Preceding Legislation, V-95 pp., 1927.
45. O'Keefe, Rev. Gerald Michael, J.C.D., Matrimonial Dispensations, Powers of Bishops, Priests, and Confessors, VIII-232 pp., 1927.
46. Quigley, Rev. Joseph A. M., A.B., J.C.D., Condemned Societies, 139 pp., 1927.
47. Zaplotnik, Rev. Johannes Leo, J.C.D., De Vicariis Foraneis, X-142 pp., 1927.
48. Duskie, Rev. John Aloysius, A.B., J.C.D., The Canonical Status of the Orientals in the United States, VIII-196 pp., 1928.
49. Hyland, Rev. Francis Edward, J.C.D., Excommunication, Its Nature, Historical Development and Effects, VIII-181 pp., 1928.
50. Reimann, Rev. Gerald Joseph, O.M.C., J.C.D., The Third Order Secular of Saint Francis, 201 pp., 1928.
51. Schenk, Rev. Francis J., J.C.D., The Matrimonial Impediments of Mixed Religion and Disparity of Cult, XVI-318 pp., 1929.
52. Coady, Rev. John Joseph, S.T.D., J.U.D., A.M., The Appointment of Pastors, VIII-150 pp., 1929.
53. Kay, Rev. Thomas Henry, J.C.D., Competence in Matrimonial Procedure, VIII-164 pp., 1929.
54. Turner, Rev. Sidney Joseph, C.P., J.U.D., The Vow of Poverty, XLIX-217 pp., 1929.
55. Kearney, Rev. Raymond A., A.B., S.T.D., J.C.D., The Principles of Delegation, VII-149 pp., 1929.
56. Conran, Rev. Edward James, A.B., J.C.D., The Interdict, V-163 pp., 1930.
57. O'Neill, Rev. William H., J.C.D., Papal Rescripts of Favor, VII-218 pp., 1930.
58. Bastnagel, Rev. Clement Vincent, J.U.D., The Appointment of Parochial Adjutants and Assistants, XV-257 pp., 1930.
59. Ferry, Rev. William A., A.B., J.C.D., Stole Fees, V-136 pp., 1930.
60. Costello, Rev. John Michael, A.B., J.C.D., Domicile and Quasi-Domicile, VII-201 pp., 1930.
61. Kremer, Rev. Michael Nicholas, A.B., S.T.B., J.C.D., Church Support in the United States, VI-136 pp., 1930.
62. Angulo, Rev. Luis, C.M., J.C.D., Legislation de la Iglesia sobre la intencion en la application de la Santa Misa, VII-104 pp., 1931.

63. FREY, REV. WOLFGANG NORBERT, O.S.B., A.B., J.C.D., The Act of Religious Profession, VIII-174 pp., 1931.
64. ROBERTS, REV. JAMES BRENDAN, A.B., J.C.D., The Banns of Marriage, XIV-140 pp., 1931.
65. RYDER, REV. RAYMOND ALOYSIUS, A.B., J.C.D., Simony, IX-151 pp., 1931.
66. CAMPAGNA, REV. ANGELO, PH.D., J.U.D., Il Vicario Generale del Vescovo, VII-205, pp., 1931.
67. COX, REV. JOSEPH GODFREY, A.B., J.C.D., The Administration of Seminaries, VI-124 pp., 1931.
68. GREGORY, REV. DONALD J., J.U.D., The Pauline Privilege, XV-165 pp., 1931.
69. DONOHUE, REV. JOHN F., J.C.D., The Impediment of Crime, VII-110 pp., 1931.
70. DOOLEY, REV. EUGENE A., O.M.I., J.C.D., Church Law on Sacred Relics, IX-143 pp., 1931.
71. ORTH, REV. CLEMENT RAYMOND, O.M.C., J.C.D., The Approbation of Religious Institutes, 171 pp., 1931.
72. PERNICONE, REV. JOSEPH M., A.B., J.C.D., The Ecclesiastical Prohibition of Books, XII-267 pp., 1932.
73. CLINTON, REV. CONNELL, A.B., J.C.D., The Paschal Precept, IX-108 pp., 1932.
74. DONNELLY, REV. FRANCIS B., A.M., S.T.L., J.C.D., The Diocesan Synod, VIII-125 pp., 1932.
75. TORRENTE, REV. CAMILO, C.M.F., J.C.D., Las Procesiones Sagradas, V-145 pp., 1932.
76. MURPHY, REV. EDWIN J., C.PP.S., J.C.D., Suspension Ex Informata Conscientia, XI-122 pp., 1932.
77. MACKENZIE, REV. ERIC F., A.M., S.T.L., J.C.D., The Delict of Heresy in its Commission, Penalization, Absolution, VII-124 pp., 1932.
78. LYONS, REV. AVITUS E., S.T.B., J.C.D., The Collegiate Tribunal of First Instance, XI-147 pp., 1932.
79. CONNOLLY, REV. THOMAS A., J.C.D., Appeals, XI-195 pp., 1932.
80. SANGMEISTER, REV. JOSEPH V., A.B., J.C.D., Force and Fear as Precluding Matrimonial Consent, V-211 pp., 1932.
81. JAEGER, REV. LEO A., A.B., J.C.D., The Administration of Vacant and Quasi-Vacant Episcopal Sees in the United States, IX-229 pp., 1932.
82. RIMLINGER, REV. HERBERT T., J.C.D., Error Invalidating Matrimonial Consent, VII-79 pp., 1932.
83. BARRETT, REV. JOHN D. M., S.S., J.C.D., A Comparative Study of the Councils of Baltimore and the Code of Canon Law, IX-223 pp., 1932.
84. CARBERRY, REV. JOHN J., PH.D., S.T.D., J.C.D., The Juridical Form of Marriage, X-177 pp., 1934.
85. DOLAN, REV. JOHN L., A.B., J.C.D., The Defensor Vinculi, XII-157 pp., 1934.

86. Hannan, Rev. Jerome D., A.M., S.T.D., LL.B., J.C.D., The Canon Law of Wills, IX-517 pp., 1934.
87. Lemieux, Rev. Delise A., A.M., J.C.D., The Sentence in Ecclesiastical Procedure, IX-131 pp., 1934.
88. O'Rourke, Rev. James J., A.B., J.C.D., Parish Registers, VII-109 pp., 1934.
89. Timlin, Rev. Bartholomew, O.F.M., A.M., J.C.D., Conditional Matrimonial Consent, X-381 pp., 1934.
90. Wahl, Rev. Francis X., A.B., J.C.D., The Matrimonial Impediments of Consanguinity and Affinity, VI-125 pp., 1934.
91. White, Rev. Robert J., A.B., LL.B., S.T.B., J.C.D., Canonical Ante-Nuptial Promises and the Civil Law, VI-152 pp., 1934.
92. Herrera, Rev. Antonio Parra, O.C.D., J.C.D., Legislacion Ecclesiastica sobra el Ayuno y la Abstinencia, XI-191 pp., 1935.
93. Kennedy, Rev. Edwin J., J.C.D., The Special Matrimonial Process in Cases of Evident Nullity, X-165 pp., 1935.
94. Manning, Rev. John J., A.B., J.C.D., Presumption of Law in Matrimonial Procedure, XI-111 pp., 1935.
95. Moeder, Rev. John M., J.C.D., The Proper Bishop for Ordination and Dismissorial Letters, VII-135 pp., 1935.
96. O'Mara, Rev. William A., A.B., J.C.D., Canonical Causes for Matrimonial Dispensations, IX-155 pp., 1935.
97. Reilly, Rev. Peter, J.C.D., Residence of Pastors, IX-81 pp., 1935.
98. Smith, Rev. Mariner T., O.P., S.T.Lr., J.C.D., The Penal Law for Religious, VIII-169 pp., 1935.
99. Whalen, Rev. Donald W., A.M., J.C.D., The Value of Testimonial Evidence in Matrimonial Procedure, XIII-297 pp., 1935.
100. Cleary, Rev. Joseph F., J.C.D., Canonical Limitations on the Alienation of Church Property, VIII-141 pp., 1936.
101. Glynn, Rev. John C., J.C.D., The Promoter of Justice, XX-337 pp., 1936.
102. Brennan, Rev. James H., S.S., M.A., S.T.B., J.C.D., The Simple Convalidation of Marriage, VI-135 pp., 1937.
103. Brunini, Rev. Joseph Bernard, J.C.D., The Clerical Obligations of Canons 139 and 142, X-121 pp., 1937.
104. Connor, Rev. Maurice, A.B., J.C.D., The Administrative Removal of Pastors, VIII-159 pp., 1937.
105. Guilfoyle, Rev. Merlin Joseph, J.C.D., Custom, XI-144 pp., 1937.
106. Hughes, Rev. James Austin, A.B., A.M., J.C.D., Witnesses in Criminal Trials of Clerics, IX-140 pp., 1937.
107. Jansen, Rev. Raymond J., A.B., S.T.L., J.C.D., Canonical Provisions for Catechetical Instruction, VII-153 pp., 1937.
108. Kealy, Rev. John James, A.B., J.C.D., The Introductory Libellus in Church Court Procedure, XI-121 pp., 1937.

109. McManus, Rev. James Edward, C.SS.R., J.C.D., The Administration of Temporal Goods in Religious Institutes, XVI-196 pp., 1937.
110. Moriarty, Rev. Eugene James, J.C.D., Oaths in Ecclesiastical Courts, X-115 pp., 1937.
111. Rainer, Reg. Eligius George, C.SS.R., J.C.D., Suspension of Clerics, XVII-249 pp., 1937.
112. Reilly, Rev. Thomas F., C.SS.R., J.C.D., Visitation of Religious, VI-195 pp., 1938.
113. Moriarty, Rev. Francis E., C.SS.R., J.C.D., The Extraordinary Absolution from Censures, XV-334 pp., 1938.
114. Connolly, Rev. Nicholas P., J.C.D., The Canonical Erection of Parishes, X-132 pp., 1938.
115. Donovan, Rev. James Joseph, J.C.D., The Pastor's Obligation in Prenuptial Investigation, XII-322 pp., 1938.
116. Harrigan, Rev. Robert J., M.A., S.T.B., J.C.D., The Radical Sanation of Invalid Marriages, VIII-208 pp., 1938.
117. Boffa, Rev. Conrad Humbert, J.C.D., Canonical Provisions for Catholic Schools, VII-211 pp., 1939.
118. Parsons, Rev. Anscar John, O.M.Cap., J.C.D., Canonical Elections, XII-236 pp., 1939.
119. Reilly, Rev. Edward Michael, A.B., J.C.D., The General Norms of Dispensation, XII-156 pp., 1939.
120. Ryan, Rev. Gerald Aloysius, A.B., J.C.D., Principles of Episcopal Jurisdiction, XII-172 pp., 1939.
121. Burton, Rev. Francis James, C.S.C., A.B., J.C.D., A Commentary on Canon 1125, X-222 pp., 1940.
122. Miaskiewicz, Rev. Francis Sigismund, J.C.D., Supplied Jurisdiction According to Canon 209, XII-340 pp., 1940.
123. Rice, Rev. Patrick William, A.B., J.C.D., Proof of Death in Prenuptial Investigation, VIII-156 pp., 1940.
124. Anglin, Rev. Thomas Francis, M.S., J.C.D., The Eucharistic Fast, VIII-183 pp., 1941.
125. Coleman, Rev. John Jerome, J.C.D., The Minister of Confirmation, VI-153 pp., 1941.
126. Downs, Rev. John Emmanuel, A.B., J.C.D., The Concept of Clerical Immunity, XI-163 pp., 1941.
127. Esswein, Rev. Anthony Albert, J.C.D., Extrajudicial Penal Powers of Ecclesiastical Superiors, X-144 pp., 1941.
128. Farrell, Rev. Benjamin Francis, M.A., S.T.L., J.C.D., The Rights and Duties of the Local Ordinary Regarding Congregations of Women Religious of Pontifical Approval, V-195 pp., 1941.
129. Feeney, Rev. Thomas John, A.B., S.T.L., J.C.D., Restitutio in Integrum, VI-169 pp., 1941.
130. Findlay, Rev. Stephen William, O.S.B., A.B., J.C.D., Canonical Norms Governing the Deposition and Degradation of Clerics, XVII-279 pp., 1941.

131. GOODWINE, REV. JOHN, A.B., S.T.L., J.C.D., The Right of the Church to Acquire Property, VIII-119 pp., 1941.
132. HESTON, REV. EDWARD LOUIS, C.S.C., PH.D., S.T.D., J.C.D., The Alienation of Church Property in the United States, XII-222 pp., 1941.
133. HOGAN, REV. JAMES JOHN, A.B., S.T.L., J.C.D., Judicial Advocates and Procurators, XIII-200 pp., 1941.
134. KEALY, REV. THOMAS M., A.B., LITT.B., J.C.D., Dowry of Women Religious, IX-152 pp., 1941.
135. KEENE, REV. MICHAEL JAMES, O.S.B., J.C.D., Religious Ordinaries and Canon 198, V-164 pp., 1941 (printed 1942).
136. KERIN, REV. CHARLES A., S.S., M.A., S.T.B., J.C.D., The Privation of Christian Burial, XVI-279 pp., 1941.
137. LOUIS, REV. WILLIAM FRANCIS, M.A., J.C.D., Diocesan Archives, X-101 pp., 1941.
138. MCDEVITT, REV. GILBERT JOSEPH, A.B., J.C.D., Legitimacy and Legitimation, X-247 pp., 1941.
139. MCDONOUGH, REV. THOMAS JOSEPH, A.B., J.C.D., Apostolic Administrators, X-217 pp., 1941.
140. MEIER, REV. CARL ANTHONY, A.B., J.C.D., Penal Administrative Procedure Against Negligent Pastors, XI-240 pp., 1941.
141. SCHMIDT, REV. JOHN ROGG, A.B., J.C.D., The Principles of Authentic Interpretation in Canon 17 of the Code of Canon Law, XII-331 pp., 1941.
142. SLAFKOSKY, REV. ANDREW LEONARD, A.B., J.C.D., The Canonical Episcopal Visitation of the Diocese, X-197 pp., 1941.
143. SWOBODA, REV. INNOCENT ROBERT, O.F.M., J.C.D., Ignorance in Relation to the Imputability of Delicts, IX-271 pp., 1941.
144. DUBÉ, REV. ARTHUR JOSEPH, A.B., J.C.D., The General Principles for the Reckoning of Time in Canon Law, VIII-299 pp., 1941.
145. MCBRIDE, REV. JAMES T., A.B., J.C.D., Incardination and Excardination of Seculars, XX-585 pp., 1941.
146. KRÓL, REV. JOHN T., J.C.D., The Defendant in Ecclesiastical Trials, XII-207 pp., 1942.
147. COMYNS, REV. JOSEPH J., C.SS.R., A.B., J.C.D., Papal and Episcopal Administration of Church Property, XIV-155 pp., 1942.
148. BARRY, REV. GARRETT FRANCIS, O.M.I., J.C.D., Violation of the Cloister, XII-260 pp., 1942.
149. BOLDUC, REV. GATIEN, C.S.V., A.B., S.T.L., J.C.D., Les Études dans les Religious Cléricales, VIII-155 pp., 1942.
150. BOYLE, REV. DAVID JOHN, M.A., J.C.D., The Juridic Effects of Moral Certitude on Pre-Nuptial Guarantees, XII-188 pp., 1942.
151. CANAVAN, REV. WALTER JOSEPH, M.A., LITT.D., J.C.D., The Profession of Faith, XII-143 pp., 1942.
152. DESROCHERS, REV. BRUNO, A.B., PH.L., S.T.B., J.C.D., Le Premier Concile Plénier de Québec et le Code de Droit Canonique, XIV-186 pp., 1942.

153. DILLON, REV. ROBERT EDWARD, A.B., J.C.D., Common Law Marriage, X-148 pp., 1942.
154. DODWELL, REV. EDWARD JOHN, PH.D., S.T.B., J.C.D., The Time and Place for the Celebration of Marriage, X-156 pp., 1942.
155. DONNELLAN, REV. THOMAS ANDREW, A.B., J.C.D., The Obligation of the Missa pro Populo, VII-131 pp., 1942.
156. ELTZ, REV. LOUIS ANTHONY, A.B., J.C.D., Cooperation in Crime, XII-208 pp., 1942.
157. GASS, REV. SYLVESTER FRANCIS, M.A., J.C.D., Ecclesiastical Pensions, XI-206 pp., 1942.
158. GUINIVEN, REV. JOHN JOSEPH, C.SS.R., J.C.D., The Precept of Hearing Mass, XIV-188 pp., 1942.
159. GULCZYNSKI, REV. JOHN THEOPHILUS, J.C.D., The Desecration and Violation of Churches, X-126 pp., 1942.
160. HAMMILL, REV. JOHN LEO, M.A., J.C.D., The Obligations of the Traveler According to Canon 14, VIII-204 pp., 1942.
161. HAYDT, REV. JOHN JOSEPH, A.B., J.C.D., Reserved Benefices, XI-148 pp., 1942.
162. HUSER, REV. ROGER JOHN, O.F.M., A.B., J.C.D., The Crime of Abortion in Canon Law, XII-187 pp., 1942.
163. KEARNEY, REV. FRANCIS PATRICK, A.B., S.T.L., J.C.D., The Principles of Canon Law 1127, X-162 pp., 1942.
164. LINAHEN, REV. LEO JAMES, S.T.L., J.C.D., De Absolutione Complicis in Peccato Turpi, V-114 pp., 1942.
165. McCLOSKEY, REV. JOSEPH ALOYSIUS, A.B., J.C.D., The Subject of Ecclesiastical Law According to Canon 12, XVII-246 pp., 1942 (printed 1943).
166. O'NEILL, REV. FRANCIS JOSEPH, C.SS.R., J.C.D., The Dismissal of Religious in Temporary Vows, XIII-220 pp., 1942.
167. PRINCE, REV. JOHN EDWARD, A.B., S.T.B., J.C.D., The Diocesan Chancellor, X-136 pp., 1942.
168. RIESNER, REV. ALBERT JOSEPH, C.SS.R., J.C.D., Apostates and Fugitives from Religious Institutes, IX-168 pp., 1942.
169. STENGER, REV. JOSEPH BERNARD, J.C.D., The Mortgaging of Church Property, 186 pp., 1942.
170. WALDRON, REV. JOSEPH FRANCIS, A.B., J.C.D., The Minister of Baptism, XII-197 pp., 1942.
171. WILLETT, REV. ROBERT ALBERT, J.C.D., The Probative Value of Documents in Ecclesiastical Trials, X-124 pp., 1942.
172. WOEBER, REV. EDWARD MARTIN, M.A., J.C.D., The Interpellations, XII-161 pp., 1942.
173. BENKO, REV. MATTHEW ALOYSIUS, O.S.B., M.A., J.C.D., The Abbot *Nullius*, XVI-148 pp., 1943.
174. CHRIST, REV. JOSEPH JAMES, M.A., S.T.L., J.C.D., Dispensation from Vindicative Penalties, XIV-285 pp., 1943.
175. CLANCY, REV. PATRICK M. J., O.P., A.B., S.T.Lr., J.C.D., The Local Religious Superior, X-229 pp., 1943.

176. Clarke, Rev. Thomas James, J.C.D., Parish Societies, XII-147 pp., 1943.
177. Connolly, Rev. John Patrick, S.T.L., J.C.D., Synodical Examiners and Parish Priest Consultors, X-223 pp., 1943.
178. Drumm, Rev. William Martin, A.B., J.C.D., Hospital Chaplains, XII-175 pp., 1943.
179. Flanagan, Rev. Bernard Joseph, A.B., S.T.L., J.C.D., The Canonical Erection of Religious Houses, X-147 pp., 1943.
180. Kelleher, Rev. Stephen Joseph, A.B., S.T.B., J.C.D., Discussions with Non-Catholics: Canonical Legislation, X-93 pp., 1943.
181. Lewis, Rev. Gordian, C.P., J.C.D., Chapters in Religious Institutes, XII-169 pp., 1943.
182. Marx, Rev. Adolph, J.C.D., The Declaration of Nullity of Marriages Contracted Outside the Church, X-151 pp., 1943.
183. Matulenas, Rev. Raymond Anthony, O.S.B., A.B., J.C.D., Communication, a Source of Privileges, VII-225 pp., 1943.
184. O'Leary, Rev. Charles Gerard, C.SS.R., J.C.D., Religious Dismissed After Perpetual Profession, X-213 pp., 1943.
185. Power, Rev. Cornelius Michael, J.C.D., The Blessing of Cemeteries, XII-231 pp., 1943.
186. Shuhler, Rev. Ralph Vincent, O.S.A., J.C.D., Privileges of Religious to Absolve and Dispense, XII-195 pp., 1943.
187. Ziolkowski, Rev. Thaddeus Stanislaus, A.B., J.C.D., The Consecration and Blessing of Churches, XII-151 pp., 1943.
188. Heneghan, Rev. John Joseph, S.T.D., J.C.D., The Marriages of Unworthy Catholics: Canons 1065 and 1066, XVI-213 pp., 1944.
189. Carroll, Rev. Coleman Francis, M.A., S.T.L., J.C.L., Charitable Institutions.
190. Ciesluk, Rev. Joseph Edward, Ph.B., S.T.L., J.C.D., National Parishes in the United States, VI-178 pp., 1944.
191. Coburn, Rev. Vincent Paul, A.B., J.C.D., Marriages of Conscience, XII-172 pp., 1944.
192. Connors, Rev. Charles Paul, C.S.Sp., A.B., J.C.D., Extra-Judicial Procurators in the Code of Canon Law, X-94 pp., 1944.
193. Coyle, Rev. Paul Raymond, A.B., J.C.D., Judicial Exceptions, X-142 pp., 1944.
194. Fair, Rev. Bartholomew Francis, A.B., S.T.L., J.C.D., The Impediment of Abduction, XII-122 pp., 1944.
195. Gallagher, Rev. Thomas Raphael, O.P., A.B., S.T.Lr., J.C.D., The Examination of the Qualities of the Ordinand, X-166 pp., 1944.
196. Gannon, Rev. John Mark, S.T.L., J.C.D., The Interstices Required for the Promotion to Orders, XII-100 pp., 1944.
197. Goldsmith, Rev. J. William, B.C.S., S.T.L., J.C.D., The Competence of Church and State Over Marriages—Disputed Points, X-128 pp., 1944.

198. Goodwine, Rev. Joseph Gerard, A.B., S.T.B., J.C.D., The Reception of Converts, XIV-326 pp., 1944.
199. Kowalski, Rev. Romuald Eugene, O.F.M., A.B., J.C.D., Sustenance of Religious Houses of Regulars, X-174 pp., 1944.
200. McCoy, Rev. Alan Edward, O.F.M., J.C.D., Force and Fear in Relation to Delictual Imputability and Penal Responsibility, XII-160 pp., 1944.
201. McDevitt, Rev. Vincent John, Ph.B., S.T.L., J.C.L., Perjury.
202. Martin, Rev. Thomas Owen, Ph.D., S.T.D., J.C.D., Adverse Possession, Prescription and Limitation of Actions: The Canonical "Praescriptio," XX-208 pp., 1944.
203. Miklosovic, Rev. Paul John, A.B., J.C.L., Attempted Marriages and Their Consequent Juridic Effects.
204. Mundy, Rev. Thomas Maurice, A.B., S.T.L., J.C.D., The Union of Parishes, X-164 pp. 1944.
205. O'Dea, Rev. John Coyle, A.B., J.C.D., The Matrimonial Impediment of Nonage, VIII-126 pp., 1944.
206. Olalia, Rev. Alexander Ayson, S.T.L., J.C.D., A Comparative Study of the Christian Constitution of States and the Constitution of the Philippine Commonwealth, XII-136 pp., 1944.
207. Poisson, Rev. Pierre-Marie, C.S.C., A.B., Ph.L., Th.L., J.C.L., Droits Patrimoniaux des Maisons et des Eglises Religieuses.
208. Stadalnikas, Rev. Casimir Joseph, M.I.C., J.C.D., Reservation of Censures, X-141 pp., 1944.
209. Sullivan, Rev. Eugene Henry, S.T.L., J.C.D., Proof of the Reception of the Sacraments, X-165 pp., 1944.
210. Vaughan, Rev. William Edward, J.C.D., Constitutions for Diocesan Courts, X-200 pp., 1944.
211. Paro, Rev. Gino, S.T.D., J.C.D., The Right of Papal Legation, X-221 pp., 1944 (printed 1947).
212. Balzer, Rev. Ralph Francis, C.P., J.C.D., The Computation of Time in a Canonical Novitiate, X-227 pp., 1945.
213. Dougherty, Rev. John Whelan, A.B., S.T.L., J.C.D., De Inquisitione Speciali, XII-195 pp., 1945.
214. Dziob, Rev. Michael Walter, J.C.D., The Sacred Congregation for the Oriental Church, XII-181 pp., 1945.
215. Eidenschink, Rev. John Albert, O.S.B., B.A., J.C.D., The Election of Bishops in the Letters of Pope Gregory the Great, VIII-200 pp., 1945.
216. Gill, Rev. Nicholas, C.P., J.C.D., The Spiritual Prefect in Clerical Religious Houses of Study, X-140 pp., 1945.
217. Hynes, Rev. Harry Gerard, S.T.L., J.C.D., The Privileges of Cardinals, XII-183 pp., 1945.
218. McDevitt, Rev. Gerald Vincent, S.T.L., J.C.D., The Renunciation of an Ecclesiastical Office, XIV-179 pp., 1945.

219. MANNING, REV. JOSEPH LEROY, J.C.D., The Free Conferral of Offices, VII-116 pp., 1945.
220. MEYER, REV. LOUIS G., O.S.B., A.B., S.T.B., J.C.D., Alms-gathering by Religious, XII-163 pp., 1945.
221. O'DONNELL, REV. CLETUS FRANCIS, M.A., J.C.D., The Marriage of Minors, XII-268 pp., 1945.
222. PRUNSKIS, REV. JOSEPH, J.C.D., Comparative Law, Ecclesiastical and Civil, in Lithuanian Concordat, X-161 pp., 1945.
223. SWEENEY, REV. FRANCIS PATRICK, C.SS.R., J.C.D., The Reduction of Clerics to the Lay State, X-199 pp., 1945.
224. VOGELPOHL, REV. HENRY JOHN, J.C.D., The Simple Impediments to Holy Orders, XVI-190 pp., 1945.
225. BROCKHAUS, REV. THOMAS AQUINAS, O.S.B., J.C.D., Religious who are known as *Conversi*, X-127 pp., 1945.
226. GRIESE, REV. ORVILLE NICHOLAS, S.T.D., J.C.D., The Marriage Contract and the Procreation of Offspring, XVI-224 pp., 1946.
227. BOUDREAUX, REV. WARREN LOUIS, J.C.D., The *"ab acatholicis nati"* of Canon 1099, § 2, XII-110 pp., 1946.
228. BOWE, REV. THOMAS JOSEPH, A.B., J.C.D., Religious Superioresses, VIII-206 pp., 1946.
229. DIEDERICHS, REV. MICHAEL FERDINAND, S.C.J., J.C.D., The Jurisdiction of the Latin Ordinaries over their Oriental Subjects, XIV-153 pp., 1946.
230. DINGMAN, REV. MAURICE JOHN, A.B., S.T.L., J.C.L., The Plaintiff in Contentious Trials.
231. FRISON, REV. BASIL, C.M.F., M.MUS., J.C.D., The Retroactivity of Law, X-221 pp., 1946.
232. CALVIN, REV. WILLIAM ANTHONY, M.A., J.C.D., The Administrative Transfer of Pastors, XII-288 pp., 1946.
233. GORACY, REV. JOSEPH C., J.C.L., The Diriment Matrimonial Impediment of Major Orders.
234. HALE, REV. JOSEPH FRANCIS, M.A., S.T.L., J.C.D., The Pastor of Burial, X-247 pp., 1946 (printed 1949).
235. HENRY, REV. JOSEPH ARTHUR, A.B., J.C.D., The Mass and Holy Communion: Interritual Law, XII-138 pp., 1946.
236. LINENBERGER, REV. HERBERT, C.PP.S., J.C.D., The False Denunciation of an Innocent Confessor, VIII-205 pp., 1946 (1949).
237. LOWRY, REV. JAMES MARTIN, A.B., J.C.D., Dispensation from Private Vows, XII-266 pp., 1946.
238. LYNCH, REV. GEORGE EDWARD, A.B., S.T.L., J.C.D., Coadjutors and Auxiliaries of Bishops, X-107 pp., 1946 (printed 1947).
239. LYNCH, REV. TIMOTHY, M.S.SS.T., J.C.D., Contracts between Bishops and Religious Congregations, XIII-232 pp., 1946.
240. MCCLUNN, REV. JUSTIN DAVID, A.B., S.T.L., J.C.D., Administrative Recourse, VII-142 pp., 1946.

241. Lohmuller, Rev. Martin Nicholas, A.B., J.C.D., The Promulgation of Law, XII-140 pp., 1947.
242. McGrath, Rev. James, A.B., J.C.D., The Privilege of the Canon, XII-156 pp., 1946.
243. Marbach, Rev. Joseph Francis, A.B., J.C.D., Marriage Legislation for the Catholics of the Oriental Rites in the United States and Canada, XIV-314 pp., 1946.
244. Shimkus, Rev. Bernard Aloysius, A.B., J.C.L., The Determination and Transfer of Rite.
245. Smith, Rev. Vincent Michael, A.B., S.T.L., J.C.L., Ignorance Affecting Matrimonial Consent.
246. Wachtrle, Rev. Paul Anthony, A.B., J.C.L., The Baptism of the Children of Non-Catholics.
247. Crotty, Rev. Matthew Michael, J.C.D., The Recipient of First Holy Communion, X-142 pp., 1947.
248. Eagleton, Rev. George, J.C.D., The Quinquennial Faculties, Formula IV, XIV-199 pp., 1947 (printed 1948).
249. Gibbons, Rev. Marion Leo, C.M., J.C.L., Domicile of the Wife Unlawfully Separated from Her Husband, XIV-171 pp., 1947.
250. Kelly, Rev. Bernard M., S.T.L., J.C.D., The Functions Reserved to Pastors, XII-141 pp., 1947.
251. Kilcullen, Rev. Thomas J., LL.M., J.C.D., The Collegiate Moral Person as Party Litigant, X-150 pp., 1947.
252. Lafontaine, Rev. Germaine Joseph, W.F., J.C.D., Relations Canoniques entre le Missionaire et Ses Superieurs, X-117 pp., 1947.
253. Lane, Rev. Loras Thomas, A.B., S.T.L., J.C.D., Matrimonial Procedure in the Ordinary Court of Second Instance, XVI-184 pp., 1947.
254. Lover, Rev. James Francis, C.Ss.R., J.C.D., The Master of Novices, X-168 pp., 1947.
255. McNicholas, Rev. Timothy Joseph, J.C.D., The *Septimae Manus* Witness, XII-133 pp., 1947 (printed 1949).
256. Marositz, Rev. Joseph John, M.S.C., J.C.D., Obligations and Privileges of Religious Promoted to the Episcopal or Cardinalitial Dignities, XII-180 pp., 1947.
257. Murphy, Rev. Francis Joseph, J.C.D., Legislative Powers of the Provincial Council, XII-158 pp., 1947.
258. O'Brien, Rev. Romaeus William, O.Carm., J.C.D., The Provincial Superior in Religious Orders of Men, X-294 pp., 1947.
259. Pfaller, Rev. Benedict Anthony, O.S.B., J.C.D., *The ipso facto* Effected Dismissal of Religious, XII-225 pp., 1947.
260. Popek, Rev. Alphonse Sylvester, J.C.D., The Rights and Obligations of Metropolitans, XX-460 pp., 1947.
261. Ristuccia, Rev. Bernard Joseph, C.M., J.C.D., Quasi-Religious, XVI-318 pp., 1947 (printed 1949).
262. Sonntag, Rev. Nathaniel Louis, O.F.M.Cap., J.C.D., Censorship of Special Classes of Books, XII-147 pp., 1947.

263. Stadler, Rev. Joseph Nicholas, J.C.D., Frequent Holy Communion, X-158 pp., 1947.
264. Szal, Rev. Ignatius Joseph, J.C.D., The Communication of Catholics with Schismatics, XII-217 pp., 1947.
265. Wagner, Rev. Urban S., O.F.M., Conv., J.C.D., Parochial Substitute Vicars and Supplying Priests, IX-126 pp., 1947.
266. Quinn, Rev. Joseph, M.A., J.C.D., Documents Required for the Reception of Orders, XIV-207 pp., 1948.
267. Bennington, Rev. James Clement, A.B., J.C.L., The Recipient of Confirmation.
268. Blaher, Rev. Damian Joseph, O.F.M., A.B., J.C.D., The Ordinary Processes in Causes of Beatification and Canonization, XVI-290 pp., 1948 (printed 1949).
269. Clune, Rev. Robert Bell, B.A., J.C.D., The Judicial Interrogation of the Parties, XII-142 pp., 1948.
270. Courtemanche, Rev. Basil F., B.A., J.C.D., The Total Simulation of Matrimonial Consent, XX-120 pp., 1948.
271. Dlouhy, Rev. Maur John, O.S.B., A.B., J.C.L., The Ordination of Exempt Religious.
272. Donovan, Rev. John Thomas, Ph.B., S.T.L., J.C.D., The Clerical Obligation of Canons 138 and 140, XII-209 pp., 1948.
273. Freking, Rev. Frederick W., A.B., S.T.B., J.C.D., The Canonical Installation of Pastors, XII-210 pp., 1948.
274. Fulton, Rev. Thomas B., J.C.D., Prenuptial Investigation, XII-190 pp., 1948.
275. Godley, Rev. James P., J.C.D., Time and Place for the Celebration of Mass, X-206 pp., 1948 (printed 1949).
276. Kane, Rev. Thomas A., A.B., B.S., J.C.D., Jurisdiction of the Patriarchs of the Major Sees in Antiquity and in the Middle Ages, XII-111 pp., 1948 (printed 1949).
277. Kennedy, Rev. Andrew A., J.C.L., The Annual Pastoral Report to the Local Ordinary.
278. Konrad, Rev. Joseph George, J.C.D., Transfer of Religious to Another Community, VIII-284 pp., 1948 (printed 1949).
279. Kress, Rev. Alphonse, J.C.L., Contumacy in Ecclesiastical Trials.
280. McCartney, Rev. Marcellus Anthony, O.F.M., M.A., J.C.D., Faculties of Regular Confessors, XII-164 pp., 1948 (printed 1949).
281. McCaslin, Rev. Edward Patrick, M.A., S.T.L., J.C.L., The Division of Parishes.
282. McElroy, Rev. Francis J., A.B., J.C.L., The Privileges of Bishops.
283. Quinn, Rev. Stephen, M.S.SS.T., J.C.D., Relation Between the Local Ordinary and Religious of Diocesan Approval, XII-153 pp., 1948 (printed 1949).
284. Schneider, Rev. Edelhard Louis, S.D.S., B.A., J.C.L., The Status of Secularized Ex-Religious Clerics, X-155 pp., 1948.

285. Thompson, Chester J., A.B., J.C.L., The Simple Removal from Office.
286. O'Brien, Rev. Kenneth R., A.B., J.C.D., The Nature of Support of Diocesan Priests in the United States, XVI-162 pp., 1949.
287. Metz, Rev. John E., S.T.L., J.C.D., The Recording Judge in the Ecclesiastical Collegiate Tribunal, X-130 pp., 1949.
288. Reinhardt, Rev. Marion J., S.T.L., J.C.D., The Rogatory Commission, XIII-182 pp., 1949.
289. Ortega Uhiuk, Rev. Juan, S.J., J.C.L., De Delicto Sollicitationis.
290. Casey, Rev. James V., J.C.D., A Study of Canon 2222 § 1, XII-127 pp., 1949.
291. Allgeier, Rev. Joseph L., J.C.D., The Canonical Obligation of Preaching in Parish Churches, X-115 pp., 1949 (printed 1950).
292. Cahill, Rev. Daniel R., J.C.D., The Custody of the Holy Eucharist, XVI-178 pp., 1949 (printed 1950).
293. Carr, Rev. Aiden, O.F.M., Carm., S.T.D., J.C.L., Vocation to the Priesthood: Its Canonical Concept.
294. Knopke, Rev. Roch F., O.F.M., J.C.D., Reverential Fear in Matrimonial Cases in Asiatic Countries: Rota Cases, XII-112 pp., 1949.
295. Lavelle, Rev. Howard D., J.C.D., The Obligation of Holding Sacred Missions in Parishes, XVI-142 pp., 1949.
296. Mickells, Rev. Anthony B., J.C.L., The Constitutive Elements of Parishes.
297. Noone, Rev. John J., J.C.D., Nullity in Judicial Acts, X-147 pp., 1949 (printed 1950).
298. Sheehan, Rev. Daniel E., J.C.L., The Minister of Holy Communion.
299. Statkus, Rev. Francis J., J.C.L., The Minister of the Last Sacraments.
300. Cook, Rev. John P., J.C.D., Ecclesiastical Communities and Their Ability to Induce Legal Customs, XII-152 pp., 1949 (printed 1950).
301. Fazzalaro, Rev. Francis J., J.C.D., The Place for the Hearing of Confessions, X-150 pp., 1949 (printed 1950).
302. Hannan, Rev. Philip M., J.C.D., The Canonical Concept of *congrua sustentatio* for the Secular Clergy, XII-237 pp., 1949 (printed 1950).
303. Quinn, Rev. Hugh G., S.T.L., J.C.L., The Particular Penal Precept.
304. Gallagher, Rev. John F., J.C.L., The Matrimonial Impediment of Public Propriety.
305. Welsh, Rev. Thomas J., J.C.L., The Use of the Portable Altar.
306. Waters, Rev. Joseph L., S.S.J., J.C.L., The Probation in Societies of Quasi-Religious.
307. Regan, Rev. Michael J., J.C.L., Canon 16.
308. Byrne, Rev. Harry J., J.C.L., Investment of Church Funds.
309. Gallagher, Rev. Thomas V., J.C.L., The Rejection of Judicial Witnesses and Testimony.
310. Chatham, Rev. Josiah G., Ph.B., S.T.L., J.C.L., Force and Fear as Invalidating Marriage: the Element of Injustice, XIV-183 pp., 1950.
311. Brown, Rev. James Victor, O.R.S.A., J.C.L., The Invalidating Effects of Force, Fear, and Fraud Upon the Canonical Novitiate.

312. DUERR, REV. CHARLES J., B.A., J.C.L., The Judicial Notary.
313. GONZALEZ, REV. FRANCISCO J., O.S.A., J.C.L., De Parocho Religioso Eiusque Superiore Locali.
314. HANNON, REV. JAMES J., J.C.L., Holy Viaticum.
315. SADLOWSKI, REV. ERWIN L., J.C.L., The Sacred Furnishings of Churches.
316. SEGO, REV. ARTHUR A., J.C.L., Dispensation From the Interpellations.
317. WATERHOUSE, REV. JOHN M., J.C.L., The Power of the Local Ordinary to Impose a Matrimonial Ban.
318. FREIN, REV. EUGENE B., J.C.L., The Discretionary Power of the Defender of the Matrimonial Bond.
319. CARTON, REV. GEORGE A., J.C.L., The Time Factor in the Gaining of Indulgences.
320. WALSH, REV. JOHN J., C.S.Sp., J.C.L., The Jurisdiction of the Inter-ritual Confessor in the United States and Canada.
321. UNTERKOEFLER, REV. ERNEST L., S.T.L., J.C.L., The Presiding Judge in Matrimonial Causes of First Instance.

www.ingramcontent.com/pod-product-compliance
Lightning Source LLC
LaVergne TN
LVHW050235080826
844660LV00012B/539
9780813224749